OPTIONS
TRADING
MADE
SIMPLE

OPTIONS TRADING MADE SIMPLE

A BEGINNER'S CRASH COURSE IN OPTIONS TRADING

INDRAZITH SHANTHARAJ

JAICO PUBLISHING HOUSE

Ahmedabad Bangalore Chennai
Delhi Hyderabad Kolkata Mumbai

DISCLAIMER

The information provided in this book is for **educational and informational purposes only** and should not be considered as financial or investment advice. Options trading involves substantial risk, and there is a possibility of significant losses. Past performance is not indicative of future results.

The author, **Indrazith Shantharaj**, and **Jaico Publications** are **not responsible** for any financial losses, damages, or liabilities incurred as a result of using the concepts or strategies discussed in this book. Readers are advised to consult with a **certified financial advisor** before making any trading or investment decisions.

By reading this book, you acknowledge that you are solely responsible for your trading actions and financial decisions.

Published by Jaico Publishing House
A-2 Jash Chambers, 7-A Sir Phirozshah Mehta Road
Fort, Mumbai - 400 001
jaicopub@jaicobooks.com
www.jaicobooks.com

© Indrazith Shantharaj

OPTIONS TRADING MADE SIMPLE
ISBN 978-93-48098-71-9

First Jaico Impression: 2025

Printed by
Thomson Press India Limited, New Delhi

*This book is dedicated to **Mr Chetan Kumar**, whose guidance and passion for trading laid the foundation of my journey into the world of trading. His invaluable lessons, wisdom, and encouragement have inspired me to explore and understand the complexities of the market. Thank you for instilling in me the belief that success in trading is possible with the proper knowledge and discipline.*

Acknowledgments

I would like to express my deepest gratitude to my amazing friends who supported me throughout the writing of this book. Sahil, your encouragement and constant belief in me kept me going during the toughest of times. Nataraj Malawade, Shalini, and Vinay Kumar, your insights and discussions on trading were invaluable, and they have shaped the contents of this book.

Harneet Singh, Rohit Katwal, and Swapnja Sharma, your support and positivity helped me stay motivated and focused. Each of you played a special role in making this book a reality, and I am forever grateful for your friendship and encouragement.

I would like to extend my heartfelt thanks to TradingView, GoCharting, Sensibull, and Opstra Define Edge for providing such comprehensive and intuitive charting platforms. The use of their charts and analysis tools played a vital role in the creation of this book, helping illustrate key concepts in options trading with clarity.

Finally, I would like to extend my heartfelt gratitude to Mr. Akash Shah and Jaico Publishing House for their invaluable patience, support and dedication in bringing my book to life. Your belief in my work and commitment to excellence have made this journey truly rewarding.

CONTENTS

INTRODUCTION

Until 2016, options trading in India was all about dealing with monthly contracts. Traders would trade with monthly options, which were available for Nifty, Bank Nifty and a few major stocks. These contracts had longer durations, giving traders time to speculate or hedge their positions over 30 days. However, the pace of trading and the prospect to adjust strategies was slower, and monthly options often required traders to wait for significant market movements. Strategies like long calls, puts, and calendar spreads were common during this time. However, the absence of weekly contracts limited flexibility in capitalising on short-term price movements.

The landscape of options trading changed dramatically with the introduction of weekly options. These shorter-term contracts allowed traders to take advantage of more frequent opportunities. The shorter expiry periods created faster price movements, increased volatility, and more trading setups. The introduction of these weekly contracts led to increased liquidity, greater participation from retail traders, and more sophisticated strategies focused on shorter-term plays.

Another significant factor that contributed to the surge in options trading was the removal of margin facilities in futures trading at intraday level. Previously, traders could use margin leverage in futures contracts, but changes in regulations around margin requirements made futures trading more capital-intensive. As a result, many traders shifted to options, which required lower upfront capital, especially with the rise of weekly options. Options trading provided an accessible alternative with less margin requirement, allowing traders to hedge or speculate with more flexibility and reduced risk.

The rise of strategies like straddles and strangles was a natural consequence of the increasing popularity of options trading. These strategies allowed traders to profit from volatility in the market without needing to predict the direction of price movement. A straddle involves buying a call and a put option at the same strike price (the price at which the option holder can buy or sell the underlying asset), while a strangle involves buying a call and put with different strike prices. Both strategies became widely used due to the nature of weekly options, where sharp price swings within a short period were more likely, making them ideal for capturing profits from market volatility.

However, with the boom in options trading came new challenges. One of the key issues traders started to face was the spike in options premiums. As weekly expiry dates approached, premiums on options would sometimes rise unexpectedly, making it harder to enter or exit positions profitably. This often led to slippage, where traders could not execute trades at their desired prices, leading to larger-than-expected losses. The speed at which options prices fluctuated became an issue for many retail traders, particularly in a fast-moving market like Bank Nifty, where prices could change dramatically within minutes.

In this book, we will explore the basics of options, important aspects of technical analysis, the opportunities and challenges this dynamic market presents today, and how you can develop strategies to navigate it. From mastering basics like straddles and strangles to managing premium spikes and slippage, this book will guide you through everything you need to know to succeed in options trading in India.

1

LET'S ADMIT IT—MOST PEOPLE SECRETLY HATE OPTIONS TRADING

Dhad-Dhad....
  Dhad-Dhad Dhad-Dhad...........
  Someone was hitting the door, abruptly waking me from a deep sleep.
  In those days, I had developed a habit of sleeping in the afternoon after a heavy lunch.
  It was a hot afternoon, and I was in a deep sleep.
  My eyes refused to open.
  Dhad-Dhad....
  Dhad-Dhad Dhad-Dhad...........
  But the knocking on the door continued.
  I became frustrated and decided to confront the person who kept persistently knocking on my room door.
  I quickly got up, unlatched the lock, and opened the door.
  My angry rant got stuck in my throat as my senior, a distant relative who was also my hostel mate, stood on the other side.

After looking at my facial expression, he realised I had been fast asleep.

Senior: 'Sorry, I woke you up from a deep sleep. But do you know the news?'
I: 'It's okay, brother. I slept just a few minutes ago. What's the matter?'
Senior: 'The second semester results are out. Did you check your results?'

After hearing this, all my anger and sleep vanished. My heart started beating rapidly. I had not done well in one subject, and my internal marks were also on the lower side. I began to think about whether I would pass that subject or not.

Senior: (In a louder voice this time) 'Hey, did you check your results?'

Only then did I come to my senses. Quickly, I put on my jeans and a T-shirt, washed my face, and ran outside to take an auto. (During our engineering days, mobiles were rare; network operators would also charge for incoming calls, so there was no question of checking results on the mobile phone. Everyone had to check the results only in cybercafes).

After five minutes, the auto stopped in front of 'My Cyber Cafe.' At that time, it was the best cybercafe in Davanagere, with lots of computer systems and airconditioning in the browsing hall.

It was already crowded, mostly with engineering students. I ran inside to see whether any of my friends were checking their results so that I could also check mine without standing in the queue and making an entry.

I found a close friend in one cabin. He was about to take a printout of his results and close the system.

I rushed in and asked him to check my results as well.

He took my registration number and entered it into the website. The cursor kept spinning....
After a few minutes, the webpage displayed my results.
I could see my registration number, but my mind was unable to register the marks due to anxiety.

I: 'What happened to my results?'

Friend: (In a low voice) 'You have failed in 2 subjects.'

I was doubtful about one subject. But I could not accept that I had failed in 2 subjects. It was also the first academic failure of my life.

I: 'Oh, I know one is SOM subject. Which is the other subject?'
Friend: 'MES'
I: 'Ok, can you give me a printout of my results?'

He took a printout and handed over a sheet with my results.
I folded it a few times and put it in my pocket.
My friend took me to a juice shop and ordered a chocolate milkshake for the both of us. He was saying something, but my mind refused to make any meaning out of his words. Therefore, I responded with a 'Hmm' after each statement.
For the first time, the chocolate milkshake seemed tasteless.
After some time, my friend dropped me off at the hostel.
Once he got to know my results, my senior told me that first-year subjects were pretty easy compared to those in the following years. As I had failed two subjects already, he predicted I would be detained the next year.
That day, I realised that society looks at you differently if you fail. I knew I had failed in two subjects, not because I could not clear them, but because I did not take studying those subjects seriously.

To cut the story short, I focused on my studies, cleared those two pending subjects, and became a topper the following semester.

You may be inspired or motivated a bit after reading this story. However, the same quality will backfire in trading.

Do you think it is strange? Let me explain.

What was your parents' advice when you were in the tenth standard? Most parents say the tenth standard is critical, and you must score good marks.

Then what was their suggestion when you were in twelfth standard? It was the same old logic, right? The same advice will continue when you study for a degree or take up any competitive exams. They do not talk about 'failure' at any point in time, which is a big sin in society. So whenever we fail, people look down on us; hence, most people try to correct it immediately by fighting against it. Do you agree?

I did the same!

However, nobody can achieve 100% success in stock market trading. So, when we experience failed trades, we aim to correct them immediately by taking more unnecessary trades, taking more risks in the next few trades, or doing both. This is called revenge trading.

I have not seen anyone who lost his trading capital slowly over 100 trading days, but I have seen a lot of people who lost their entire trading capital in one or two trading days.

You should understand that failure is a part of trading, and you cannot get away with it. But you can do these two things:

1. Lose less money in failed trades.
2. Do not get into revenge trading after facing a few failed trades.

If you realise this, you look at trading in a different way from today!

HOW DO WE SOLVE THE #1 PROBLEM IN OPTIONS BUYING?

If you are an absolute beginner to options trading, you do not have to answer this. But if you have a little exposure and experience in options trading, you must answer this question!

What is the #1 problem in options buying?

If your answer is 'time decay' or 'theta decay' (gradual loss of value as expiry date approaches) think again. Definitely, time decay plays a crucial role in option-buying trades. But we are ignoring another big devil here. Let me explain it with a few examples. Most traders buy low premium options between 50-100. So I will take a similar case to explain.

Case 1

You identified a good trade opportunity in a trading instrument. So you buy an option premium of that underlying instrument at 50. After some time, the price moves in the expected direction and your premium jumps from 50 to 100.

Now you decide to book the profits as you have doubled the capital deployed in this trade. So you close the position at 100. It shows a small pullback, and you feel happy about your exit. But after some time, the option premium jumps to 200. Now a lot of emotions come to your mind and all of them get stored in your subconscious mind.

Case 2

It is a new trading day, but your previous experience is still fresh in your mind.

You noticed a good trade opportunity today as well. So you buy a similar option premium of that underlying instrument at 50. After some time, the price moves in the expected direction and your premium jumps from 50 to 100.

Now your previous experience comes to mind. So you decide to hold the trade only to book profits at 200. But after making 100, the premium comes back and hits your stop-loss. Once again, some emotions arise and all these feelings surface and get stored in your subconscious mind.

Case 3

After experiencing case #1 and case #2, your mind works day and night to find a solution to this problem. You think keeping trailing stop-loss above your entry price is the best idea to avoid all the problems. With this in mind, you get ready to face another trading day. You noticed one more good trade opportunity and bought the option premium similar to the underlying instrument at 50. After some time, the price jumped to 100. Then you decide to place a trailing stop-loss at 90 for your position, hoping it will reach 200.

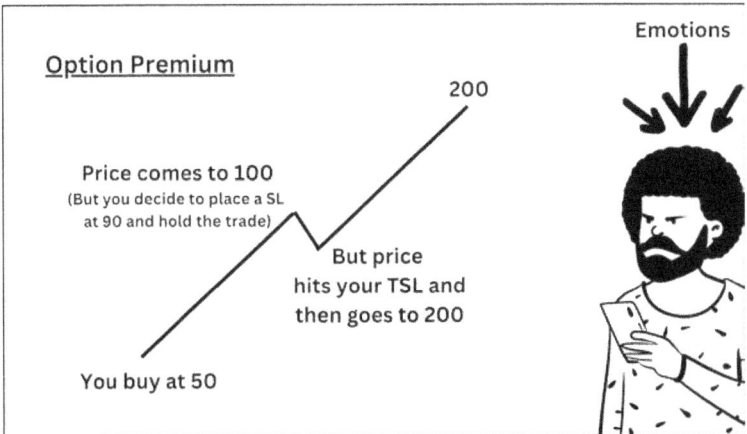

But the price comes back to 90, hits your trailing stop-loss and then jumps to 200.

Once again, this experience upsets you. It makes you recall all the posts and articles related to stop-loss hunting by big players. You curse all the big players and go to sleep.

Case 4

After all these experiences, you decide to hold the trade without placing any stop-loss in the system. You want to avoid stop-loss hunting from the big players. You get ready for the next trading day. Once again, you spot a good trading opportunity and buy an option premium at 50. You do not place stop-loss in the system this time.

After some time, the premium jumps to 100.

Because of the previous experience, you do not place even trailing stop-loss in the system. Besides, you aim to capture maximum profits on that day. But the premium comes back and becomes zero. Now you think your action in case 1 (booking profit at 100) was a better idea. Your mind becomes a mess, and once again you get upset.

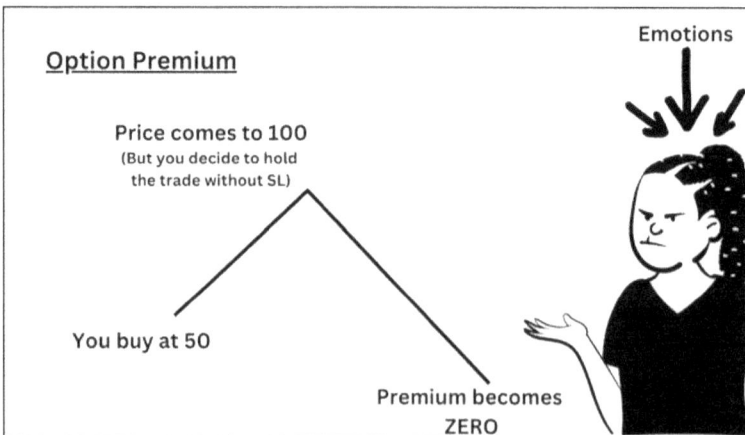

Option Premium

Price comes to 100
(But you decide to hold
the trade without SL)

You buy at 50

Premium becomes
ZERO

Emotions

These are four cherry-picked cases in buying options, which give rise to many emotions. But in reality, there will be many more cases that may upset you.

Please think for some time. Did you notice any common pattern among these 4 cases? If not, please read further.

In all these cases (case 1–case 4), you had one major problem: when to EXIT the trade!

As you know, emotions are the biggest enemy of traders, and all these cases can make you act adversely because of lack of clarity on exit.

Now the next million-dollar question—'Is there any exit technique to close the position at the top so that we stay calm through this?'

Unfortunately, the answer is a big 'NO'!

Except God and a liar, nobody can exit their position at the top.

So one has to make a proper rule to exit their position. Some of the exit rules are:

1. Booking profits at 1:2 or 1:3 risk-reward ratio
2. Trailing stop-loss using indicators like moving average, average true range (ATR), or the low of each candle, etc.
3. Book 50% profit at 1:2 risk-reward and carry the rest with entry price as trailing stop-loss

Whichever rule you pick, there will be some trades that would have made more profits if you avoided the exit. But do not alter the exit rule based on the outcome of each trade.

Hence, it is always better to follow one exit rule to avoid the most common problem of when to exit in options trading.

A COMPARISON: EQUITY VS. FUTURES VS. OPTIONS

Before explaining the differences between equity, futures, and options, I must caution you about one thing—this explanation only illustrates the leverage differences among these trading instruments. It would be best if you do not start taking trades based on this explanation. Please read the complete book before planning any trades in options.

Equity

Equity trading in the stock market refers to the buying and selling of company stocks or shares on a stock exchange.

It is one of the most popular forms of trading and investing as it offers investors the chance to generate profits from their investments by speculating on the future performance and price movements of individual stocks.

Equity traders typically buy and sell stocks based on their own investment goals, beliefs, and strategies.

Futures

Futures trading involves buying and selling contracts for an underlying asset at a predetermined future date and price.

Futures are typically used by investors looking to hedge their portfolios against potential losses from movements in market prices or to make profits by speculative traders.

A trader may enter into a long or short futures contract, depending on whether they expect the underlying asset's price to increase or decrease.

Options

There is a difference between futures contracts and option contracts. With a futures contract, there is a set price and a specific date for delivery. Both buyer and seller are obligated: the seller to deliver the asset and the buyer to accept it.

Options are more flexible. The buyer has the right, but not the requirement, to buy (call) or sell (put) the asset at a specific price by a certain date. On the other hand, the seller is obligated to fulfil the other side of the trade if the buyer decides to exercise their option.

In short, options buyers have the choices and rights, while options sellers have the obligations. A trader may buy a call option if he believes that the underlying asset price will increase in value, or enter into a put option if he anticipates that it will fall in value.

Options can also be used as part of hedging strategies as well as speculative investments.

Assume three trading accounts have the same capital Rs 1,65,000 (1.65 lakh).

All the three traders take the same trade at the same time and exit at the same time as they follow the same trading strategy (just to understand the concept).

Case 1: Equity

The first trader takes his trade in equity (image 1.1).

Entry – Rs 245 (at 9.45 am)

Exit – Rs 254 (at market)

With Rs 1,65,000, one can buy 673 shares.

Profit made due to this upside movement is Rs 6,057 (292 shares × 9 points)

Return on investment(ROI) on capital is 3.67%

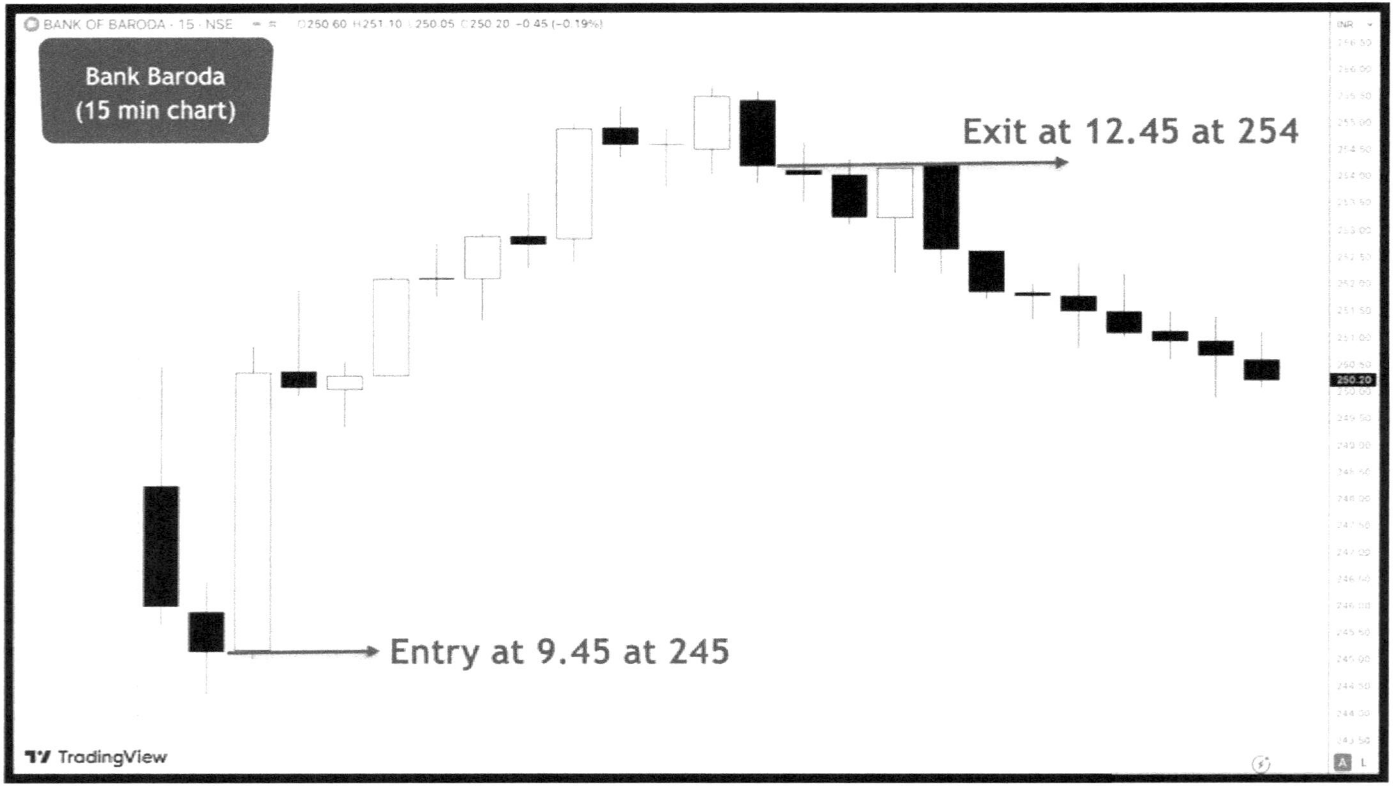

Image 1.1: 15-minute chart of Bank of Baroda equity trade

Case 2: Futures

The second trader takes his trade in futures. To take a trade in futures, we need to refer to the futures chart (image 1.2).

Entry – Rs 247 (at 9.45 am)
Exit – Rs 255.6 (at 12.45 pm)

But with a capital of Rs 1,65,000, a trader can buy 1 lot (2925 shares) in futures (image 1.3).
So the total profit made is Rs 25,155 (2925 shares × 8.6)
ROI on capital is 15.2%

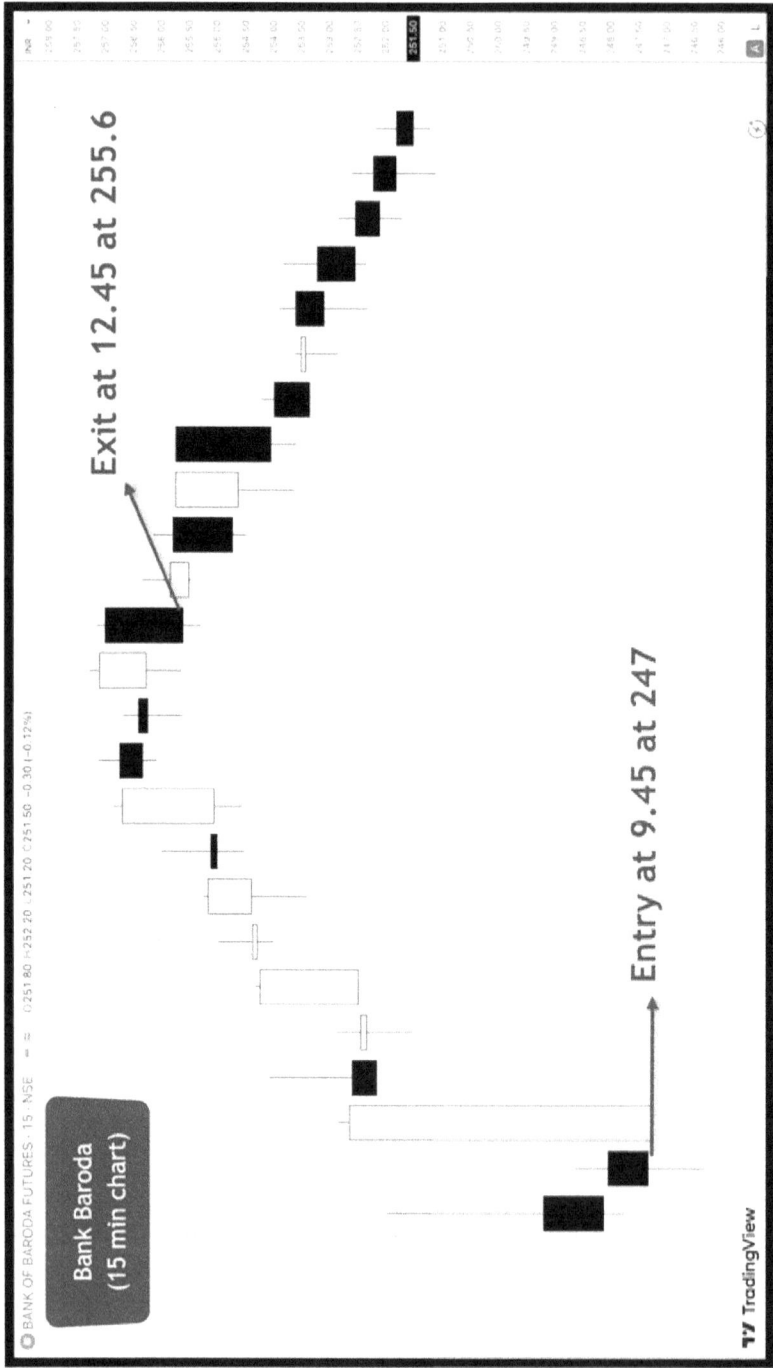

Image 1.2: 15-minute chart of Bank of Baroda showing futures trade

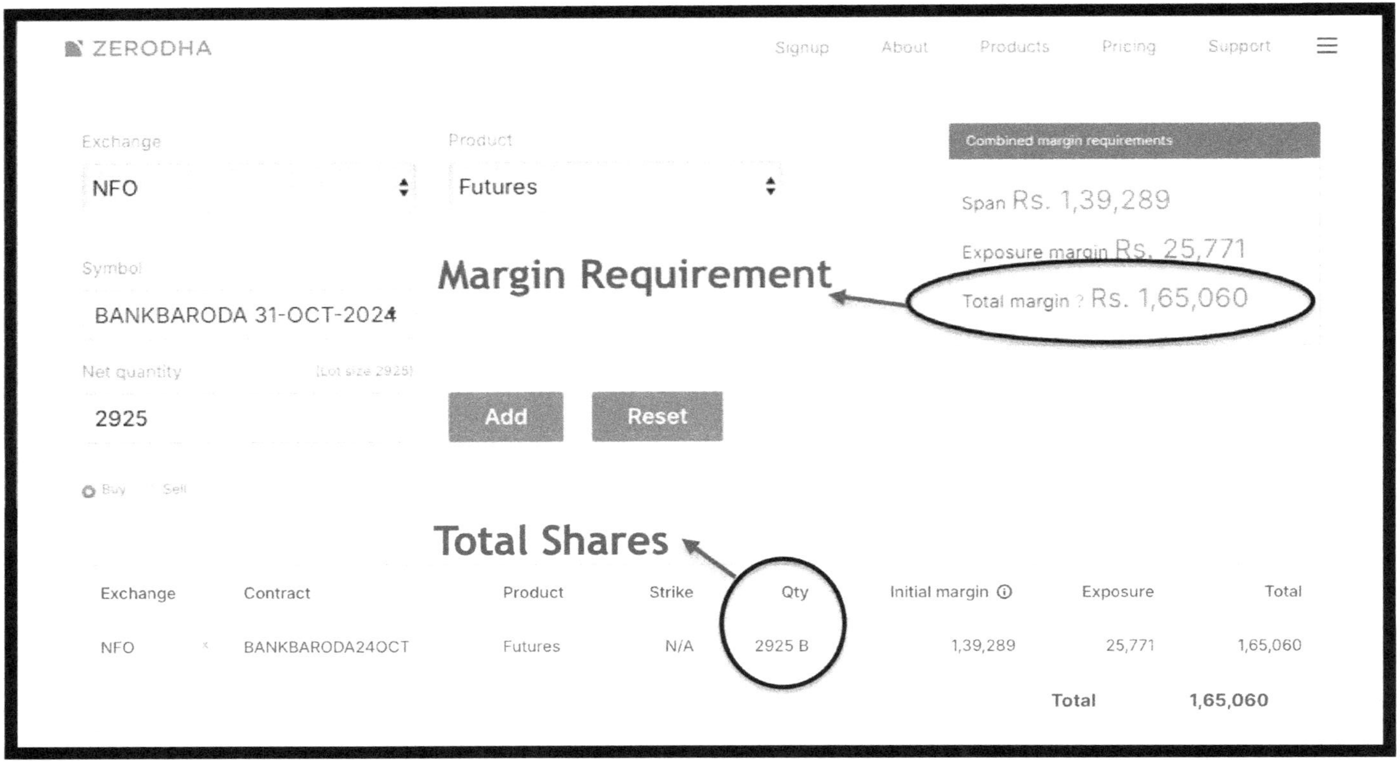

Image 1.3: Margin requirement of Bank of Baroda futures trading

Case 3: Options

The third trader takes his trade with options. He buys call option (255 Call option (CE)).

(Please note, this is just for illustration purpose. All the strategies including option selling are covered in the subsequent chapters. Also do not get excited after seeing these numbers. It is just a cherry-picked example to show the impact of leverage).

Image 1.4 shows the options chart of Bank Baroda 255 CE.
   Entry – 4.35 (at 9.45 am)
   Exit – 7.65 (at 12.45 pm)
   But with a capital of Rs 1,65,000, a trader can buy 12 lots (35,100 quantity) in options (255 CE).
   So, total profit made is Rs 1,15,830 (35,100 QTY × 3.3)
   ROI on capital is 70.2%

CONCLUSION

Never think that all the option-buying trades result in the same rate of return. Usually, profitable option buying trades yield more ROI, but they come with less success rate.

Option selling comes with high accuracy, but they usually result in less ROI. All these things vary based on the strike price we choose to trade (either for buying or selling).

Options trading instruments provide a wide range of flexibility and versatility to traders. Options allow traders to construct strategies around their risk tolerance and market outlook. They can also be used to hedge existing positions or take advantage of leverage in order to increase potential profits.

Therefore, my sincere request is to read the book until the end before arriving at any conclusions in your mind.

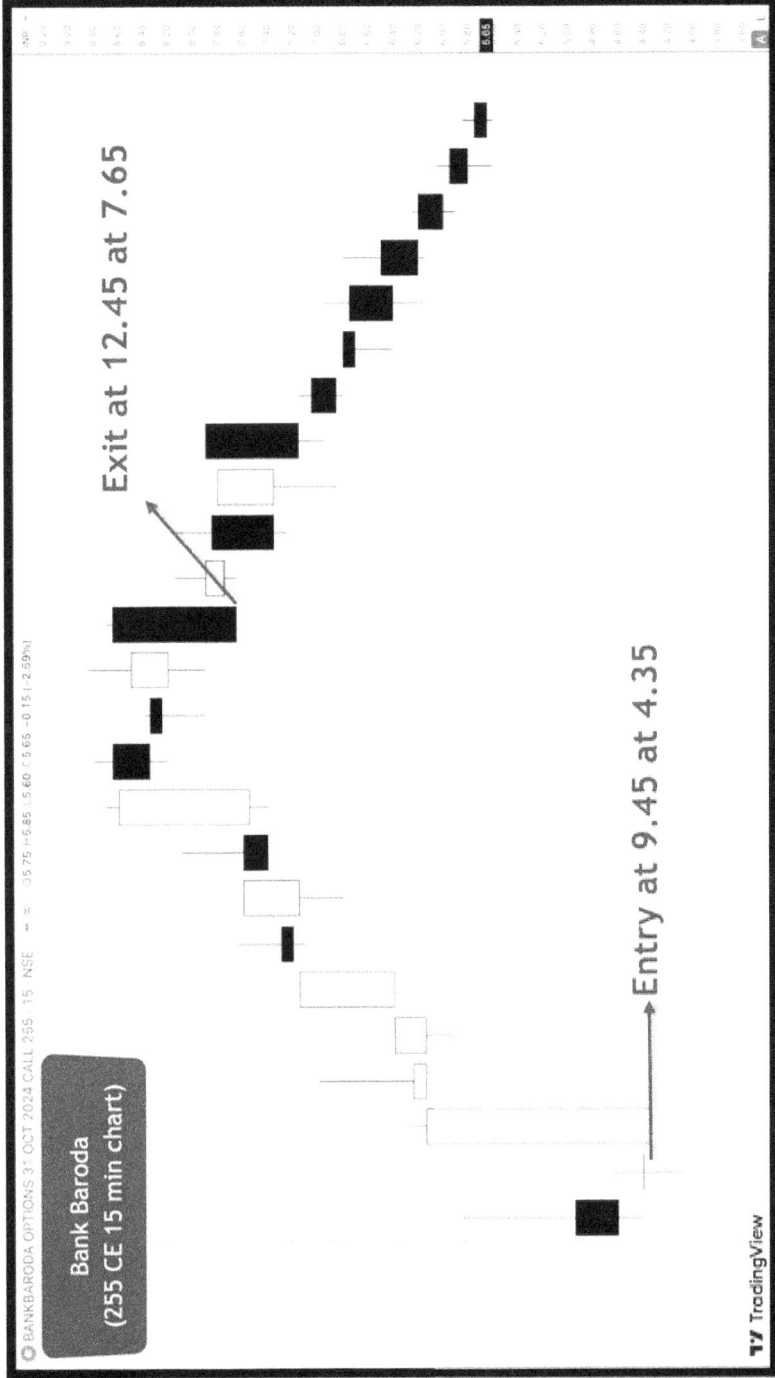

Image 1.4: 15-minute chart of Bank of Baroda showing options trade

2

A BRIEF INTRODUCTION TO OPTIONS TRADING

Recently I caught up with a friend over coffee. It had been a few years since we last met, and recalling old memories was fun. It was a pleasant surprise when I came to know that my friend also started trading options recently and was doing well. I was curious to know how he got into options trading and his trading style with options. He used a simple price action trading setup and bought options based on the direction.

Options buying comes with less success rate but with more profits if the trade goes in your favour. So I dug further. I was shocked when I came to know that he risks 10% of his capital per trade. This is not good in terms of money management rules in trading.

Let us assume there is a trading system with 50% accuracy. It means out of 100 trades, 50 trades give profits, and the remaining 50 trades result in losses.

But most beginners assume these profitable trades and losing trades are distributed evenly, that is,

WLWLWLWLWLWL......

where   W - Winning Trade
        L - Losing Trade

But the reality is different. You can also think about tossing a coin. Do you think 'head' and 'tail' appear alternately every time you toss the coin? At some point, there is a possibility of losing trades in one stretch. Similarly, you may win trades in one stretch.

Statistically, even a 50% accurate trading system can get 8–9 losing trades in one stretch. It means,

WLWLLLLLLLLLLWL...... (9 losing trades in one stretch)

What would happen to my friend if he faced this situation (as he risks 10% capital per trade)? His entire capital would get wiped out, and there is a high possibility of losing the whole capital even if he faced 5–6 losing trades in one stretch due to revenge trading.

I tried to explain this to him. However, he explained that it was working for him, so he planned to continue with this strategy.

I wished him all the best and ended the conversation.

Two months later, I received a call from him. He said my explanation was correct, as he lost his entire capital after facing a few losing trades in one stretch. Besides, he also did some revenge trading. I advised him to consider the loss as the fee paid to the market to learn this lesson and follow proper money management rules from that day on.

WHAT IS AN OPTION?

An option is a contract that gives the buyer the right to buy or sell an underlying stock or index at a specific price, known as 'strike price', within a deadline, known as 'expiry'.

If a person enters a contract to buy ABC company shares at 100 by the end of the month, he is not obligated to buy ABC shares at 100. But he retains the right (to buy) till the end of the month. Hence, it is called an 'option' rather than a 'mandatory' action.

However, this right comes with a small fee, which is called premium.

There are two types of contracts:

1. **Call Options (CE)** give the right to buy a stock at a specified price within the expiry
2. **Put Options (PE)** give the right to sell a stock at a specified price within the expiry date

Let us take a real-life example to understand options in a better way. Owning a house is the dream for most people in India. Suppose you finalise a flat in an apartment with a reputed builder in an excellent residential area in a metro city. The builder plans to deliver the flat only after 2 years, and quotes Rs 70 lakhs for the flat. A person can buy the flat by paying 70 lakhs in advance in the current setup.

But the builder may not complete the building within 2 years for some reason (a slight risk). Besides, what could possibly happen if someone files a legal case on the entire project? (another risk). These are only hypothetical situations, but they bring some risk. However, you do not want to lose the flat because the Metro transport project is coming up nearby, and there is a higher probability that the apartment cost may double after two years.

Now, what if a builder comes up with an agreement or contract saying you can retain the right to buy the flat at Rs 70 lakh anytime within the two years, but you do not own the flat in this contract period, and you need to pay only Rs 70,000 to get these rights?

I hope you happily accept the offer and sign the agreement, right? Because just by spending Rs 70,000 you retain the right to buy the flat at Rs 70 lakhs for the next two years.

The story is not over yet. As you do not own the flat yet, if there are any issues, you can always opt out of the agreement to buy the flat. You will lose only Rs 70,000 if you choose to opt-out. If there are no issues, and if the metro transport project comes nearby, then the price of the flat will go up. For the sake of explanation, let us say that the price is Rs 1,00,00,000 (1 crore) now, and you have the right to buy the same apartment at Rs 70 lakhs.

What do you do?

You will buy the flat for sure, right?

Let us go one step further now.

Assume that you do not have Rs 70 lakh capital to buy the flat. Besides, you do not want to take any loan to buy the apartment. What is your action plan in this case? You can sell the contract you had to another person, isn't it? (Because they can buy the flat at Rs 70 lakhs, but the current price is 1 crore).

Now, do you think you will sell the contract at only Rs 70,000? I am sure any fool will not do that.

You will sell the contract at a higher price. The person who is buying the rights is also happy to buy the contract at a higher price as he can save Rs 30 lakhs (as he gets the right to buy the flat at 70 lakhs).

If we look at this example in terms of options trading, then it looks like specifics mentioned below:

Options Type: Call Options (CE)
Strike Price: Rs 70 Lakh
Expiry: 2 years
Premium: Rs 70,000

This is what happens with options trading.

Most options traders do not buy or sell the underlying stock (except a few hedge funds or institutions) on their own. They mostly buy or sell the rights (options contracts) to make money in the market.

OPTIONS PREMIUM

In an options market, just like any other market, buyers and sellers compete to determine the price of an option, also known as the premium. They do this by placing bids and offers until a price is agreed upon.

This premium comprises two parts: intrinsic value and time value. Intrinsic value is the amount that would be credited to the option holder's account if you exercised the option right now at the current market price.

Let us say gold is trading at Rs 7,035 per gram, and you have a call option to buy gold at Rs 7,000 per gram. The intrinsic value would be Rs 35 per gram. This is because if you exercise the option (buy at Rs 7,000) and immediately sell at the market price (Rs 7,035), you would make a profit of Rs 35 per gram.

So, the higher the market price of gold goes compared to the strike price (your buy price in the option), the greater the intrinsic value.

An option's intrinsic value depends on the relationship between its exercise (strike) price and the current market price of the underlying asset.

- A call option has intrinsic value only if its strike price is LOWER than the current market price. The amount of intrinsic value is the difference between these two prices.
- A put option has intrinsic value only if its strike price is HIGHER than the current market price. Similar to calls, the intrinsic value is the difference between the strike price and the current market price.

Essentially, options cannot have negative intrinsic value.

An option's price in the market is typically higher than its actual value (intrinsic value). This extra cost is called time value, also known as time premium or extrinsic value.

Traders are willing to pay this premium because options offer advantages over simply buying or selling the underlying asset. These advantages come from the right, but not the obligation, to buy or sell at a specific price by a certain date.

Any option with a positive intrinsic value is considered an in-the-money (ITM) option. An option with no intrinsic value is recognised as an out-of-the-money (OTM) option. I will cover more about this topic in the following session.

ALL POPULAR OPTIONS JARGONS EXPLAINED

The option market is a bustling place where traders and investors with various motivations come together. Some participants believe they know which way prices will go, while others aim to shield their existing holdings from price swings. Some look to exploit price differences between similar products. Additionally, some players act as intermediaries, buying and selling to facilitate trades for others, profiting from the spread between the buying and selling prices.

Regardless of their goals, all options traders need to start by learning the terminology and the rules of the game. Understanding the terms used in options trading allows traders to communicate their buying and selling intentions in the market clearly. Without understanding the options contract details and their rights and obligations, traders cannot take full advantage of options or be prepared for the inherent risks involved.

To help demystify some of these terms, I have compiled a brief guide to understanding the jargon in options trading. Please note these are only small explanations about the terms, and most of these topics are covered in detail in the subsequent chapters.

Call Option: A call option is an agreement between two parties that gives the buyer (holder) the right to buy a specific asset at a predetermined price within a specified period of time. This option is typically used when a trader wants to speculate on the potential increase in the value of an underlying asset.

Put Option: A put option works similar to a call option, except it gives the buyer (holder) the right to sell a specific asset at a predetermined price within a specified period of time. This option is usually used when a trader wants to speculate on the potential decrease in the value of an underlying asset.

Options Premium: The premium is the price paid by the buyer for acquiring a call or put option to the option seller. This cost is determined by several factors, including the underlying asset's current value, the expected volatility of the asset, and the time remaining until expiry.

Strike Price: The strike price is the predetermined price at which an option can be exercised, either through buy or sell. It is also known as the exercise price or striking price.

For example, Nifty Bank is trading at 37,500. A trader thinks it will go above 38,000 in a week. Hence, he will buy 38,000 CE, assuming he will make money. Here, 38,000 is exercised price. Similarly, the security will have different strike prices to facilitate the trades between option buyers and option sellers.

Expiry Date: The expiry date is the date at which an option will expire and can no longer be exercised. This date is typically set when the option is purchased.

American Option: It is a type of option that can be exercised on any date before the expiry.

European Option: It is a type of option that can be exercised only on the expiry day. All the options instruments in India support only European options (hence the name CE and PE).

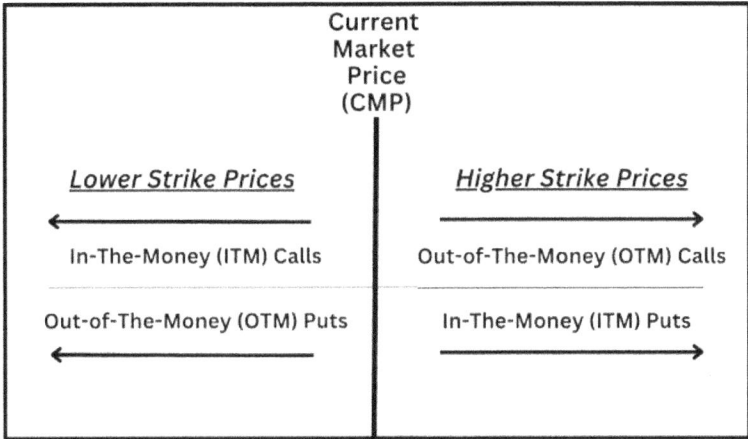

In-the-money (ITM): Options are said to be "in-the-money" when the value of their underlying asset has increased beyond the option's strike price.

For example, Nifty Bank is trading at 34,000, and you anticipate it will go to 35,000, so you buy 35,000 CE. After a week, Nifty Bank reaches 36,000, now 35,000 CE becomes in-the-money (ITM) option.

Out-of-the-money (OTM): Options are said to be "out-of-the-money" when the value of their underlying asset has decreased below the option's strike price.

For example, Nifty Bank is trading at 34,000 and you anticipate it will go to 35,000, so you buy 35,000 CE. After a week, Nifty Bank stays at 34,000, so 35,000 CE is still out-of-the-money (OTM) option.

At-the-money (ATM): Options are said to be 'at-the-money' when the option's strike price is equal to the current market price of its underlying asset.

For example, Nifty Bank is trading at 34,000, and you buy 34,000 CE. In this case, 34,000 CE is at-the-money (ATM) option.

Volatility: Volatility refers to how quickly or slowly an underlying asset's value is changing or expected to change in a given period of time.

Theta: Theta is a measure of how much money a trader loses due to the passing of time and is most commonly used when measuring the risk associated with holding options contracts.

Implied Volatility (IV): Implied volatility is a measure of the future expected volatility of an underlying asset and can be used as an indicator of market sentiment. It is derived from the price of currently traded options on that asset.

Delta: Delta is a measure of how much the option's value will change with a one-unit change in the price of its underlying asset. It can help traders to determine their risk exposure to any given position.

Gamma: Gamma measures how quickly delta changes as the price of its underlying asset fluctuates. It shows traders the amount of exposure they would have to the underlying asset if it were trading at or near the strike price of their option.

Time Value: Time value is a measure of an option's premium that is solely related to the remaining time until expiry. As expiry approaches, the time value will decrease, resulting in a lower overall premium for the option.

These are just a few terms traders need to understand when trading options. Knowing and understanding these terms can help you better evaluate the risk associated with any trade and make more informed decisions.

A detailed explanation of most of these terms is provided in the subsequent chapters.

3

THE #1 THING PEOPLE GET WRONG ABOUT OPTIONS TRADING

I started to learn options trading a decade ago. Back then, I struggled to understand the terms of options trading. Compared to buying or selling equity shares, additional tabs like 'CE/PE' and 'Strike Price' consistently increased my confusion about taking a trade in options.

I decided to understand these concepts and started reading a book about options written by a foreign author. After reading 50% of the book, I understood these terms and was confident about taking a trade with options.

The next day, I thought Nifty would go up, so I bought some call options. Nifty went up on that day, and I made some profits. I thought I had mastered options trading and felt like a genius. The day after that too, I made some profits by buying options. So I decided to buy options every day. I thought I would make a huge amount of money by the end of the month. But at the end of the month, I lost all my capital and did not know where I had made a mistake.

Most people go through a similar experience when they start with options trading. Hence they always advocate not trading with options. There is no doubt that options trading brings a little high risk, but if you learn how to deal with this risk, you will also be eligible to get good rewards.

LONG POSITION VS. SHORT POSITION IN TRADING

Let us assume a person decides to trade in stocks.

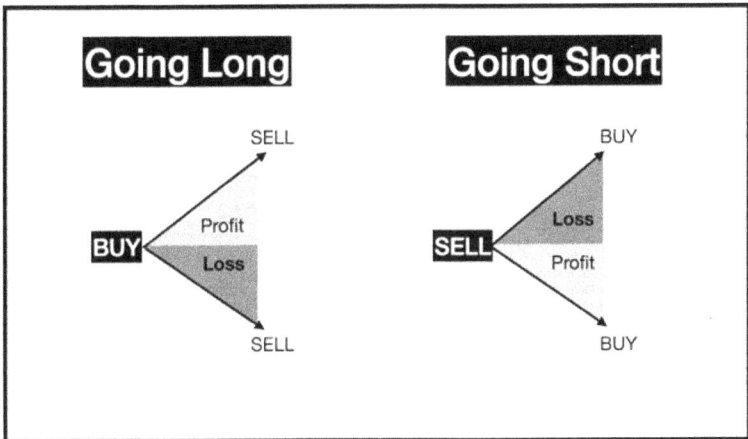

Image 3.1: Long position vs. short position in trading

Long Position

When a person buys some shares of a stock anticipating an increase in the price in the future, it is called a long position. In trading, it is essentially a bet that an asset's price will increase over time. This type of trading involves buying an asset and holding it for some time, expecting its value to rise. In this strategy, a trader purchases an asset at a lower price and then sells it at a higher price in order to generate a profit.

For example, let us say you believe that the price of gold will increase in the near future due to geopolitical tensions in the Middle East. You decide to buy a gram of gold at its current market price of Rs 5,000 and hold on to it until geopolitical tensions subside. If the price rises to Rs 6,000, you would have made Rs 1,000 in profit.

Short Position

In contrast, when a trader sells some stock shares first (without having any position in the same stock), anticipating the price will fall in the future, it is called a short position.

Short selling, also known as 'shorting' or 'going short,' is a trading technique used by investors and traders to speculate on the decline in the price of a particular asset. Short selling aims to generate profits when the asset's price falls by purchasing it back at a lower price.

Let us say that Ram believes that XYZ's stock price will decline over the coming weeks. He sells 100 shares of XYZ for Rs 500 each. On the next day, the value of XYZ dropped to Rs 400 per share, so Ram buys back the same number of shares he sold from Jim. The difference between the amount he received when he sold (Rs 500) and the amount he paid to buy back the shares (Rs 400) is Jim's profit of Rs 100 per share.

WHAT IS LONG VS. SHORT IN OPTIONS, ANYWAY?

Most beginners are only interested in buying options because they assume it is the only choice they have. It looks desirable because (1) They can buy more quantity with less capital, and (2) They can make big profits when the price moves in their direction.

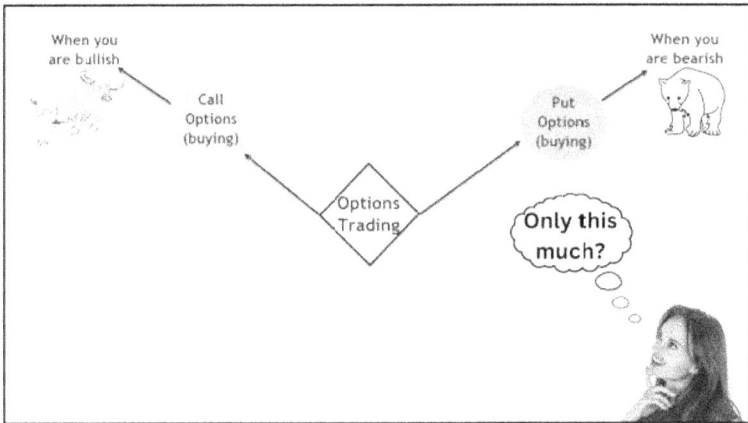

Image 3.2: Options buying (call and put)

Because of limited knowledge most beginners end up buying only options (either call or put). This is known as long position in options.

But most people forget that there should be an opposite party to complete a transaction. If you are buying something, then there should be someone who is selling the same thing at the agreed level. This is called short position in options.

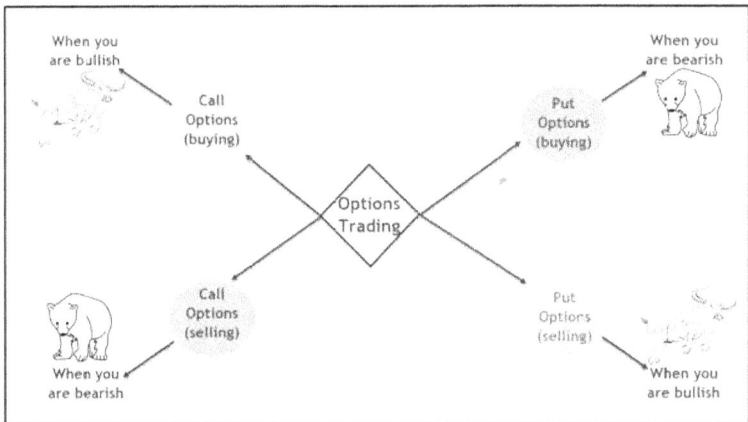

Image 3.3: Options trading (buying and selling)

When the market overview is bullish, a beginner will buy a call option. But in this case we can also sell a put option to make profits. When the underlying price moves up, the premium of the put option reduces and hence it yields some profits.

Similarly, when the market overview is bearish, most people will buy a put option. But we can also sell a call option to make profits in this case. When the underlying price moves down, the premium of the call option reduces and hence it yields some profits.

However, risk-reward, accuracy, and profit size varies between options buying and options selling. Besides, the result also depends on the options greeks which play a crucial role in options trading. All these topics are covered in subsequent chapters and chapter 7 provides more information about options buying and options selling.

MARGIN REQUIREMENTS IN OPTIONS

The critical difference between margin requirements for buying and selling options lies in the level of risk involved.

Buying options (limited risk)

When you buy an option (call or put), you have the right, but not the obligation, to buy or sell the underlying asset at a specific price by a certain date. Your maximum loss is limited to the premium you paid for the option.

Suppose you buy a call option for Rs 100 with a strike price of Rs 1,000. The most you can lose is Rs 100 (the premium) even if the stock price drops to zero.

Margin for buying: Since your risk is limited, brokers typically require a minimal margin for buying options. For example, if you wish to buy a call option of Nifty-50 at a Rs 90 premium for 25 shares. Then your margin requirement becomes Rs 90 (premium) × 25 (shares) = Rs 2,250 (approximately).

Selling options (unlimited risk)

When you sell an option (put or call), you take on an obligation. If the buyer exercises their right, you must buy or sell the underlying asset at the strike price. This exposes you to potentially unlimited losses if the price moves against you.

Suppose you sell a call option with a strike price of Rs 1,000. If the stock price goes up significantly, you must sell the stock at Rs 1,000 even if the market price is much higher. This could lead to substantial losses.

Margin for selling: Due to the unlimited risk, brokers require a higher margin for selling options than buying. This margin acts as a security deposit to ensure you have enough capital to fulfil your obligation if the trade goes against you.

Extra Margin Blocking

There might be situations where even the standard margin for selling options is not enough. This can happen in scenarios like:

i. **Deep out-of-the-money (OTM) options:** Options with strike prices far away from the current market price are considered out-of-the-money (OTM). Selling such options carries a lower likelihood of the buyer exercising the option. However, the potential loss can be significant if the price unexpectedly moves. Brokers might require additional margin for such options to manage their own risk.

ii. **Overnight positions:** Options held overnight are generally subject to higher margin requirements compared to day trades. This is because the market can fluctuate significantly outside trading hours, potentially increasing your risk.

iii. **Volatile markets:** When markets are volatile, the underlying asset price can swing dramatically. This increases the potential for significant losses in options selling strategies.

To manage this risk, brokers require higher margin deposits for option sellers during volatile periods. This extra cushion ensures you have the capital to meet your obligations if the market moves against you unexpectedly.

In essence, margin blocking for option selling protects you, the broker, and the system. It ensures you have some 'skin in the game' to discourage reckless trades and helps the broker manage the risk of you defaulting on your obligation if the trade goes south.

4

EMBRACE THESE BASIC STRATEGIES TO START OPTIONS TRADING

Anjali, a bright young girl, asked her uncle Ramesh, a bank employee, about insurance one day. Her simple doubt was that insurance companies collect a small premium but pay hefty compensation if things go wrong; hence, it would be tough for those companies to make profits.

With a wide smile on his face, Ramesh explained, "These smart insurance companies collect money (as premium) from a large pool of people (policyholders). By setting the premiums appropriately, these insurance companies aim to collect more money in premiums than they pay out in claims, leaving a profit."

Anjali: "Could you please elaborate, uncle?"

Ramesh: "Sure, for example, do you know about term insurance policies? Insurance companies pay only when the client dies within the policy period."

Anjali: "Yes, I know."

Ramesh: "Let us consider a simplified scenario:
    Total insured people under the policy = 2,00,000 people
    Policy term = 20 years
    Annual premium = Rs 15,000 per person
    Death Benefit = Rs 1,00,00,000 (1 crore)
    Mortality rate (probability of death per year) = 0.1% (This is
    for illustration purposes only. Actual mortality rates would
    be different)

Calculations

Total premium collected per person per year
    = Rs 15,000 × 2,00,000
    = Rs 3,00,00,00,000 (300 crores)
Total deaths based on 0.1% mortality rate
    = 2,00,000 × 0.001
    = 200 people
Total death claims to be paid
    = Rs 1,00,00,000/person × 200 people
    = Rs 2,00,00,00,000 (200 crores)

Profit Potential

Total premium collected = Rs 300 crores
Total death claims paid = Rs 200 crores
So the total profit in the first year is Rs 100 crores.

Anjali, please note this is a simplified scenario, and you can consider the points mentioned below as well:

i.   Insurance premiums vary based on many factors, like age,
     health, and other demographics.
ii. Those insurance companies also manage their operating
     expenses like employee salaries, marketing, and
     administrative costs.

iii. Investment is the income earned on premiums. Insurance companies, in turn, invest the premiums collected in other markets like bond markets and money markets, and they generate some amount as constant returns every year."

Anjali: "Thanks uncle, this example made a lot of sense to me."

Insurance and options trading share a core concept—risk management. Both offer ways to protect yourself from potential financial losses due to unforeseen events.

Insurance: In traditional insurance, you pay a premium to the insurance company in exchange for coverage against a specific risk (like fire, theft, or death). If the event occurs, the insurance company compensates you for your loss up to a specified limit.

Options Trading: Options contracts give you the right, but not the obligation, to buy or sell an asset at a specific price by a certain date. This allows you to hedge your holdings in the underlying asset.

Similarities

i. **Limited downside:** Both options buying and some insurance policies limit your potential downside. In options buying, your loss is limited to the premium paid. In some kinds of insurance (like term life insurance), your payout is capped at a specific amount.

ii. **Hedging against risk:** Both can be used to hedge against potential losses. Options allow you to hedge your stock holdings by giving you the right to sell at a specific price if the stock price falls. Similarly, some insurance policies (like property insurance) hedge against potential losses due to unforeseen events.

Differences

i. **Focus:** Insurance focuses on protecting against specific events, while options offer more flexibility in terms of what you can hedge and the timing.

ii. **Cost:** Insurance premiums are typically fixed, while option prices can fluctuate based on various factors.

iii. **Obligation:** Insurance policies do not require you to take any action. Options give you the right to buy or sell but not the obligation.

To make it simple, both insurance and options trading provide tools to manage financial risk, but they cater to different needs and risk profiles. So, you need to study how different options strategies can be constructed to cater to your specific needs.

For example, the below options are available in this monthly expiry (current monthly expiry and not weekly expiry) for Nifty with only 13 trading days before the expiry day.

Current Market Price (CMP) of Nifty is Rs 22,055 (image 4.1).

Let us understand how the buying and selling of different call options and put options can vary our profits and losses.

(The profit and loss figures shown in the examples below are generated by Sensibull. They are for informational purposes only and should not be considered absolute guarantees. The real market may produce slightly different results.)

CMP is Rs 22,055

Strikes	21,800	21,900	22,000	22,100	22,200	22,300	22,400
Call Premium (in Rs)	476	408	347	288	238	190	153
Put Premium (in Rs)	147	181	218	260	310	364	425

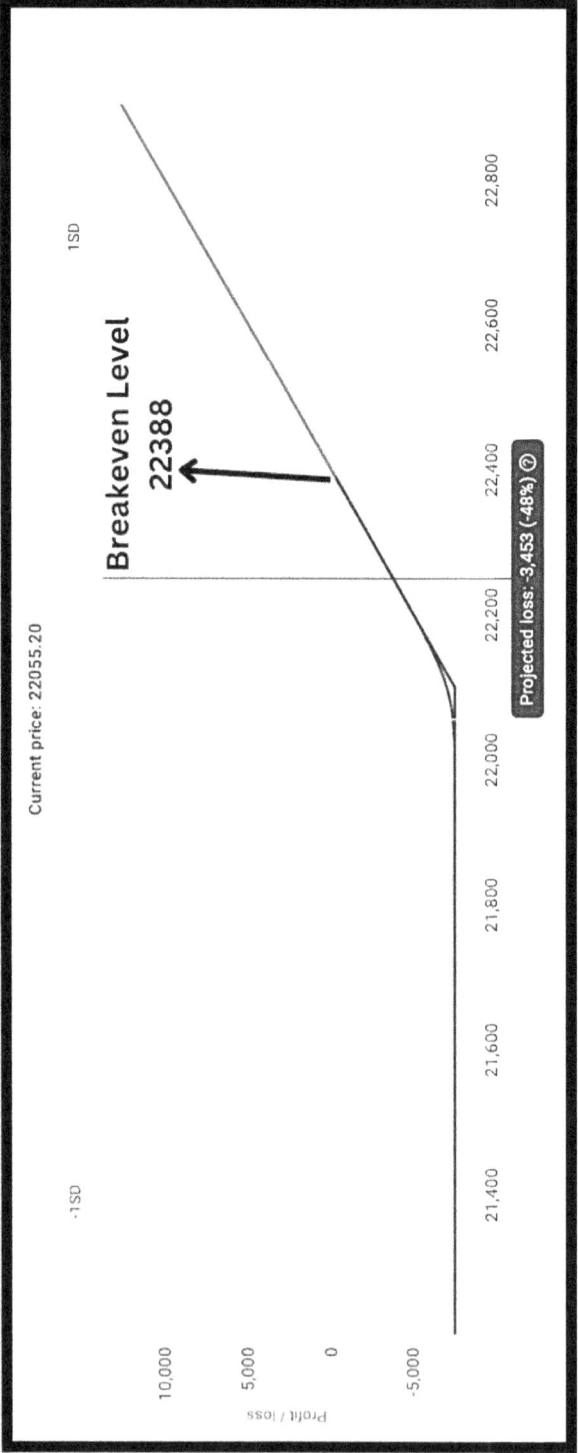

Image 4.1: Payout graph of Nifty 22,100 CE (when Nifty expires at 22,250)

BUYING CALL OPTION

I. Suppose a trader believes that Nifty will rise to at least 22,250 before the expiry. So, he will purchase a Nifty 22,100 CE at Rs 288.

So the total investment is

288 (premium value) × 25 (quantity per lot) = Rs 7, 200 (per lot)

You believe he will make profits in this trade, but the reality may be different!

Based on the payout graph, even if Nifty closes at 22,250 on expiry, this trader will lose Rs 3,453 approximately because he has paid Rs 288 as premium to buy Nifty 22,100 CE. So his real profit starts when Nifty closes above 22,388 (Strike price is 22,100 + premium paid is 288).

Let us assume instead of 22,250, Nifty expired at 22,500 on the last day of the expiry. The results will be different as shown in image 4.2. He will make Rs 2,796 profits in this trade. It means this trader has generated 39% returns on the capital (with an original investment of Rs 7,200 per lot).

Now let us go back to the beginning.

Suppose the same trader buys 22,400 CE (instead of 22,100 CE) at Rs 153.

So, the total investment is 153 (premium value) × 25 (quantity per lot) = Rs 3,825 (per lot)

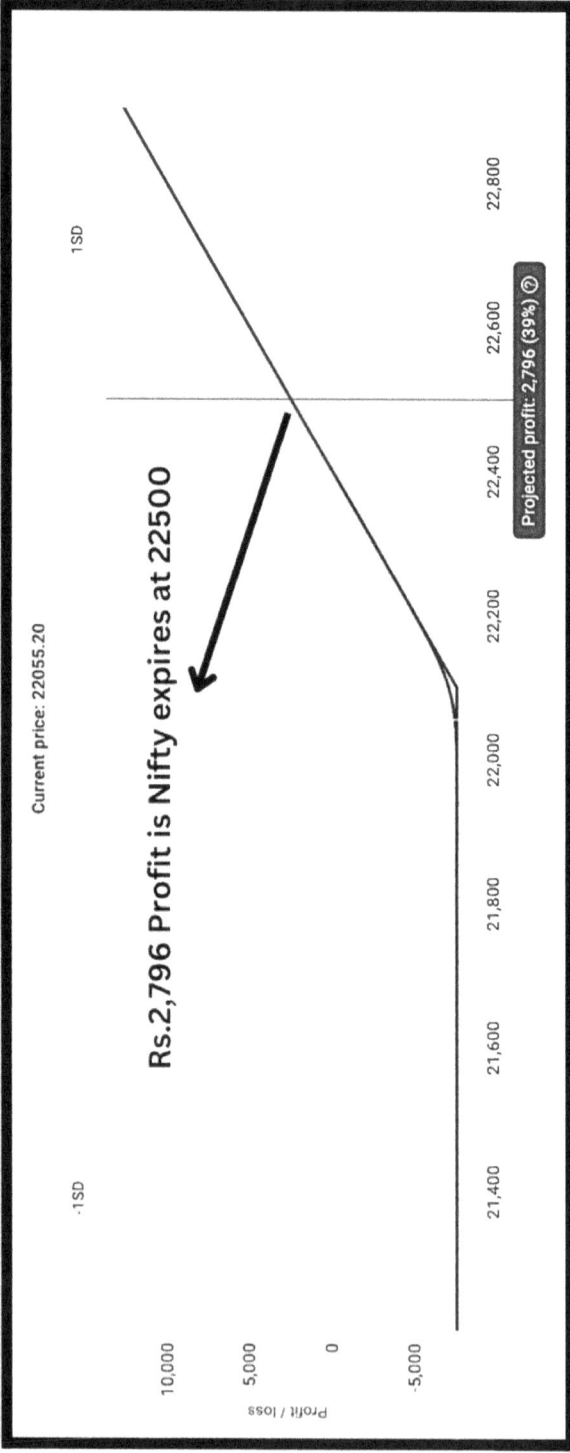

Image 4.2: Payout graph of Nifty 22,100 CE (when Nifty expires at 22500)

II. If Nifty expires at 22,250

As per the payout graph, even if Nifty closes at Rs 22,250 on expiry, this trader will lose Rs 3,823 approximately because he paid Rs 153 as premium to buy Nifty 22,400 CE (image 4.3).

So, his real profit starts when Nifty closes above 22,553 (Strike price is 22,400 + premium paid is 153).

III. If Nifty expires at 22,700

As per the payout graph, when Nifty expires at Rs 22,700 on the last day, this trader will make Rs 3,685 profits approximately (image 4.4).

It means this trader has generated 96.3% returns on the capital (original investment is Rs 3,825 per lot).

After observing these profit and loss scenarios, we can conclude the following points:

i. **Lower upfront cost:** Choosing a strike price further away from the current market price (out-of-the-money) often comes with a lower premium compared to closer strike prices. This can be attractive for options buyers seeking lower upfront costs.

ii. **Need for a bigger move:** However, to turn a profit, the underlying asset's price needs a significant move in your favour. This move must not only push the price past the strike price but also cover the premium you paid for the option.

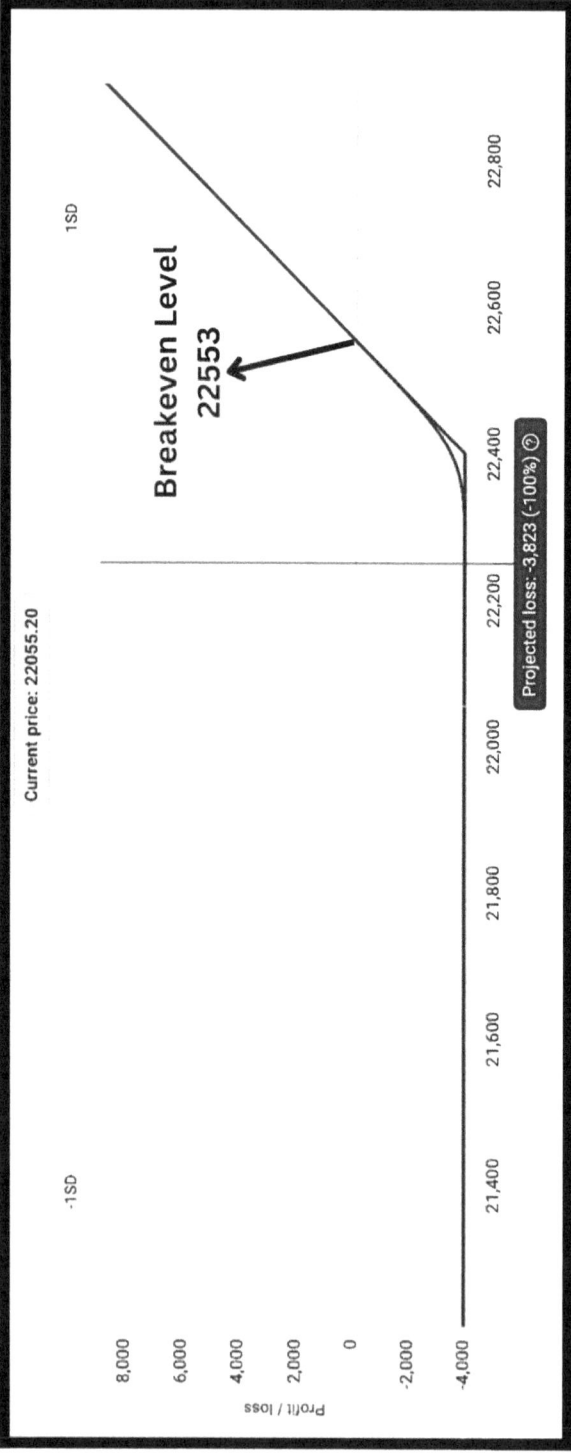

Image 4.3: Payout graph of Nifty 22,400 CE (when Nifty expires at 22,250)

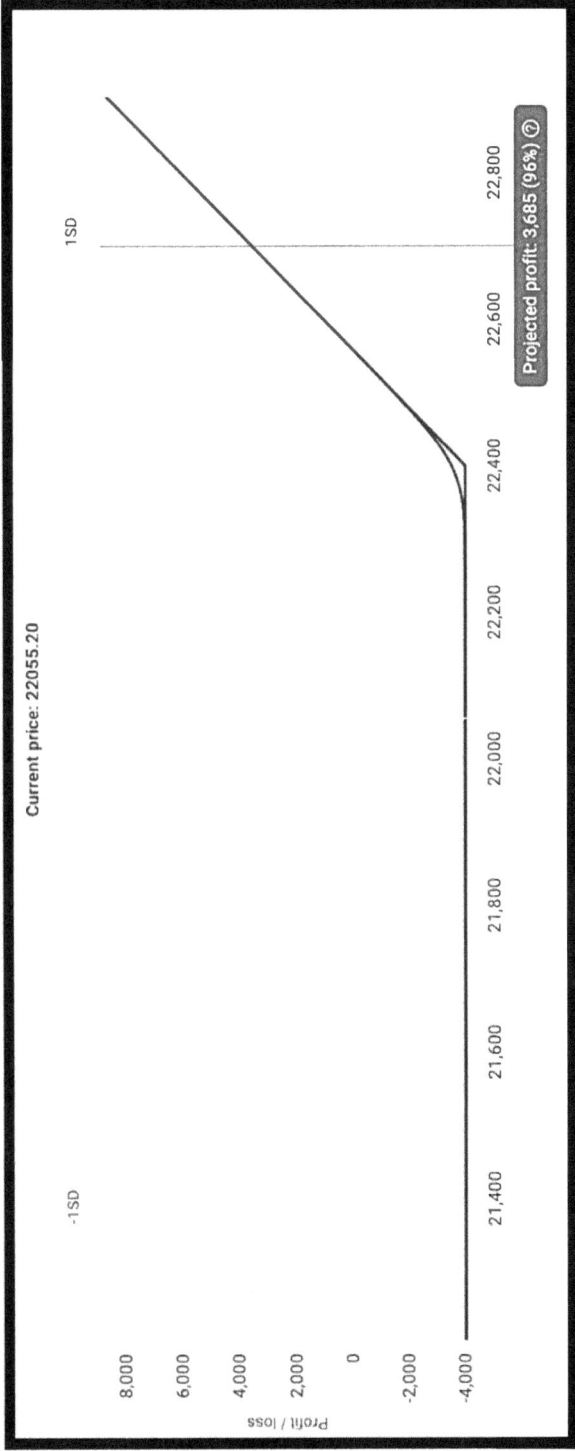

Image 4.4: Payout graph of Nifty 22,400 CE (when Nifty expires at 22,700)

   iii. **Probability of profits:** Options buying generally carries a lower probability of profits. This is because the price needs to move in your favour by a specific amount above the strike price to overcome the premium paid.

Remember: Far out-of-the-money options offer lower upfront costs but also have a lower probability of profitability because they require a more significant price movement.

SELLING CALL OPTION

Options sellers might seem like the underdogs in the options trading world. Unlike buyers chasing potentially large profits, sellers typically aim for smaller, more frequent wins.

Imagine you are renting out a bicycle on a beach for travellers to take photographs with. You will not make a huge profit each day, but the income adds up if you have a steady stream of renters. Options sellers take a similar approach, seeking consistent returns by capitalising on time decay and small price movements in their favour.

Options buyers and sellers are on opposite sides when predicting price movements. Options buyers depend on the asset's price moving a lot in their favour—up for call options and down for put options—to make a profit. Their primary focus is on guessing 'where the price will go.'

On the other hand, options sellers benefit from stability. They make money as time passes (because of time decay) or when the asset's price stays within a specific range. They care about 'where the price will not go' and can still earn premiums even if the price moves against them, as long as the movement is not too large.

Let us study the same examples to understand how option selling works.

Nifty current market price – 22,055

Strikes	21800	21900	22000	22100	22200	22300	22400
Calls	476	408	347	288	238	190	153
Puts	147	181	218	260	310	364	425

An option seller thinks Nifty will not expire above 22,400 (13 trading days pending before expiry). So, he decides to sell Nifty 22,400 CE.

Case 1

There are additional margin requirements for options sellers because they carry high risk compared to options buyers. In this case (image 4.5), this trader needs Rs 55,121 to sell 1 lot of Nifty 22,400 CE (25 quantity) (please note, it keeps on changing depending on the rules set by the regulatory bodies and market volatility).

Capital needed = Rs 55,121
Maximum profit is Rs 3,824 if Nifty expires below 22,400.
Loss starts from 22,553 (strike price 22,400 + premium collected
                                                        153 points)
Maximum returns on the capital (if Nifty closes below 22,400) is 7%

Case 2

Another trader is a bit aggressive with his approach and thinks Nifty will not expire above 22,300. He prefers to sell Nifty 22,300 CE and his payoff graph looks like image 4.6.

Capital needed = Rs 57,513
Maximum profit is Rs 4,750 if Nifty expires below 22,300.
Loss starts from 22,490 (strike price 22,300 + premium collected
        190 points)
Maximum returns on the capital (if Nifty closes below 22,300) is 9%

Compared to case 1, the margin requirement is high in this case as the trader is taking a little extra risk. But as the premium collected is higher than the previous case, the returns on capital are also high.

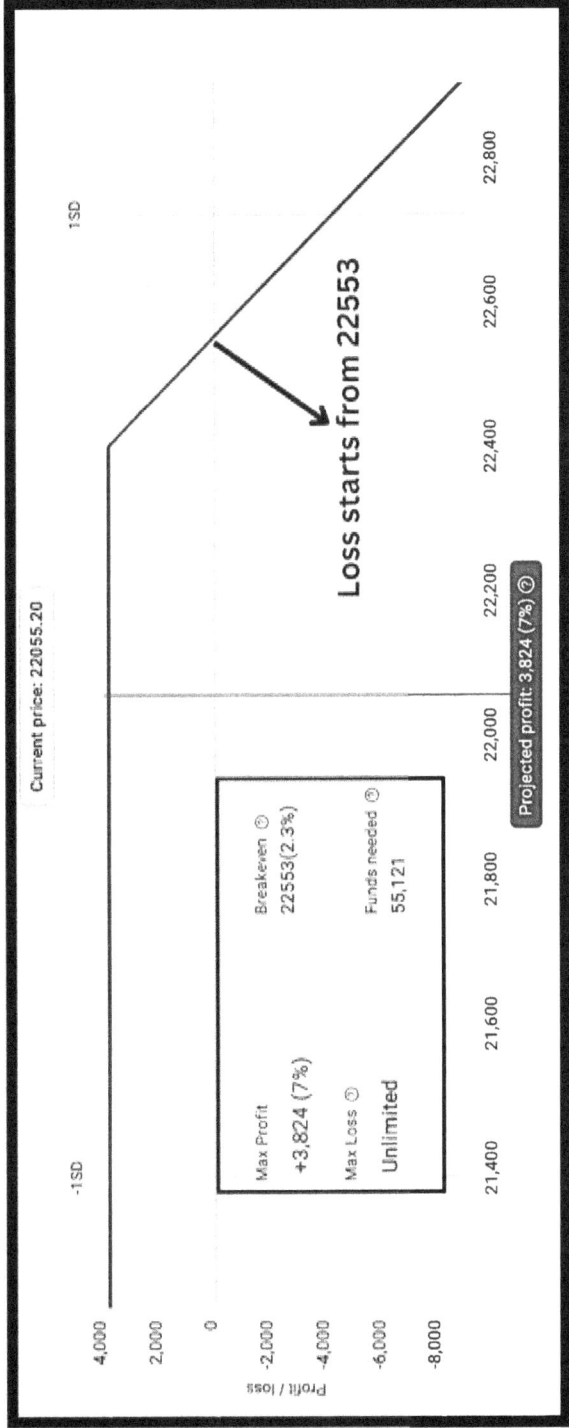

Image 4.5: Payout graph of Nifty 22,400 CE (options selling)

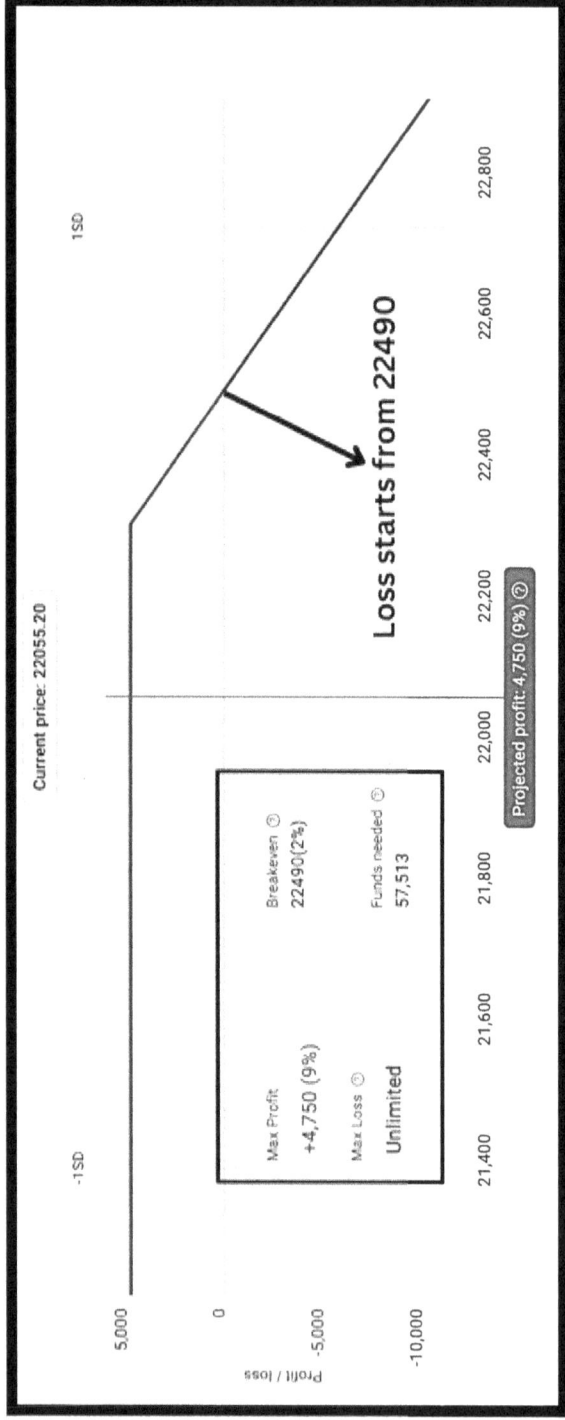

Image 4.6: Payout graph of Nifty 22,300 CE (options selling)

Options sellers need to strike a balance between return on investment (ROI) and probability of profit when selling call options, especially during strike price selection.

Here is a breakdown:

I. Selling calls with nearby strike prices

i. **Higher ROI potential:** The premium you receive is generally higher when you sell a call option with a strike price close to the current market price (at-the-money or slightly out-of-the-money). This translates to a potentially more significant return on investment if the option expires worthless (when the underlying price stays below the strike price for a call).

ii. **Lower probability of profit:** However, the closer the strike price is to the current market price, the higher the chance of the buyer exercising the option if the price moves up even slightly. This is because it becomes profitable for them to buy the stock at the lower strike price you offered (through the call option) and immediately sell it at the higher market price. Hence the probability of profit reduces.

II. Selling calls with far away strike prices

i. **Lower ROI potential:** The probability of the option expiring worthless is higher when you choose a strike price far away from the current market price (far out-of-the-money), so the premium you receive is generally lower. This translates to a potentially smaller ROI.

ii. **Higher probability of profit:** The benefit is that the underlying asset's price has more room to move before the option becomes profitable for the buyer (goes in-the-money). This increases your chances of the option expiring worthless and capturing the entire premium as profit.

Understanding the Trade-off

The key is to find a balance between lower ROI potential and higher probability of profit. Here is what you need to consider:

i. **Market volatility:** In a more volatile market, the underlying asset's price is likely to fluctuate more. This makes selling calls with a nearby strike price riskier, as the price might jump and trigger the option. Choosing a slightly farther strike price can offer protection in such scenarios.

ii. **Time to expiry:** The closer the option gets to expiry, the less time there is for the price to move against you (upward for call sellers). So, if you are looking for a higher probability of profiting, choosing a farther strike price might be better as it gives the price more time to stay below the strike.

iii. **Your risk tolerance:** Are you comfortable with the possibility of a higher loss if the price moves significantly against you (stock price goes much higher for call sellers)? Or are you more interested in a higher probability of smaller, consistent gains?

BUYING PUT OPTION

Big investors often favour buying put options as a form of portfolio insurance, but it is not always the case. Here is why puts act like insurance and when big investors might use them:

Puts as Portfolio Insurance

Imagine a big investor holds a significant amount of stock in a company they believe in long-term. However, the market is unpredictable, and short-term dips can occur. This is where put options come in.

i. **Protection against downside:** By buying a put option, the investor gets the right, but not the obligation, to sell the stock at a predetermined price (strike price) by a specific date (expiry). This acts like insurance.

ii. **Limited downside risk:** If the stock price falls, investors can exercise the put option and sell their shares at the strike price, limiting their losses. Even if the stock price plummets, their loss is capped at the difference between the purchase price and the strike price, minus the premium paid for the put option.

Benefits for big investors

i. **Hedge existing holdings:** Puts allow big investors to hedge their existing stock positions without selling them entirely. This is crucial when they believe in the long-term potential of the stock but want to protect against short-term volatility.

ii. **Maintain portfolio value:** By mitigating downside risk, puts can help big investors maintain the overall value of their portfolio during market downturns. This stability can be crucial for institutions managing large sums of money.

iii. **Peace of mind:** Puts offer peace of mind, allowing investors to focus on long-term investment strategies without worrying about short-term price fluctuations.

However, puts are not always preferred due to the following reasons.

i. **Cost:** Put options cost money upfront (premium), which reduces potential returns from the underlying stock.

ii. **Limited upside:** If the stock price increases significantly, the put option expires worthless, and the investor loses the premium paid.

In essence, buying put options is a kind of portfolio protection strategy that the big investors use to hedge against downside risk in their existing holdings. It is a balancing act between cost, potential returns, and peace of mind.

Let us study the same examples to understand how put option buying works.

Case 1

A trader believes Nifty can show some fall and hence he will buy 22,000 PE at Rs 218.35.

So total investment is

Rs 218.35 (premium value) × 25 (quantity per lot)

= Rs 5,458.75 (per lot)

As per the payout graph, even if Nifty closes at 21,900 on expiry, this trader will lose Rs 2,959 approximately because he as paid Rs 218.35 as premium to buy Nifty 22,000 PE (image 4.7).

So, his real profit starts when Nifty closes below 21,781.65,

(Strike price is 22,000 – premium paid is Rs 218.35).

Nifty current market price – 22,055

Strikes	21800	21900	22000	22100	22200	22300	22400
Calls	476	408	347	288	238	190	153
Puts	147	181	218.35	260	310	364	425

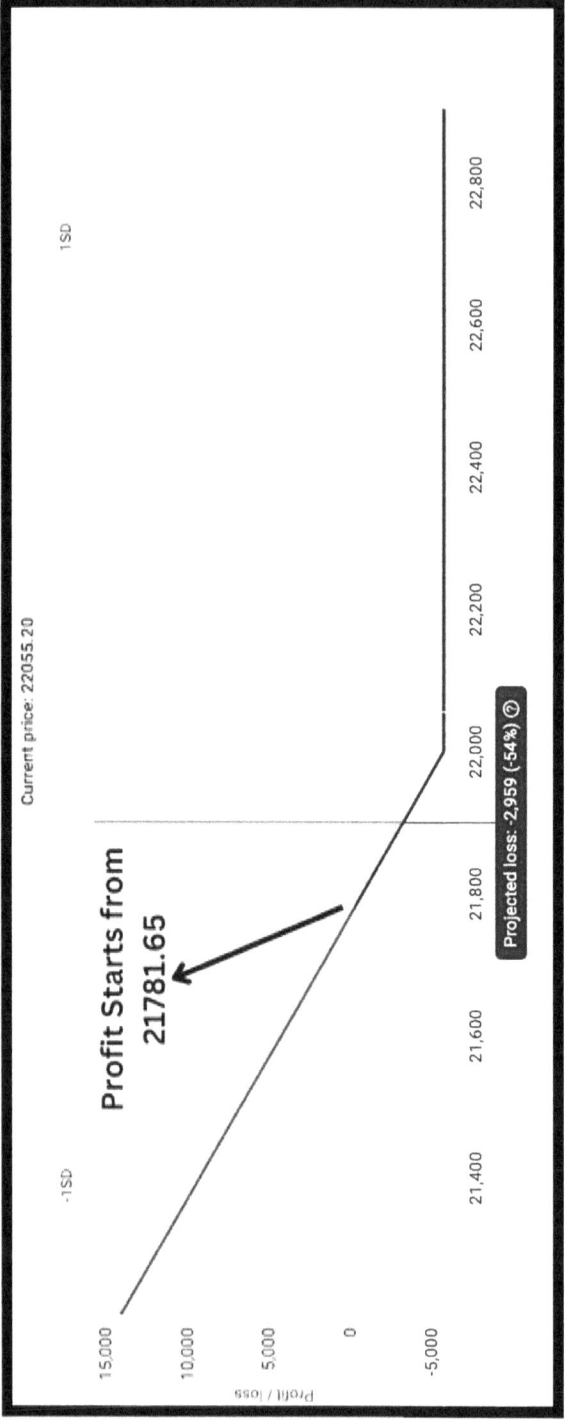

Image 4.7: Payout graph of Nifty 22,000 PE

Case 2

Another trader also has a bearish view on Nifty, but he prefers to buy 21,800 PE at Rs 147.

So total investment is Rs 147 (premium value) × 25 (quantity per lot) = Rs 3,675 (per lot)

Let us assume Nifty expired at 21,600 on the expiry day. Then the results are different as shown in image 4.8.

This trader will make Rs 1,325 profits in this trade. It means this trader has generated 36% returns on the capital (original investment is Rs 3,675 per lot).

SELLING PUT OPTION

Traders will consider selling put options when they have a neutral or slightly bullish outlook on the underlying asset's price to generate small returns. If the price stays flat or rises moderately, the option will expire worthless, and the seller will keep the entire premium.

Case 1

A trader sells Nifty 21,900 PE at 181 (image 4.9). In this case, this trader needs Rs 56,318 to sell 1 lot of Nifty 21,900 PE (25 quantity).

Capital needed: Rs 56,318

Maximum profit is Rs 4,543 if Nifty expires above 21,900.

Loss starts from 21,719 (strike price 21,900, premium collected 181 points)

Maximum return on the capital (if Nifty closes above 21,900) is 9%

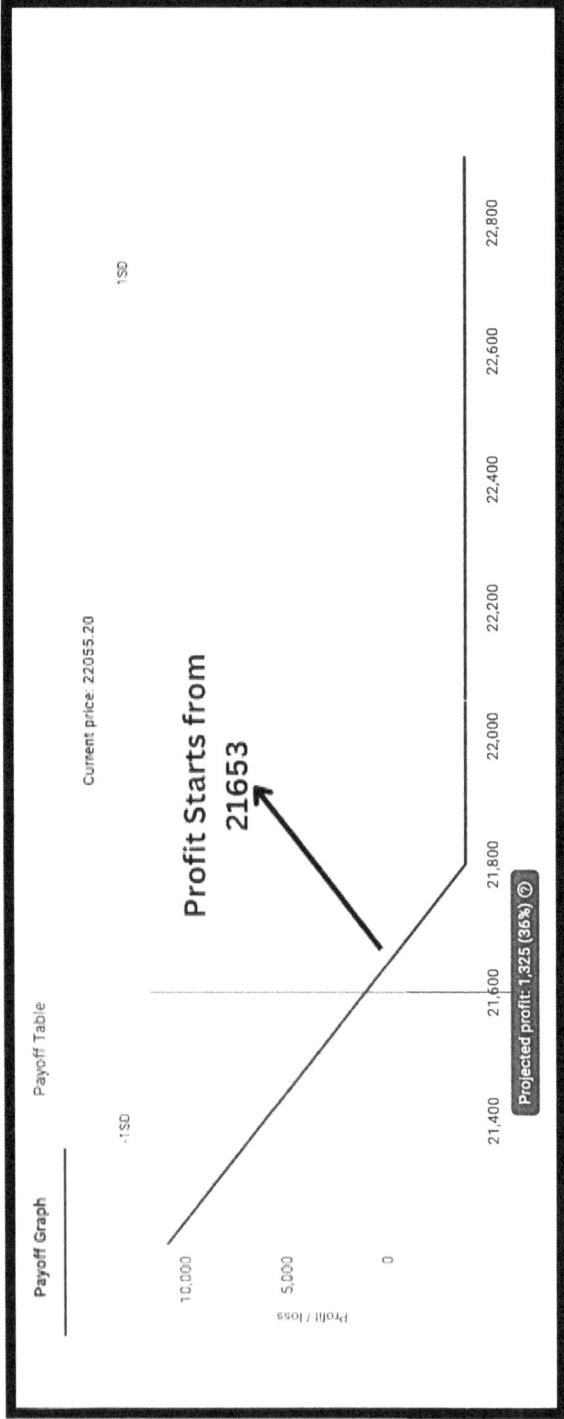

Image 4.8: Payout graph of Nifty 21,600 PE

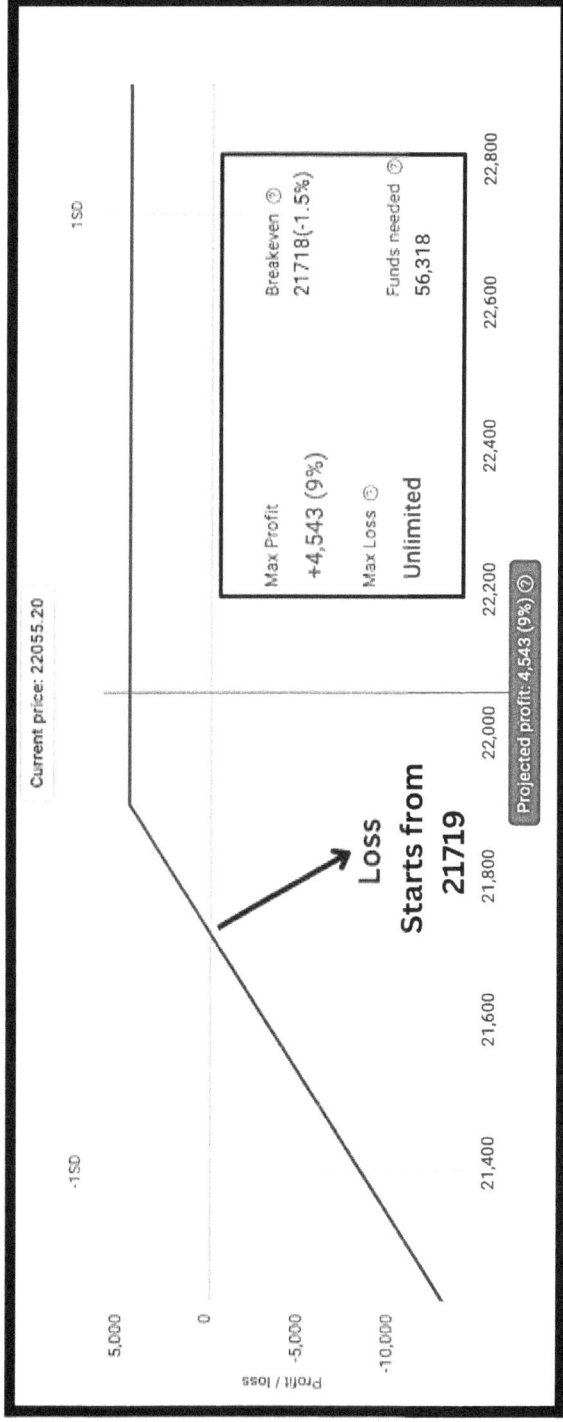

Image 4.9: Payout graph of Nifty 21, 900 PE (options selling)

Case 2

Another trader sells Nifty 21,800 PE at 147 (image 4.10). In this case, this trader needs Rs 53,875 to sell 1 lot of Nifty 21,800 PE (25 quantity).

Capital needed is Rs 53,875

Maximum profit is Rs 3,675 if Nifty expires above 21,800.

Loss starts from 21,653 (strike price 21,800, premium collected 147 points)

Maximum return on the capital (if Nifty closes above 21,900) is 7%

There is a trade-off between profitability (ROI) and success rate when selling put options. Here is a breakdown.

Selling puts close to the money (ATM)

i.   **Higher ROI potential:** Since the strike price is near the current market price, the premium you collect for selling the put option is generally higher. This translates to a potentially larger ROI if the stock price stays above the strike price by expiry.

ii. **Lower success rate:** There is a greater chance of the put option being exercised by the buyer if the stock price dips even slightly below the strike. This is because the put becomes very valuable for the buyer.

Selling puts far out-of-the-money (OTM)

i.   **Lower ROI potential:** The premium you receive for selling a put with a strike price far below the current market price is generally lower. This limits your potential return.

ii. **Higher success rate:** The put option becomes valuable to the buyer only if the stock price falls significantly below

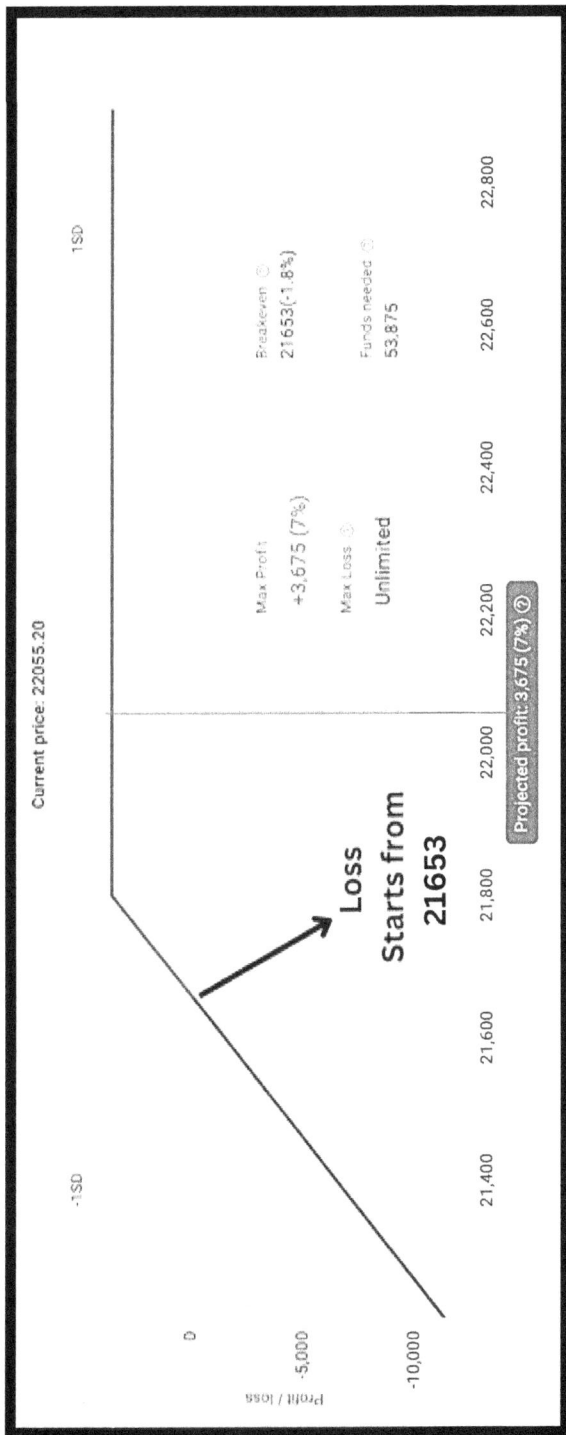

Image 4.10: Payout graph of Nifty 21,800 PE (options selling)

the strike price by expiry. Since this is a less likely scenario, there is a higher chance of the option expiring worthless, capturing your premium as profit.

You need to delve deeper to truly navigate the world of advanced options strategies. Understanding options greeks and how they interact with option moneyness (ITM, ATM, and OTM) will be your compass.

So, you can study these topics in the subsequent chapters and then dive into advanced options strategies.

5

OPTIONS GREEKS MADE SIMPLE—WHAT YOU NEED TO KNOW

During an options trading workshop, the trainer was explaining options greeks, and a participant suddenly interrupted him and asked a question.

Participant: "Sir, many traders say there is no need to learn options greeks. They advise keeping trading simple and not using these options greeks while taking trades in options. What are your thoughts about this?"

Trainer: "A good question. I want to take a simple example to explain this. So, I need to ask a few questions. Are you okay with answering those questions?"

Participant: "Sure sir, please go ahead."

Trainer: "Where is your native place?"

Participant: "I am basically from Naregalla, a small village in North Karnataka. But now I have settled in Bangalore."

Trainer: "Good. Let us say one person from your village plans to sell his house, and you also plan to buy a house in your native place. How would you proceed?"

Participant: "It is simple sir. We will finalise the price in front of 2–3 people from the same village and then register the house by paying the agreed upon amount."

Trainer: "Okay, now let us assume you plan to buy a flat in Bangalore. What are the precautions you take?"

(Answered after thinking for some time)

Participant: "I will verify the builders' reputation and all the papers with lawyers. I will also check with friends who stay in the same locality, and whether the flat comes within my budget or not."

Trainer: "Interesting, you did not take all these precautions when you planned to buy a house in your native place. But you are taking all these precautions to buy a flat in Bangalore. Why?"

Participant: "In my village, I know most people, and nobody dares to cheat a person. But buying a flat in Bangalore has some risks, so I take all the precautions."

Trainer: "Wonderful! A similar logic applies to options greeks as well. If you aim to buy only options, then knowing greeks may not be necessary. But if you desire to step up your game, learning options greeks is a must. In fact, naked option buyers also should know option greeks because time decay works against them, and they should know how to mitigate it."

Participant: "I got your point sir; now I am curious to learn options greeks."

1. Delta

It measures the rate of change of options premium concerning change in the underlying price. In simple words, how much does the option premium go up or down as the price underlying security goes up or down.

Delta is one of the important greeks and appears as a decimal number. It varies between 0 to 1 for call options and the premiums of the call options are expected to go up as the price of the underlying security goes up.

Delta varies between -1 to 0 for put options and the premiums of the put options are expected to go up as the price of the underlying security goes down.

For example,

Nifty is trading at 17,400.

17,450 call option (CE) premium is at 80.

Delta of 17,450 CE is '**0.5**'

It means if Nifty moves upside by 20 points, then premium of the 17,450 CE will go up by 10 points (50% move) that is, the premium will be at 90.

2. Gamma

It is the change in option delta per unit change in the underlying security. In simple words, it measures the rate of change of delta. Gamma varies between 0 to 1.

Let us take the same example of Nifty 17,450 CE. The gamma of 17,450 CE is 0.10. It means if Nifty goes up by 10 points, then the delta of 17,450 CE goes up by 1.

If the gamma is high, delta is highly sensitive to option prices. Among OTM, ITM, and ATM options, ATM options will have the highest gamma as their delta is most sensitive to small changes in the underlying asset's price.

Gamma is a beneficial tool for options traders because delta value can change over time. So if you find two trading instruments with the same delta, then a look at gamma will help you decide which trading instrument to choose (low gamma instrument if you are an options seller and high gamma instrument if you are an options buyer).

3. Theta

It measures the impact on the option premium concerning the time remaining for expiry. It describes how much the option premium changes every day until expiry. Theta will always be a negative number as options premiums lose their value as the expiry date comes close.

An options instrument with a theta of -10 would decrease by an average of 10 rupees every day (assuming all other parameters are constant).

We will take the same Nifty 17, 450 CE and the premium of 17,450 CE is 80.

The theta of 17,450 CE is −10. It means every day the premium of 17,450 CE will come down by 10 points (first day it will be 70, second day it will be 60, etc.) assuming all other parameters remain constant.

4. Vega

It is the rate of change in the premium concerning change in the volatility. If the option's vega is high (either positive or negative), the option premium values are highly sensitive to any changes in the volatility.

In simple words, it measures how much the option premium value changes based on a 1% change in the volatility of the underlying instrument.

If vega increases, the premium of both the call options and put options will increase.

5. Rho

It measures the rate of change concerning interest rate. In simple words, it measures the rate of change in an option's premium value based on a 1% change in the interest rate.

For example, if an option instrument has a rho of .25, then the value of the option would increase or decrease by an average of 25 cents when the interest rate increases or decreases by 1%.

6

THREE TYPES OF STRIKE PRICES, DEBUNKED IN THREE MINUTES

A few years ago, I was part of a small group of intraday traders. We would sit together during live market hours and take trades together. We would discuss our views and ideas with each other.

I shared my view on Nifty one expiry day, and took the corresponding trade with options. We all shared the same view on Nifty, and hence, most of us took trades in the same direction.

Nifty moved as we expected, and most of us profited that day. However, one group member told us that he took the same trade but made losses.

When we checked his trade, we realised that he had taken one leg far away from the strike price, and Nifty closed below his strike price. Hence, his trade ended with a loss instead of giving profits.

We took this as an opportunity to discuss the different strike price types and how they can impact our trading results.

Image 6.1: Option Moneyness

ITM, ATM, and OTM are terms used to describe the relationship between a security's market price and its strike price.

The terms in-the-money (ITM), at-the-money (ATM), and out-of-the-money (OTM) refer to the relative position of the asset's current market price in relation to its strike price.

    i.   If the current market price of an underlying asset is higher than its strike price, then it is considered ITM (for calls).
   ii.   If it is lower than its strike price, then it is OTM (for calls).
  iii.   If it is equal to its strike price, then the option or derivatives contract is said to be ATM (for both calls and puts).

For example, if Nifty spot current market price is 17,000, then:

- Nifty 16,500 CE is in the in-the-money (ITM) option
- Nifty 17,000 CE is at-the-money (ATM) option and
- Nifty 17,500 CE is out-of-the-money (OTM) option.

For put options (PE), it works a bit differently. If Nifty Bank spot is at 35,000, then:

- Bank Nifty 35,500 PE is in-the-money (ITM) option
- Bank Nifty 35,000 PE is at-the-money (ATM) option and
- Bank Nifty 34,500 PE is out-of-the-money (OTM) option.

INTRINSIC VALUE

It is nothing but the value of the option that the option buyer makes from the option.

Call option (CE) Intrinsic value = Spot price – Strike Price

Put option (PE) Intrinsic value = Strike Price – Spot price

Intrinsic value of an option is always either zero or a positive number and it is never a negative number.

For example, Nifty spot is trading at 17,425, the strike price is 17,400 CE, and you have the right to exercise this option.

Hence,

Intrinsic value = Spot price – strike price

$$= 17,425 - 17,400$$
$$= 25 \text{ points.}$$

Therefore, if you exercise this option contract, you would make a profit of Rs 25 (ignoring other factors).

In the same example, if you take 17,500 CE, it will not have any intrinsic value.

Image 6.2 shows cashflow variations for ITM, ATM, and OTM for call options.

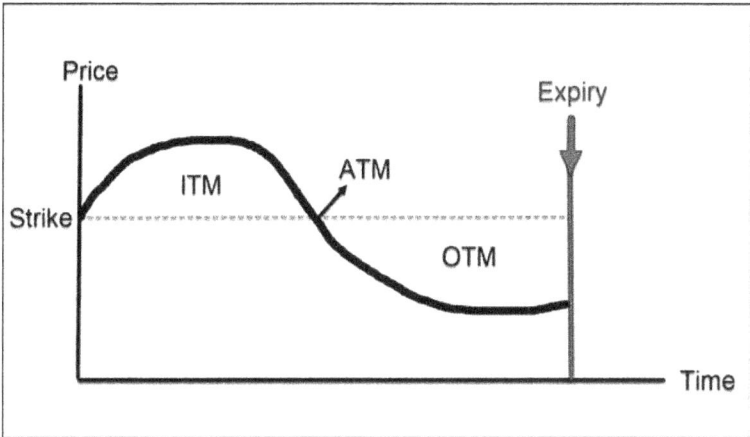

Image 6.2: ITM, ATM, OTM for Call Option (CE)

Image 6.3 shows cashflow variations for ITM, ATM, and OTM for put options.

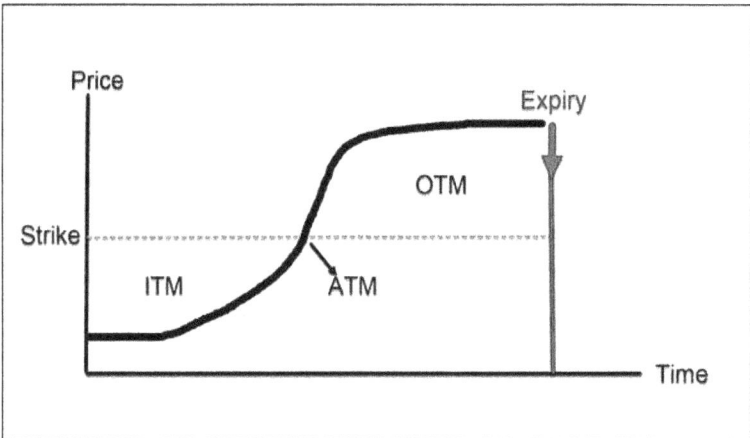

Image 6.3: ITM, ATM, OTM for Put Option (PE)

IN-THE-MONEY (ITM) OPTION

ITM option results in positive cash flow to the holder (due to positive intrinsic value) if it is exercised immediately.

For CE: When the spot price is higher than the strike price.
For PE: When the spot price is lower than the strike price.

AT-THE-MONEY (ATM) OPTION

ATM option results in zero cash flow to the holder if it is exercised immediately.

For CE: When the spot price = strike price.
For PE: When the spot price = strike price.

OUT-OF-THE-MONEY (OTM) OPTION

OTM option results in negative cash flow to the holder (no intrinsic value) if it is exercised immediately.

For CE: When the spot price is lower than the strike price.
For PE: When the spot price is higher than the strike price.

OTM options have no intrinsic value and are entirely dependent on the security's price movement in the direction of the option before expiry. Generally, OTM options are the least expensive of the three types of options, as they have the lowest probability of being profitable (buying perspective).

In conclusion, understanding how ITM, ATM, and OTM options affect your trading strategy is critical to making better trading decisions and maximising your returns.

- ITM options provide you with immediate profits but come with a higher upfront cost.
- ATM options allow you to profit from both upward and downward price movements but have a lower probability of being profitable.
- OTM options are the least expensive but come with a high risk of loss.

HOW ITM, ATM AND OTM OPTIONS IMPACT YOUR TRADING

Options trading strategies can be complex, and it is important to understand the impact of different options strike prices on your overall strategy.

In-the-money (ITM) options are typically more expensive than out-of-the-money (OTM) or at-the-money (ATM) options because they offer greater potential gains. Many traders use ITM options when they expect strong movement in either direction in an asset's price; therefore, these options are often used as part of directional trading strategies.

OTM options are less expensive than their ITM counterparts, but they offer a lower probability of profit. OTM options are typically used when traders expect minimal movement in an asset's price and want to buy insurance on their position at a lower cost than that of ITM options.

Let us take a simple example to understand these concepts in a practical manner.

Image 6.4 is the Nifty 15-min chart. We will make two assumptions to know OTM, ITM and ATM in a better way.

1. Three different traders plan to opt for a **short trade** at 11.30 a.m.
2. Today is weekly expiry day.

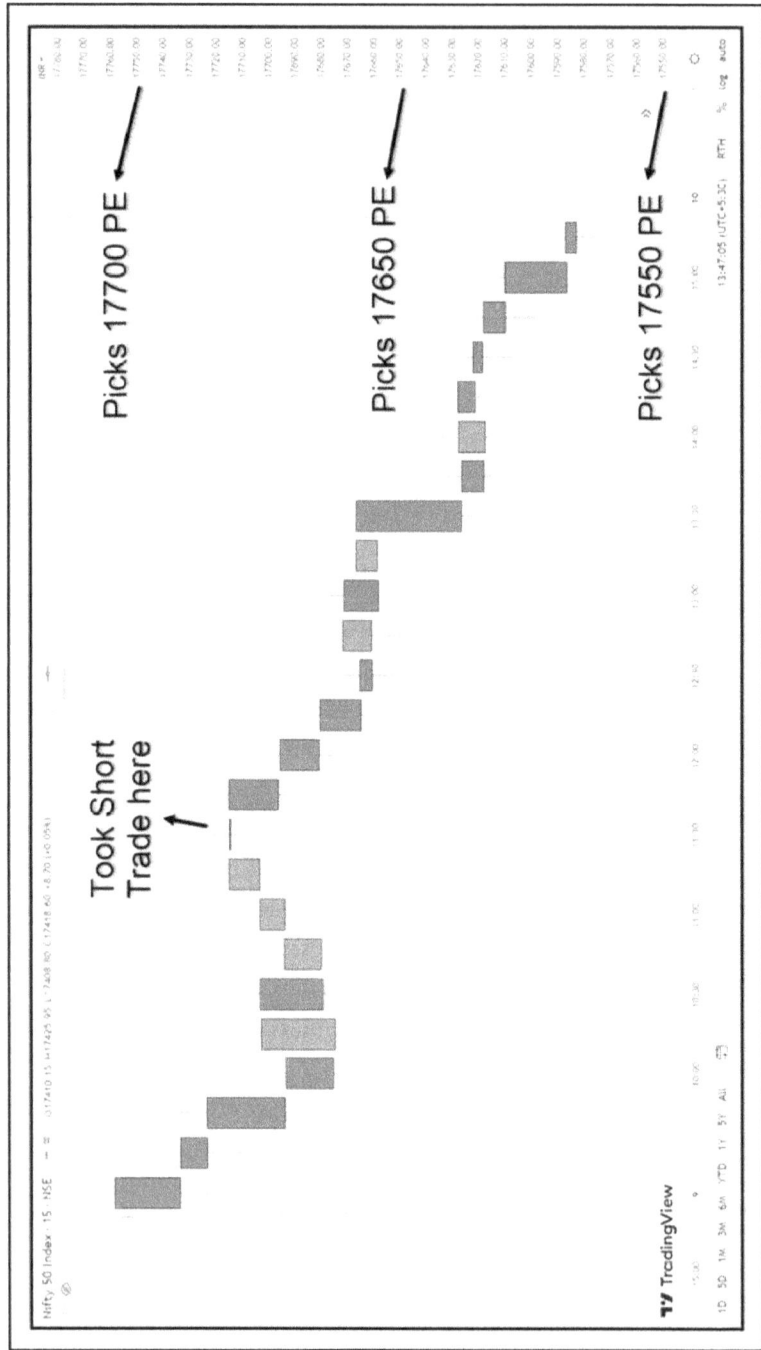

Image 6.4: Impact of strike prices in trading

Trader 1 decides to buy 17,700 PE (in-the-money option) at 160.

Trader 2 decides to buy 17,650 PE (slight out-of-the-money option) at 80.

Trader 3 decides to buy 17,550 PE (deep out-of-the-money option) at 20.

Nifty fell over 130 points in their expected direction.

However, do you think all these traders made profit?

Only trader 1 will make profits and both trader 2 and trader 3 end up making losses.

Because trader 1 has bought ITM options, the impact of time decay is less and delta is high. Hence, he benefitted from the fall.

Trader 2 has bought slight OTM options. The impact of time decay is high and delta is medium with this option. Hence, most of the advantage gained by the fall (delta advantage) will be negated by the erosion of time decay. So he will make a breakeven or a very small amount of profits.

Trader 3 bought deep OTM options. The impact of time decay is very high and delta is less with this option. Also price closed above his strike price. Hence he will lose all the premium amount in this trade.

7

OPTIONS BUYING VS. OPTIONS SELLING

Ajay and Vijay were colleagues in an IT company. Both were passionate about trading. They attended a few trading workshops together and started to take trades simultaneously.

Ajay was attracted to options buying as a single good trade can bring massive profits. In contrast, Vijay was fascinated with the high success rate of options selling. So, Ajay started to take option buying trades with stock options in monthly options, and Vijay began to write weekly options with Nifty and Nifty Bank.

Once in a while, Ajay made enormous profits, and would share the details with Vijay only when he made profits. But Vijay made small profits on most days, and he was a bit reluctant to share this with Ajay thinking this was a small profit compared to his.

After a few days, Ajay started to buy weekly options in Nifty. The liquidity was good with indices in weekly options, but he still could not replicate the same success which he had with monthly options in stocks. Even a small sideways move in Nifty hit his stop-loss. He tried his level best but lost all his trading capital in a few days.

Vijay continued with weekly options selling trades, but big profits like Ajay's was what he wanted to get. However, he was not able to figure out how to make such profits in selling options.

With this thought process, one day, he was bullish on Nifty Bank and sold put options in Nifty Bank. He was sure about the movement and did not place a stop-loss for his trade in the system.

After a while, he went to attend an office meeting. When he returned, Nifty Bank fell over 2% from his entry price, which wiped out most of his trading capital.

WHO IS RIGHT—OPTIONS BUYER OR OPTIONS SELLER?

When it comes to options buying, traders will pay a small premium for the right to purchase an underlying asset at a pre-agreed strike price. If the price moves quickly in their anticipated direction, they make big profits. In all other cases, they lose money.

On the other side of the coin, when it comes to options selling, sellers take on the opposite side of the contract and accept a small premium for giving up their right to buy or sell an underlying asset at the predetermined price. Hence, they make money when the price moves sideways or in the direction they expect it to move. They lose money only when the underlying instrument moves big quickly in a short period of time.

In the story, Ajay became greedy and started to buy weekly options. The impact of time decay is high with weekly options (compared to monthly options) and he was not equipped enough to deal with it.

Vijay was making small profits with his option selling trades. But he turned greedy for more profits like Ajay. Besides, he also made the mistake of not placing a stop-loss in the system. He ignored the fact that option selling comes with infinite risk (if we do not hedge or place stop-loss) and paid a heavy price for his mistake.

Options buying and options selling both have their own set of risks and rewards, so it is crucial to thoroughly understand each strategy before entering any contract. In addition, understanding how different factors can affect options premiums is also essential for success in this arena.

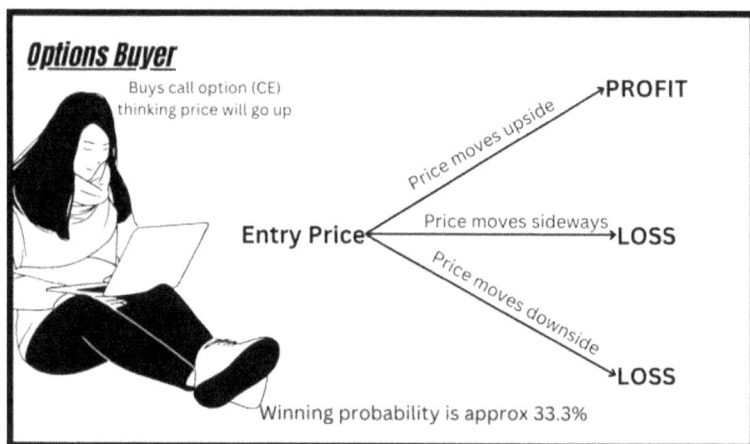

Image 7.1: Winning probability in options buying

Let us assume a person is bullish on a scrip and decides to buy the call option of that underlying instrument. In this case, they will make profits only when the price moves quickly upside. In the remaining cases, such as sideways and downside, they will lose money. So we can say that the winning probability with options buying is approximately 33.33% (1 out of 3). It also varies slightly based on the technical concept they deploy to manage their trades.

Image 7.2 is the 15 min chart for Nifty Financial Services (spot) on 14 March 2023 (expiry day). Before that, it was in a downtrend. So you plan to opt for a short trade after seeing the bearish pin bar (second candle). A bearish pin bar is a candlestick pattern that shows a small body at the bottom of the price range, with a long upper wick, signalling a potential reversal to the downside. It indicates

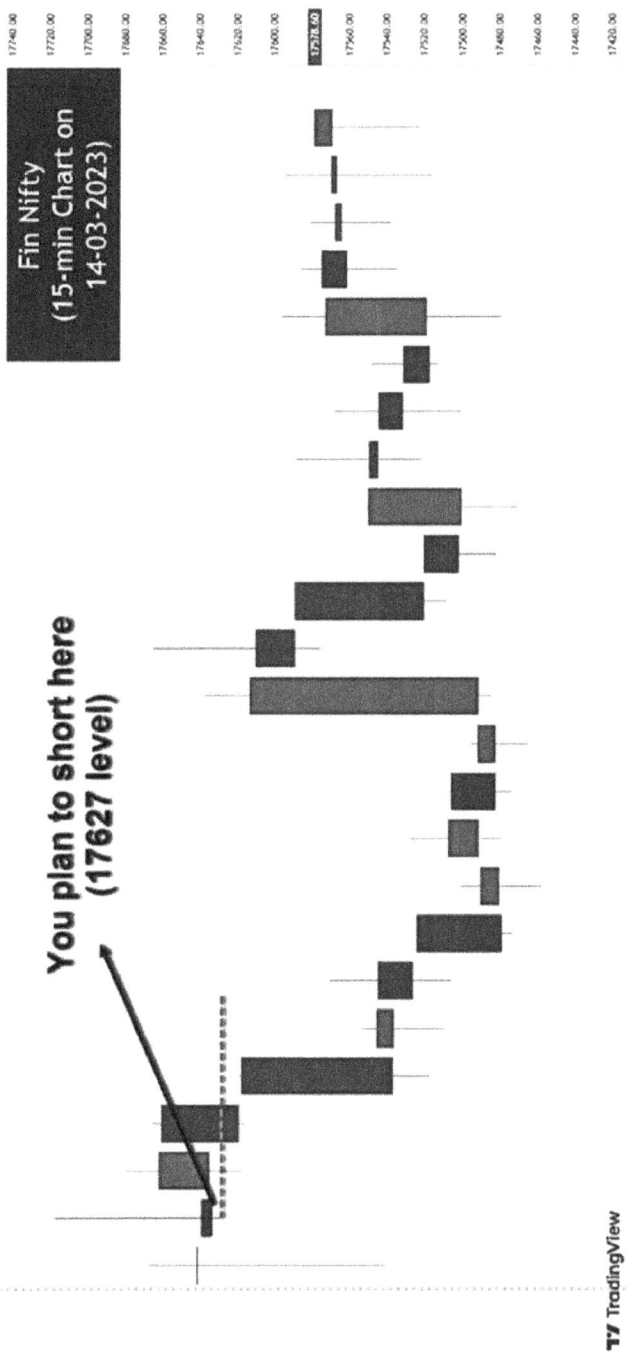

Image 7.2: Option buying for Nifty Financial Services

that buyers tried to push the price up but were overpowered by sellers, suggesting a shift in momentum.

Nifty Financial Services was trading around 17,627 at that time. You plan to buy 17,500 put options anticipating you make some profits.

When you decide to take entry, 17,500 PE was trading at 21.5. Nifty Financial Services (spot) fell immediately after your entry, but later moved in a sideways direction (image 7.2). It moved 49 points downwards and you hope to make some profits.

Now observe the 17,500 PE chart carefully (image 7.3). From your entry price 21.5, it moved to zero when the market was closed. It means even though the price moved in your direction by 49 points, you made a loss in this trade. Herein lies the risk with options buying. You make profits only when the price displays a quick move in the expected direction. In the above trade, you would have made some profits only when Nifty Financial Services closed below 17,478.5 (17,500 strike price with a 21.5 premium that you paid).

For the same example of a long trade, another trader is also bullish on the scrip which may be a stock or security. But instead of buying call options, he sells put options.

In such a scenario, he will make profits if the price goes up. He will also make profits when the price moves sideways (due to time decay). He will lose money only when the price moves downside. So we can say that the winning probability with options selling is approximately 66.66% (2 out of 3, as shown in image 7.4). Success rate also varies based on the technical concept he deploys to manage his trades.

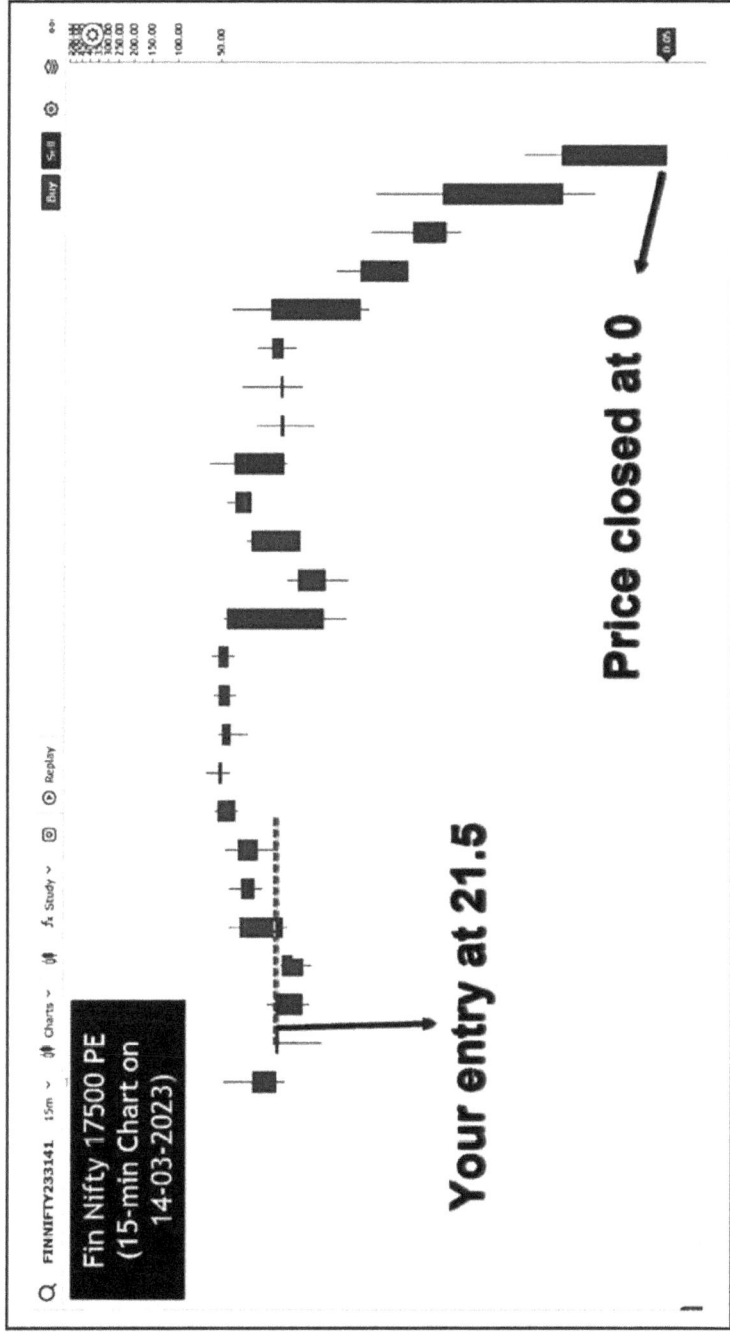

Image 7.3: Option buying trade result for Nifty Financial Services

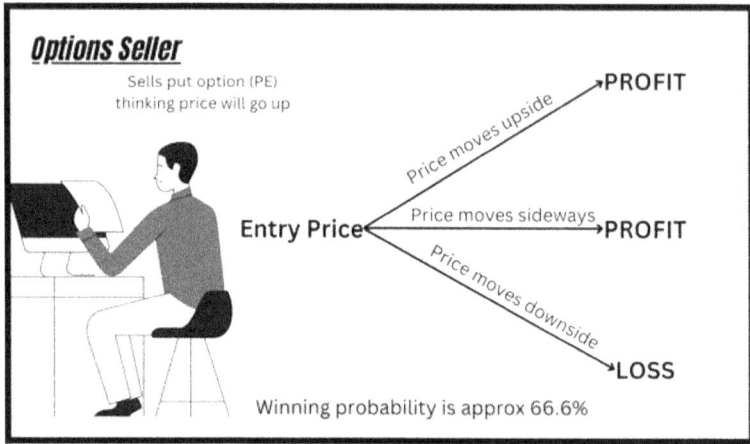

Image 7.4: Winning probability in options selling

Let us take the same example of Nifty Financial Services (image 7.2). An option seller turns bearish exactly after seeing the bearish pinbar. But he decides to sell call options (CE), instead of buying put options (PE) (image 7.5).

He will sell 17,600 CE at 75.

In this case, Nifty Financial Services moves only 49 points in the expected direction. But the premium of 17,600 CE becomes zero when the market closes. So time decay worked in your favour.

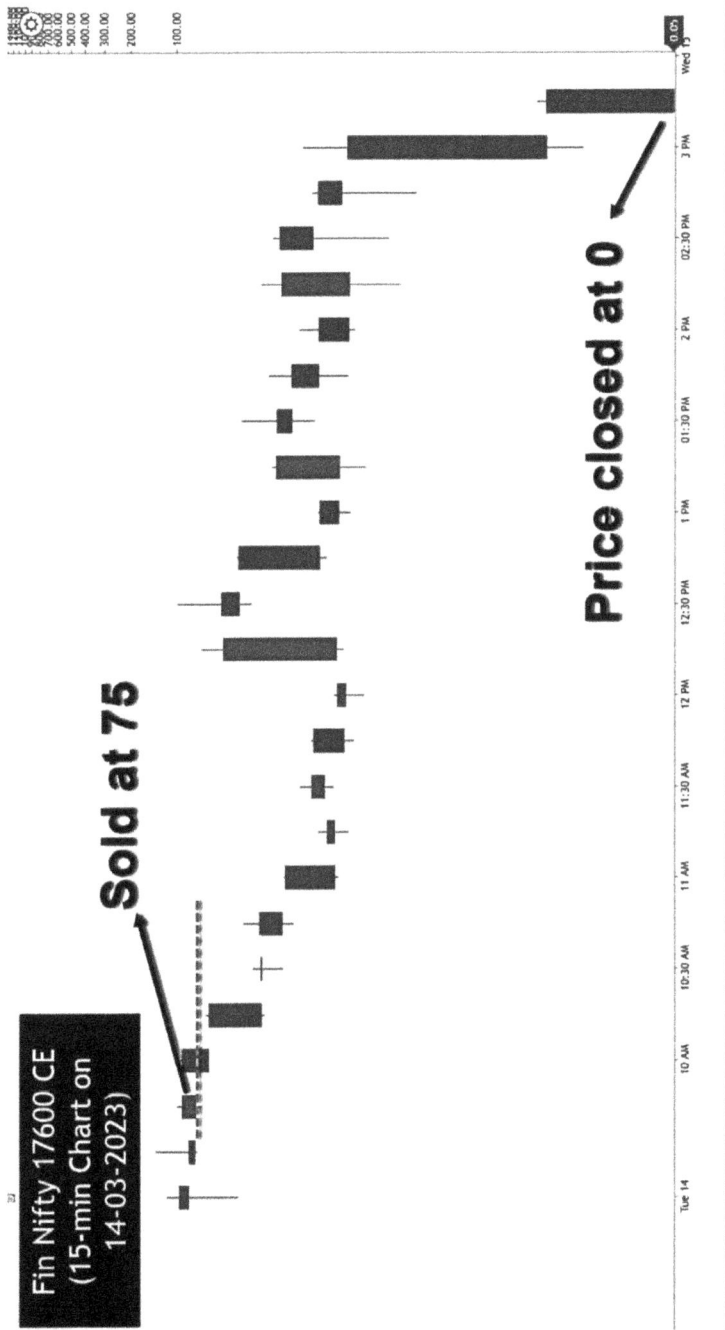

Fin Nifty 17600 CE (15-min Chart on 14-03-2023)

Sold at 75

Price closed at 0

Image 7.5: Options selling example result in Nifty Financial Services

OPTIONS BUYING VS. OPTIONS SELLING

Let us assume you are an amateur boxer who started to learn boxing six months earlier. A national-level boxing championship is happening, and you have registered for the event. The boxing championship schedule is announced, and you face the previous year's champion in your first match.

How do you feel?

If you feel fear in your heart or are dead scared for your first match, do not worry; you are a normal person. But if you are not scared, then either you are stupid or overconfident about your abilities.

> "Champions aren't made in gyms. Champions are made from something they have deep inside them—a desire, a dream, a vision. They have to have the skill, and the will. But the will must be stronger than the skill."
>
> —Mohammed Ali (1942–2016)

Even if you are scared, you want to prepare well and give tough competition to the last champion. If you have a good coach, do you know the aspects he will focus on training you more apart from your regular workout routines?

He will focus on two main aspects—the champion opponent's strength and weakness. If the champion's strength is uppercut, then your coach will deploy an hour in your workout schedule for you to face and block only uppercut. This practice builds muscle memory and helps you stand against the opponent for a long time. Similarly, suppose your champion lost matches after facing a solid hook punch by an opponent, your coach will ask you to practise more hook punches as it increases the probability of winning against the champion. The rest depends on your practice, willpower, and presence of mind to execute these tactics in the match.

You might lose or win the match, but if you practised according to the strength and weaknesses of the champion, there is a high possibility that you will be able to give them tough competition in the game.

Now let us come back to options trading.

Before picking options for buying or selling, have you studied their strengths and weaknesses?

Let us discuss options buying first, as most people prefer trading in this style.

What are the advantages of options buying?

1. It helps you to make more profits compared to any other trading instrument (higher ROI).
2. You know how much money you are going to lose if the trade idea fails.

Because of these two advantages, most people straightaway jump into options buying, ignoring the negative aspects of trading with it.

Then what are the disadvantages of options buying?

1. There is no such thing as an ideal exit.
2. Time decay always works against you.

Managing exits in options buying

For some reason you decide to buy Nifty 16,900 CE at Rs 134.5 (as shown in image 7.6). In this case, you do not know how far the premium can go on the upside. Based on the Nifty spot movement and volatility, it can go to 500, 1,000, 2,000, or even higher.

If a person has sold 16,900 CE at Rs 134.5, then they can plan to hold only until the premium becomes zero. In this case (option selling), the target is very clear.

So nobody can define an ideal exit for option buying trades. Each exit with option buying trades brings some emotions. After some time, your mind will get messed up with different thought processes, and you will commit more mistakes. The only solution to this problem is to define your exit mechanism so that it brings the least disturbances, irrespective of any move. You could opt for any one of the following strategies for your exit rule:

   i. It can be a 1:2 or 1:3 risk-reward ratio exit.
  ii. Carry all the positions with trailing stop-loss.
 iii. Book profits for 50% position at 1:2 risk-reward ratio and carry the remaining 50% position with trailing stop-loss.

After defining your exit rule, you must follow it for all your options buying trades religiously.

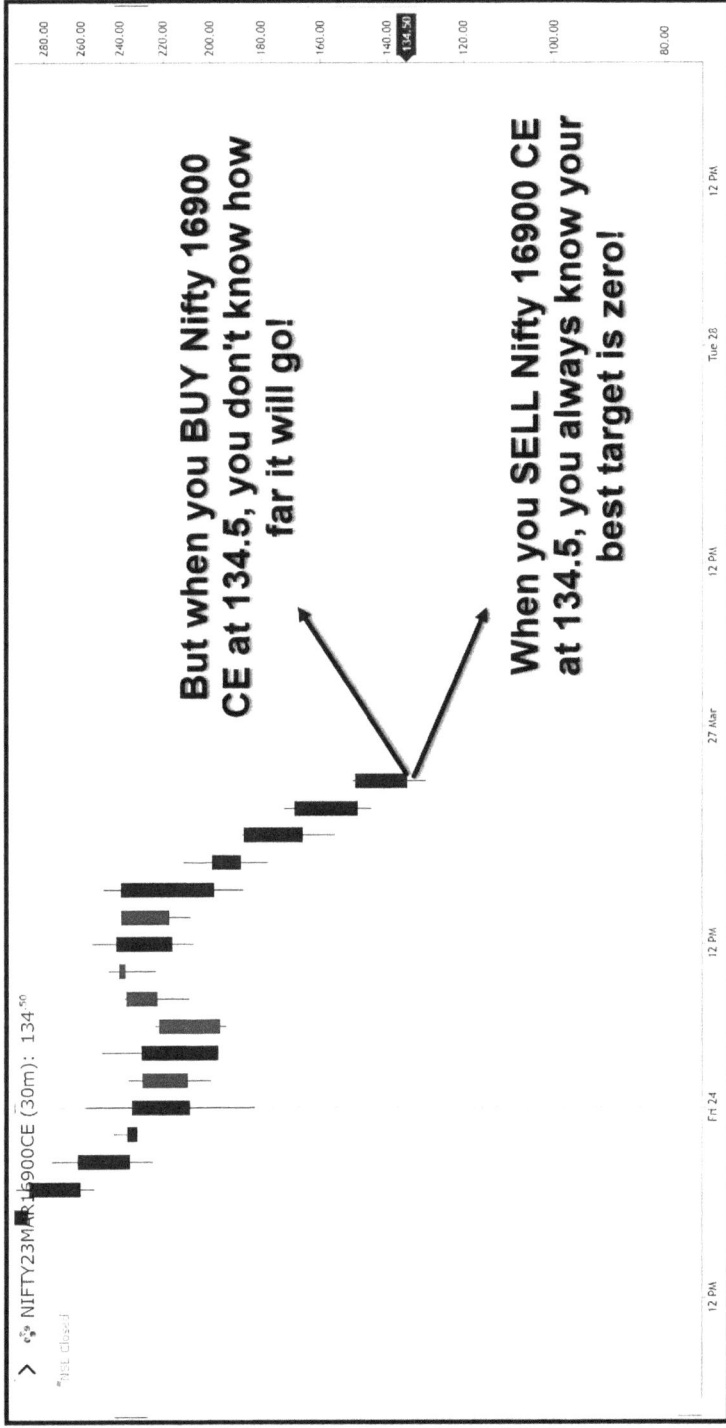

Image 7.6: Exit in options buying vs. options selling

Managing time decay in options buying

Image 7.7 shows the 15-min charts of the Nifty spot chart and corresponding option chart Nifty 17,000 PE on 24 March 2023.

After the first candle's formation, let us assume you turn bearish and plan to take a short trade. The first candle closed at 17,020. So, you plan to take the nearest strike 17,000 PE. In simple terms, you buy 17,000 PE hoping you make good profits.

Your trade logic fails when the Nifty spot trades above the first candle's high because you had a bearish view in the first candle and price trading above the high of the first candle negates the bearish view . But the price did not break the first candle high throughout the day and fell rapidly in the second half.

But if you observe the Nifty 17,000 PE chart, the price traded below the first candle's low a few times. If you kept stop-loss at the low of the first candle, then it would get hit a few times. This is due to the time decay impact. Remember, time decay always works against options buyers. So if you are an options buyer, you need to design your trading system so that it will possess quick entry and exit.

Also, please note, 24 March 2023, Friday is the first day of the weekly options. On the first day, the impact of the time decay will be less. Its impact will be aggressive close to expiry (Wednesday and Thursday).

Now we move on to options selling.

What are the advantages of options selling?

1. Accuracy will be higher with options selling.
2. Time decay always works in favour of options writers (sellers).

Most trades only observe these points and they do not prepare well for negative aspects of options selling.

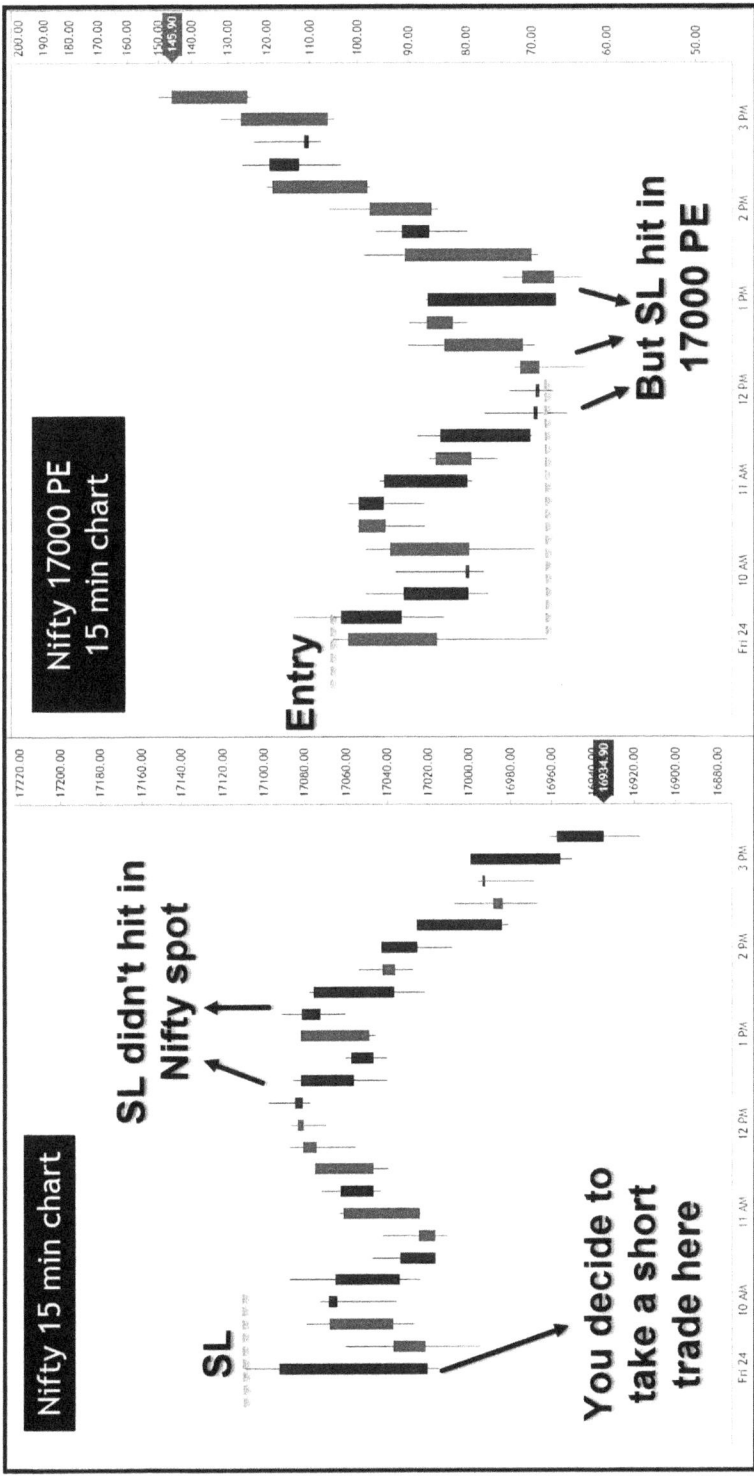

Image 7.7: Time decay impact in options buying trade

Then what are the two disadvantages of options selling?

1. Even though it has good accuracy, the profits are always smaller (less ROI).
2. You could lose more money if the price moves against you and you have not kept a stop-loss in the system, or in case of no hedging.

How to deal with less ROI

It is an open fact that options selling results in lower profits (lower ROI) compared to options buying. This is because when you sell an option, you receive a premium upfront, but your potential profit is limited to the premium you received. Also, your potential losses can be substantial.

However, there are several ways to deal with this and potentially increase your profits:

1. **Sell options with a lower strike price:** If you sell options with a strike price that is close to the current market price (1–2 legs away OTM instead of far OTM), you can receive a higher premium, increasing your potential profits. For example, if Nifty current market price is 24,000, then selling 24,050 or 24,100 call option would bring more returns compared to selling 24,300 call option (if the view on Nifty is bearish).
2. **Sell options with a longer expiration date:** Options with a more extended expiration date generally have a higher premium, which can increase your potential profits.
3. **Use strategies that combine options selling and buying:** For example, you could use a covered call strategy, which involves buying a stock and selling a call option against it (explained in detail in chapter 9). This can limit your potential losses and increase your potential profits.

Overall, while options selling can sometimes result in lower profits compared to option buying, there are strategies you can use to increase your earnings and manage your risk potential.

How to deal with unlimited loss

When selling options, there is always a risk of unlimited losses if the underlying asset's price moves significantly against you. However, there are several strategies you can use to manage this risk:

1. **Use stop-loss orders:** You can use stop-loss orders to automatically close out your position if the underlying asset's price moves against you. This can limit your losses to a predetermined amount.
2. **Set realistic profit targets:** When selling options, it is important to set realistic profit targets and close out your position once you have reached your target or keep trailing stop-loss at that level. This can help prevent you from holding on to a losing position for too long.
3. **Use hedging strategies:** You can use hedging strategies, such as buying options on the opposite side of the market or using futures contracts, to help offset the risk of unlimited losses.
4. **Monitor the trade closely:** It is important to monitor your options selling trades closely and be prepared to take action if the price of the underlying asset moves against you. This may involve closing out the position or adjusting your strategy.

Managing the risk of unlimited losses when selling options requires a combination of risk management strategies, position sizing, and carefully monitoring your trades.

WHY ARE MOST OPTIONS TRADERS OBSESSED WITH TIME DECAY?

Nowadays, most options traders are obsessed with time decay because it is a fundamental component of options pricing and plays a crucial role in weekly options.

Time decay, also known as theta, refers to the rate at which the value of an option decreases as the expiration date approaches. When you buy an option, time decay works against you as the value of the option decreases over time. However, when you sell an option, time decay works in your favour, as you can benefit from the decrease in the option's value.

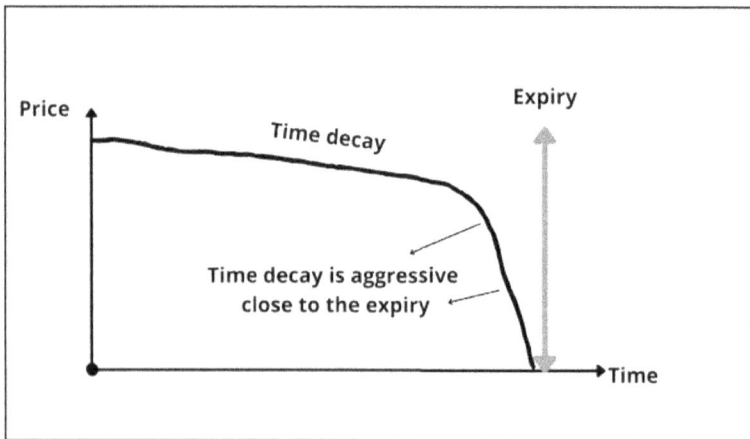

Image 7.8: Impact of time decay

As an option approaches its expiry, time decay accelerates. This means that the value of the option decreases at a faster rate, which can benefit options sellers who have chosen short options contracts.

If the underlying asset's price remains stable or moves in the options sellers' favour, they can benefit from the accelerated time decay and potentially realise a profit.

Overall, the role of time decay in options selling on the expiry day is crucial. Hence, many traders prefer to do only options selling on the expiry day (sometimes even one day before the expiry).

Hence, many weekly options expiry contracts are introduced in the market on different trading days as both the exchanges and government bodies aim to make more revenue.

Deciding whether to buy or sell options depends on your trading goals, risk tolerance, and mindset.

Here are some key points to consider when choosing between buying and selling options:

Options Buying

i. **Potential for unlimited profit:** When buying options, your potential profit is theoretically unlimited, as you can benefit from large moves in the underlying asset's price.

ii. **Limited risk:** The premium you pay is the most you can lose when buying an option.

iii. **More straightforward:** Buying options is generally considered a more straightforward strategy, as you only need to focus on the direction of the underlying asset's price movement.

iv. **Higher probability of losing trades:** When you buy options, you need the underlying asset's price to move in your favour before the option expires. This means your trades may have a higher probability of losing than winning.

Options Selling

i. **Limited profit potential:** When selling options, your potential profit is limited to the premium you received when selling the option.

ii. **Unlimited risk:** The most you can lose when selling an option is theoretically unlimited, as the underlying asset's price can move against you.

iii. **More complex:** Selling options is generally considered a more complicated strategy, as you must consider factors such as implied volatility and the greeks.

iv. **Higher probability of winning trades:** When you sell options, you can benefit from time decay and other factors that work in your favour. This means your trades may have a higher probability of winning than losing.

Both buying and selling options can be profitable strategies, depending on your trading goals and risk tolerance. It is essential to research, understand the risks involved, and develop a trading plan that suits your needs.

8

OPTIONS STRATEGIES FOR ALL MARKET CONDITIONS

In options trading, there are two main approaches—directional trading and non-directional trading. The choice between these two approaches depends on your individual goals and risk tolerance.

1. Directional Trading

This approach involves using options strategies to profit from a specific price movement of the underlying asset.

Trader's view: Traders have a firm conviction that the price will either go up (bullish) or down (bearish).

Options used: Directional strategies typically involve buying or selling calls, puts, spreads, etc.

Suitability: Traders with a strong conviction about the price movement and a willingness to take higher risk for potentially higher profits will find this approach more apt for their style.

2. Non-Directional Trading

This approach focuses on collecting premiums by selling options contracts, regardless of the direction the underlying asset's price takes.

Trader's view: Traders do not necessarily have a strong directional view of the price movement. They might believe the price will stay relatively flat or move within a specific range.

Options used: Non-directional strategies often involve selling options spreads (combinations of buying and selling options). Examples include short strangles, iron condors, and covered calls. An iron condor and a short straddle both involve selling options to profit from low volatility, but the key difference is that an iron condor has a defined risk by buying further out-of-the-money options, creating a limited loss potential. In contrast, a short straddle involves selling both a call and a put at the same strike price, which has unlimited risk if the price moves significantly in either direction.

Profit potential: Profits are generally lower than directional strategies but can be more consistent, especially in low-volatility markets.

Suitability: Traders who are comfortable with lower but more consistent profits and want to limit their risk exposure will find this approach beneficial.

A combination of both directional and non-directional strategies can offer decent profits in all market conditions.

Now, we will explore a range of options strategies, focusing on both directional and non-directional approaches. Directional strategies are designed to profit from price movements in a specific direction, while non-directional strategies aim to capitalise on price stability or low volatility.

BULL CALL SPREAD

Imagine you are moderately optimistic about a stock's future but not super bullish. You think it will go up a bit but not skyrocket. This is where the bull call spread comes in. It is like a two-legged bet that lets you profit from a gentle rise in the stock price, limiting your risk and capping your gains.

Here is how it works:

Buy a call option: You buy a call option with a strike price below or same as the current market price (ATM). This gives you the right, but not the obligation, to buy the stock at that lower price by expiry.

Sell a call option: You simultaneously sell another call option on the same stock with a higher strike price and the same expiry date. Think of it as a kind of hedge.

Key to trading profitably: You spend money upfront to buy the first call (debit) but recoup some of that cost by selling the second call (credit). The net cost is usually lower than buying a single call outright.

How you win: If the stock price goes up modestly but stays below the higher strike price you sold, you can still exercise your first (lower) call option and potentially buy the stock at a discount to sell it for a profit later or simply close the first (lower) call option to book profits.

Let us say a stock is currently trading at Rs 50. You buy a call option with a strike price of Rs 50 (long ATM call) for a premium of Rs 5. You sell a call option with a strike price of Rs 55 (short OTM call) for a premium of Rs 2. You actually paid a net of Rs 3 (Rs 5 – Rs 2) for this spread because you received a credit for selling the short call.

The outcome in different scenarios would be as follows:

i. **Stock goes to Rs 60:** Your long call is way in-the-money and would be worth more than Rs 50 if exercised. You would exercise the long call (buy the stock at Rs 50) and immediately sell it at Rs 60 for a profit. However, remember you also sold the short call at Rs 55, so you would be obligated to sell the stock at Rs 55, limiting your profit. In this scenario, your maximum profit would be Rs 2 (price increase(10) – net cost(3) – difference between strike prices(5)), which is capped by the difference between the strike prices of your options.

ii. **Stock stays below Rs 50:** Both options expire worthless, and you lose only the Rs 3 net cost of the spread.

iii. **Stock stays between Rs 50 and Rs 55, assume at Rs 53:** Your long call will be in-the-money and would be worth Rs 3 if exercised. But the short call will expire worthless and you will capture the complete premium of Rs 2 which you got earlier. So, you will be at break-even as you lost Rs 2 in long call and you captured Rs 2 in short call.

Here is the catch:

i. **Limited profits:** Since you sold the higher strike call, your profit is capped at the difference between the strike prices minus the net cost of the spread.

ii. **Time decay:** The longer you hold the spread, the more time value (potential profit) erodes from the options.

The bull call spread is a good strategy for traders who are cautiously optimistic about the stock and want to limit their risk while still participating in some potential upside.

Bull call spread in a nutshell

- Suitable for a moderately bullish outlook on the stock price.
- Limits your risk compared to buying the stock outright.
- Profits are capped, but losses are also limited.
- Strike selection for long and short calls are very important because the profit potential is highly dependent on the strike difference.

Case 1: Trade in Nifty

Let us take the same example of Nifty to see how this strategy works.

Assume a trader is moderately bullish on Nifty. So he can deploy these legs:

Buy 22,000 CE at 347
Sell 22,400 CE at 153

This strategy demands only Rs 19,779 capital per lot in Nifty. The maximum profit is Rs 5,149 when the Nifty reaches 22,400. No matter where the Nifty will expire above 22,400, this trader will only get Rs 5,149 as his profit (image 8.1).

Similarly maximum loss in this strategy is Rs 4,851 if the Nifty falls below 22,000.

Nifty current market price – 22,055

Strikes	21800	21900	22000	22100	22200	22300	22400
Calls	476	408	347	288	238	190	153
Puts	147	181	218.35	260	310	364	425

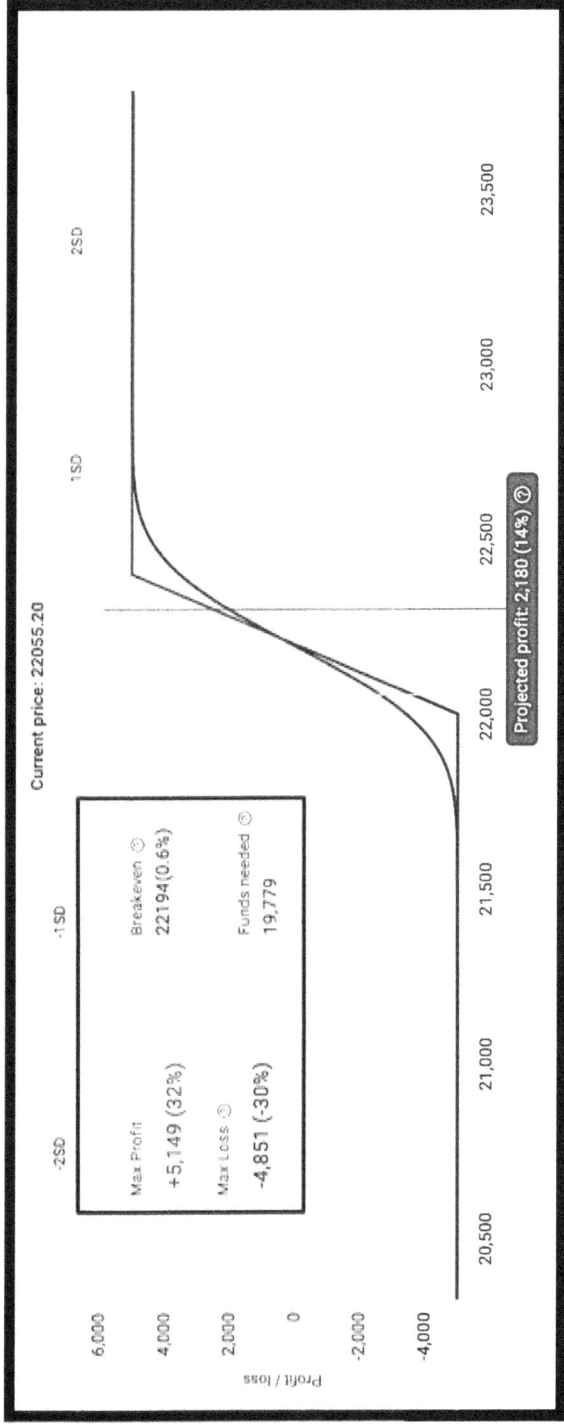

Image 8.1: Payout graph for bull call spread in Nifty

Case 2: Trade in Biocon

Image 8.2 shows the daily chart of Biocon compared with Nifty.

It is evident that Biocon performed better compared to Nifty in the past. Recently Nifty witnessed some fall, but Biocon displayed a complete sideways consolidation which indicates the strength of the investors in this stock.

So we can easily deploy bull call spread strategy for this stock.

Current Market Price (CMP) of Biocon is Rs 304.
Buy Biocon in May 2024 300 CE at Rs 15.6 and
Sell Biocon in May 2024 350 CE at Rs 2.2

To execute this trade, capital needed is Rs 92,585.

Profit starts when the price trades above 313.4 (15.6 – 2.2 + strike price 300).

The maximum profit is Rs 91,500 when the price starts to trade above 350 (image 8.3).

If the price stays exactly at the same level (Rs 304), then the trader will lose around Rs 23,002 and the maximum loss will be Rs 33,500 when the price moves below 300.

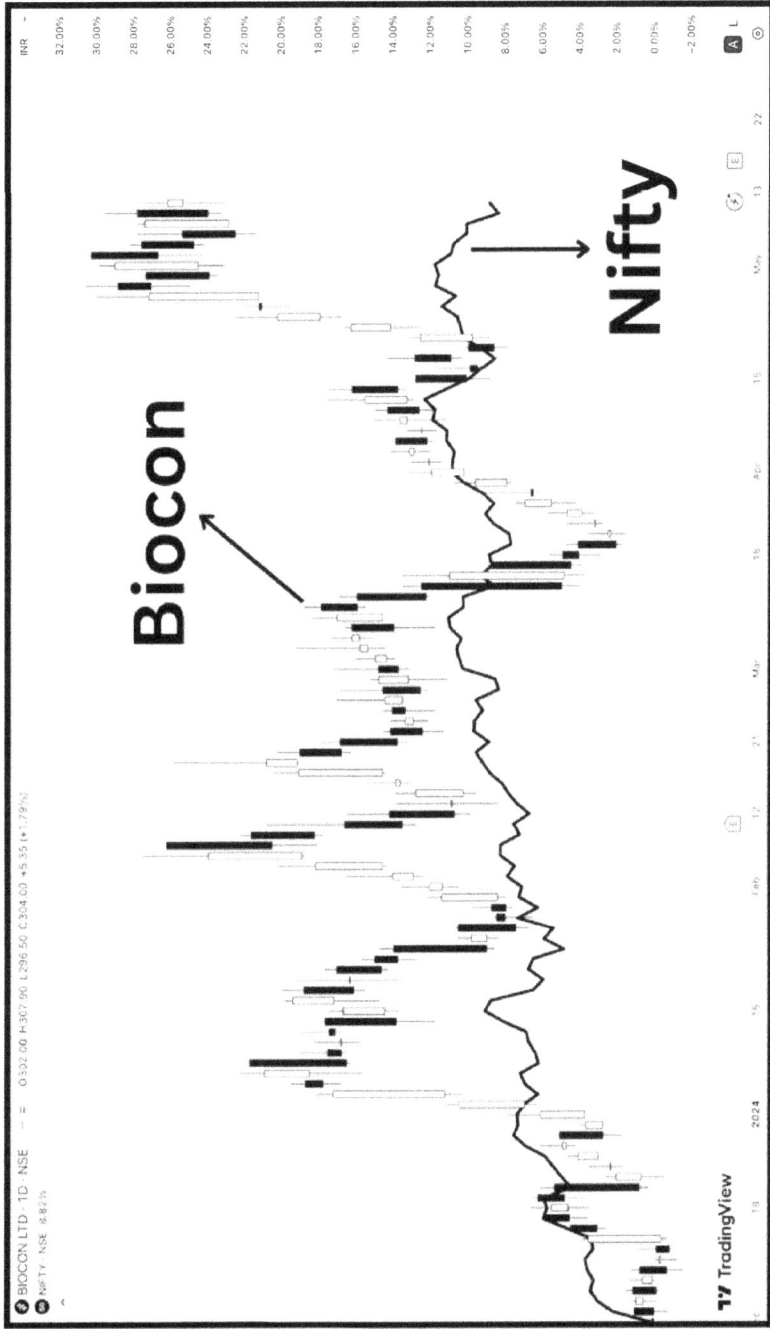

Image 8.2: Daily chart of Biocon Ltd. vs. Nifty

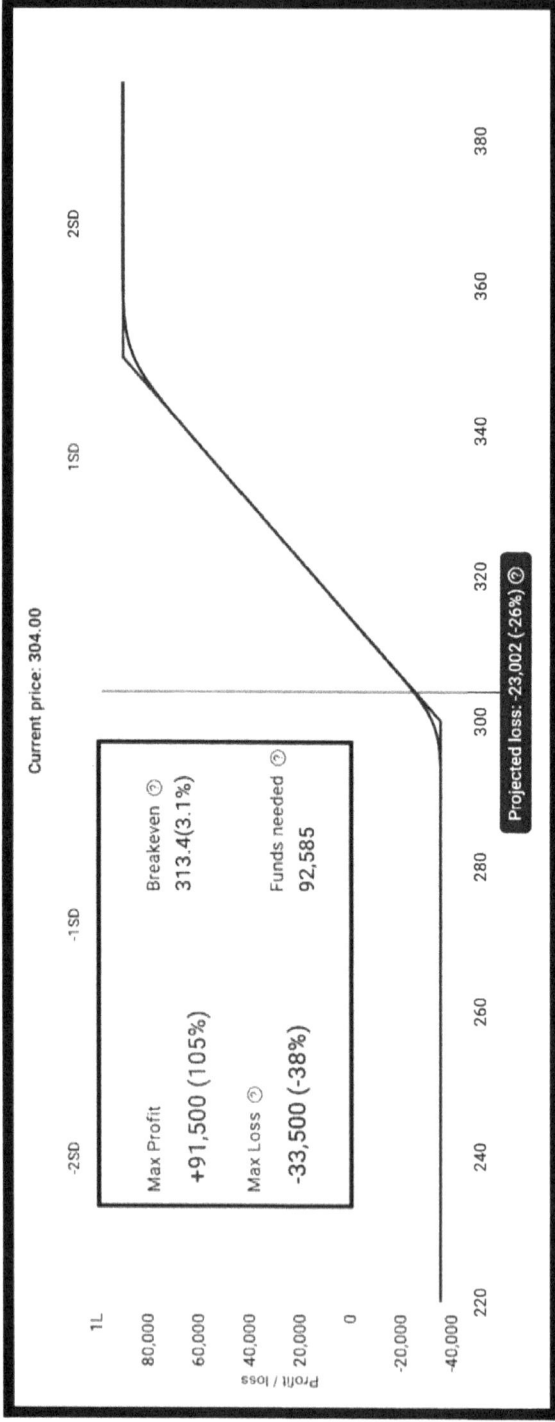

Image 8.3: Payout graph for Biocon showing a bull call spread

BEAR PUT SPREAD

Imagine you are pretty sure a stock will go down in price, but you are not 100% certain how much it will fall. This is where a bear put spread strategy comes in. It lets you profit if the stock price falls but limits your risk compared to just buying a plain put option.

Here is a breakdown of how to go about it:

i.   You buy a put option with a specific strike price (let us say Rs 100). This gives you the right, but not the obligation, to sell the stock at Rs 100 by a specific date (expiry).
ii. At the same time, you also sell a put option with a lower strike price (maybe Rs 90) and the same expiry date. By selling this put, you collect a premium (like a small fee).

Reasons for using this strategy

i.   The put you sell (lower strike) limits your potential profit. If the stock price crashes way below Rs 90, you still only profit up to the difference between the strike prices (minus the premium you paid).
ii. The key objective here is that the premium you collect by selling the lower strike put helps offset the cost of buying the higher strike put. This lowers your overall risk compared to just buying a single put option.

Suppose you buy a put option (ABC Stock) with a strike price of Rs 100 for Rs 5. (This means you pay Rs 5 upfront for the right to sell the stock at Rs 100 by expiry).

At the same time, you sell a put option (ABC Stock) with a strike price of Rs 90 for Rs 2. (This means you collect Rs 2 upfront).

Your total cost is Rs 3 (initial cost of buying the put – premium received from selling the put).

How you profit

If the stock price falls below Rs 90 by expiry, you can exercise the put you bought (sell the stock at Rs 100) and ignore the put you sold (it expires worthless). Your profit is the difference between the strike prices minus your net cost (commission fees not considered here): (Rs 100 – Rs 90) – Rs 3 = Rs 7.

Case 1: Trade in Nifty

Let us take the same example of Nifty and check how this strategy works.

Assume a trader is moderately bearish on Nifty. So, he can deploy these legs:

Buy 22,000 PE at Rs 218.35
Sell 21,800 CE at Rs 147

This strategy demands only Rs 16,560 capital per lot in Nifty.

The maximum profit is Rs 3,216 when the Nifty falls below 21,800. No matter where the Nifty will expire below 21,800, this trader will only get Rs 3,216 as his profit (image 8.4).

Similarly maximum loss in this strategy is Rs 1,784 when the Nifty rises above 22,000.

Nifty current market price – Rs 22,055

Strikes	21800	21900	22000	22100	22200	22300	22400
Calls	476	408	347	288	238	190	153
Puts	147	181	218.35	260	310	364	425

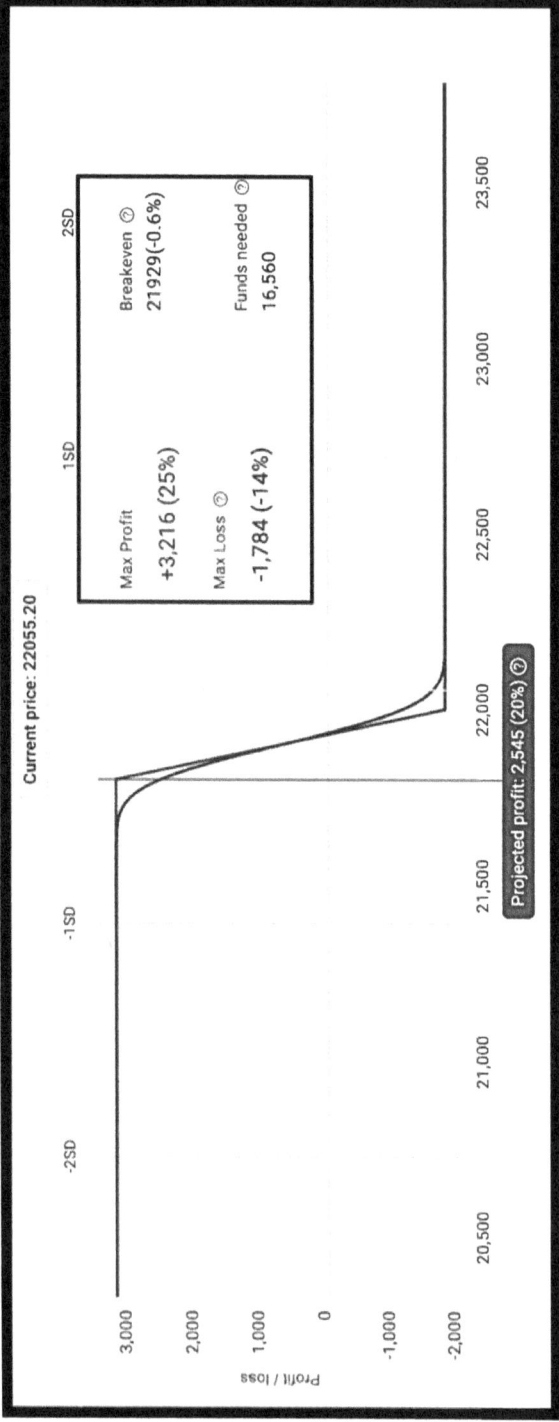

Image 8.4: Payout graph of Nifty showing a bear put spread

Case 2: Trade in Tata Consultancy Services

Image 8.5 shows the daily chart of Tata Consultancy Services (TCS) Ltd. compared to Nifty.

It is evident that TCS did not perform better compared to Nifty in the past. At the same time, it displayed further weakness recently.

So we can easily deploy bear put spread strategy for this stock.

Current Market Price (CMP) of TCS is 3,894.
Buy TCS in May 2024 3,900 PE at Rs 79.6 and
Sell TCS in May 2024 3,700 PE at Rs 15.6

To execute this trade, capital needed is Rs 37,875.

Profit starts when the price trades below 3,836 (strike price 3,900 – (79.6 – 15.6)).

The maximum profit is Rs 23,791 when the price starts to trade below 3,700 (image 8.6).

The maximum loss is Rs 11,209 when the price starts to trade above 3,900.

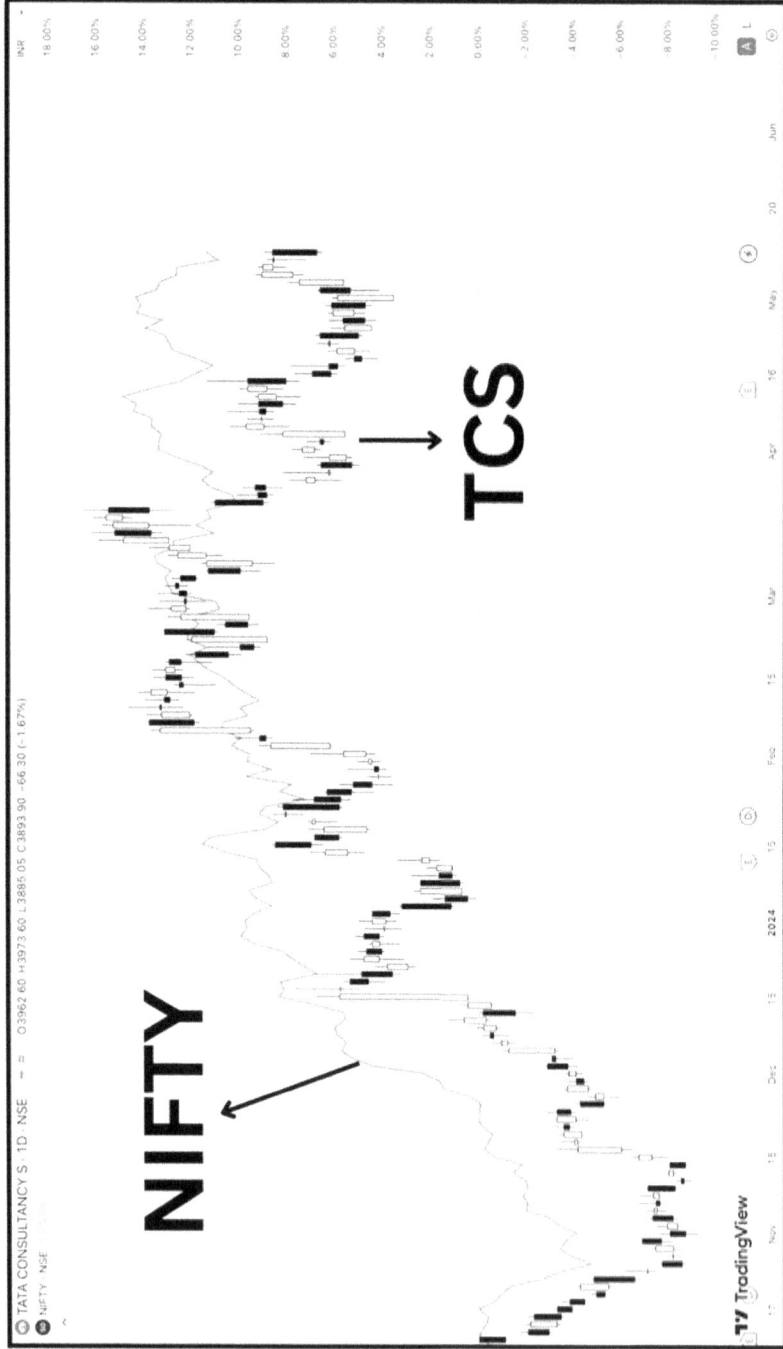

Image 8.5: Daily chart of Tata Consultancy Services Ltd. vs. Nifty for comparision

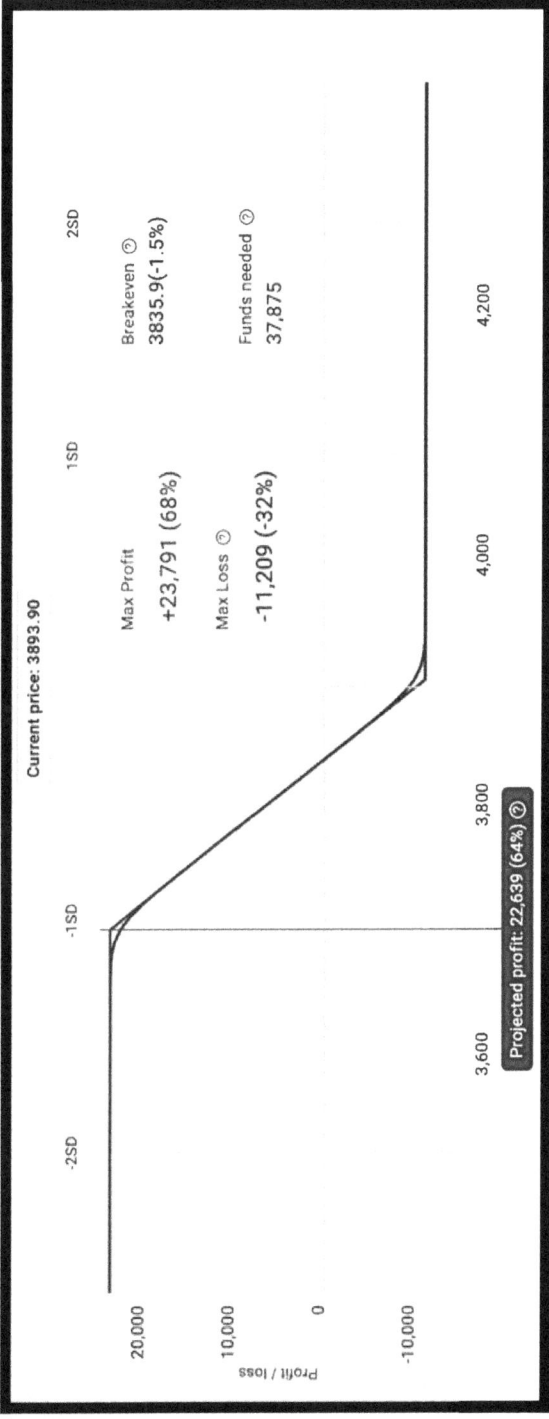

Image 8.6: Payout graph of TCS showing a bear put spread

SHORT STRANGLE STRATEGY

The short-strangle strategy is for those who believe the underlying stock price will stay relatively flat or move within a limited range. Unlike the bear put spread, which is designed to profit from a decrease, a short strangle aims to collect income if the stock price stays stagnant.

Here is how it works. You simultaneously sell two option contracts:

  i. One short call option with a strike price above the current market price.
 ii. One short put option with a strike price below the current market price.

Both options will have the same expiry date.

Reasons for using this strategy

By selling these options, you collect a premium for each (like a fee). Suppose the stock price stays between your chosen strike prices by expiry, both options expire worthless, and you keep both premiums as profit.

Let us say a stock is currently trading at Rs 100. You believe it will likely stay between Rs 90 and Rs 110 by expiry.

So, you sell a short call option with a strike price of Rs 110 and collect a premium of Rs 3.

At the same time, you sell a short put option with a strike price of Rs 90 and collect a premium of Rs 2.

Your total profit potential is Rs 5 (combined premium from both options).

How you profit

If the stock price stays between Rs 90 and Rs 110 by expiry, both options you sold expire worthless. You keep the premiums you collected (your Rs 5 profit).

Important things to remember:

    i.   If the stock price goes above Rs 110, you are obligated to sell the stock at Rs 110 (through the assigned short call exercise). This can lead to losses if the price goes significantly higher.

   ii.   Similarly, if the stock price falls below Rs 90, you are obligated to buy the stock at Rs 90 (through the assigned short put exercise). This can lead to losses if the price goes much lower.

 iii.   The short strangle profits from limited price movement and time decay (the value of options decreases as they get closer to expiry). However, it has unlimited potential losses to the upside and downside beyond the chosen strike prices.

Case 1: Trade in Nifty

Let us take the same example of Nifty and see how this strategy works.

A trader thinks Nifty will display a flat move for the next few days and hence he will deploy these legs:

Sell 22,400 CE at 153
Sell 21,800 PE at 147

This strategy demands only Rs 66,222 capital per lot in Nifty (1 lot CE and 1 lot PE)

Nifty current market price – Rs 22,055

Strikes	21800	21900	22000	22100	22200	22300	22400
Calls	476	408	347	288	238	190	153
Puts	147	181	218.35	260	310	364	425

The maximum profit is Rs 7,499 if the Nifty expires between 21,800–22,400 (image 8.7). No matter where the Nifty expires between 21,800 to 22,400, this trader will only get Rs 7,499 as his profit.

However, this strategy starts making a loss once it trades below 21,800 or trades above 22,400. There is a possibility of huge loss if the Nifty shows significant move above 22,400 or below 21,800.

Case 2: Trade in Infosys

Image 8.8 shows the daily chart of Infosys Ltd. It is very evident that this stock has been in a sideways zone since a few weeks. So there is a high possibility of a sideways move for the next few days. Hence, we can deploy short strangle strategy for this stock to make profits from the time decay.

Current Market Price (CMP) of Infosys Ltd. is 1,424.9.
Sell Infosys Ltd. in May 2024 1,520 CE at Rs 4.3, and
Sell Infosys Ltd. in May 2024 1,320 PE at Rs 3.6

To execute this trade, the capital needed is Rs 89,528.

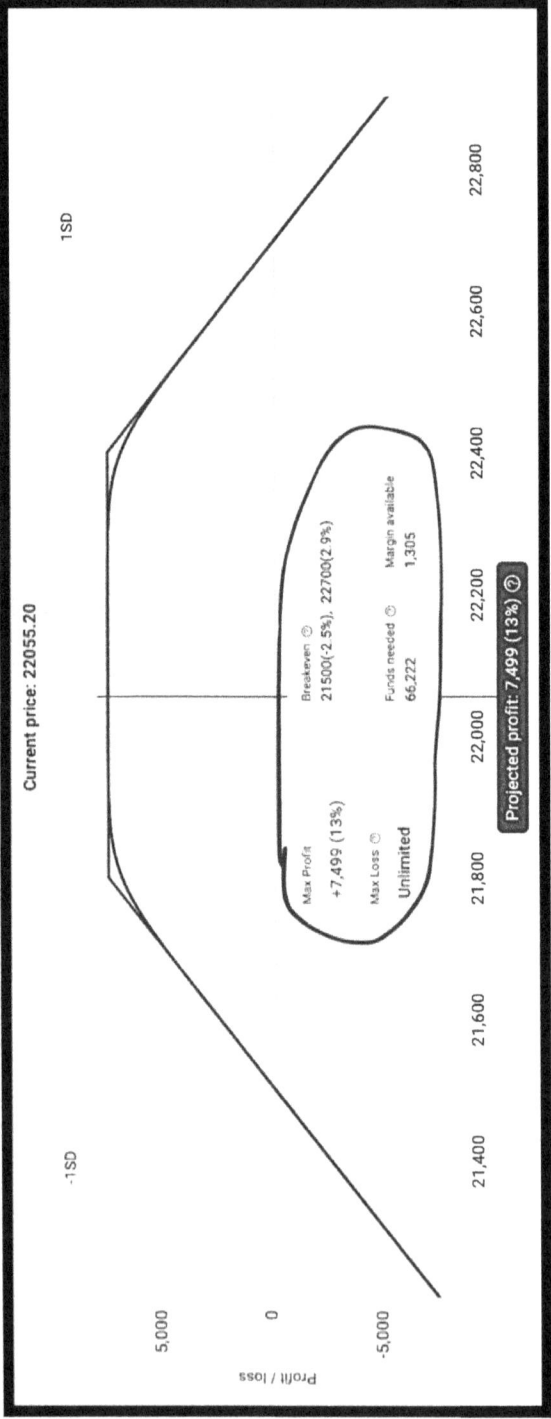

Image 8.7: Payout graph of Nifty showing a short strangle

Image 8.8: Daily chart of Infosys Ltd. showing flat moves

The maximum profit is Rs 3,160 when the price expires between the range 1,320 to 1,520 (image 8.9).

The maximum loss is unlimited when the price starts to trade above 1,520 or falls below 1,320.

SHORT STRADDLE STRATEGY

The short straddle strategy is for traders who believe the stock price will remain relatively flat with minimal movement, either up or down. It is similar to a short strangle but with a key difference. This is how it works:

  i. You simultaneously sell two option contracts with the same strike price and the same expiry date
  ii. One short call option at the strike price
  iii. One short put option at the strike price

Reasons to use this strategy

By selling these options, you collect a premium for each (like a fee). If the stock price stays very close to the strike price by expiry, both options expire worthless, and you keep both premiums as profit.

The difference between a straddle and a strangle is that you collect a higher premium from each option as you would have selected a strike price closer to the currently traded value in a straddle when compared to strike selection in case of strangle.

Imagine you set up a game where people throw balls at a target. The target has a bull's-eye (the strike price). You charge people to throw balls (selling options). If nobody hits the bull's-eye (the stock price stays exactly at the strike), you keep all the money they paid (premiums). If they hit the bull's-eye, you give them some prize money higher than the premium collected.

Let us say a stock is currently trading at Rs 100.

You believe it will stay very close to Rs 100 by expiry. So, you

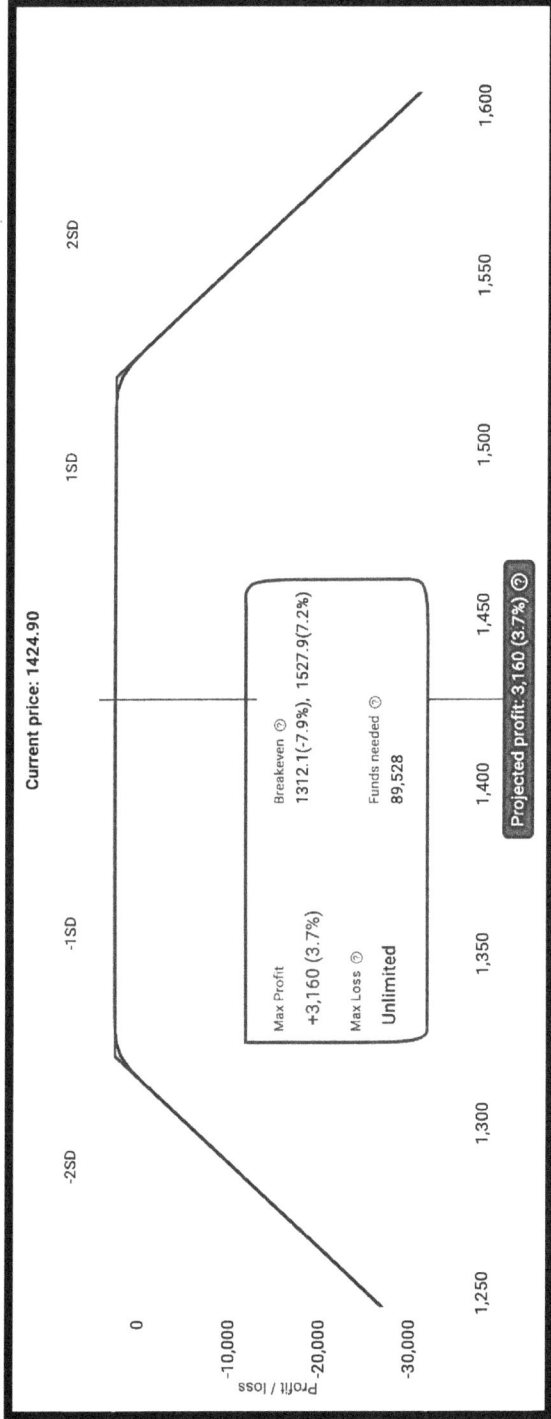

Current price: 1424.90

Max Profit ⓘ	Breakeven ⓘ
+3,160 (3.7%)	1312.1(-7.9%), 1527.9(7.2%)
Max Loss ⓘ	Funds needed ⓘ
Unlimited	89,528

Projected profit: 3,160 (3.7%) ⓘ

Profit / loss

Image 8.9: Payout graph for Infosys Ltd. showing short strangle strategy sell a short call option and a short put option, both with a strike price of Rs 100. You collect a premium of Rs 4 for the call and Rs 3 for the put.

Your total profit potential is Rs 7 (combined premium from both options).

How you profit

If the stock price stays exactly at Rs 100 by expiry, both options you sold expire worthless. You keep the premiums you collected (your Rs 7 profit).

Short Straddle vs. Short Strangle

Short strangle profits from a wider range of price movements (as long as it stays within the chosen strike prices). However, profits are capped on the upside. On the other hand, short straddle profits only from a very narrow price movement around the strike price. But it offers the potential to collect a larger premium than a short strangle with similar strike prices.

Suitability

This strategy is suitable for advanced options traders who are comfortable with high risk but also understand the limitations on profits. It requires precise timing and a high degree of confidence that the stock price will remain very stable.

Case 1: Trade in Nifty

Let us take the same example of Nifty and see how this strategy works.

Usually when options trades involve two or more trades representing one trade, it is known as 'legs'. A trader thinks Nifty will display a flat move for the next few days and hence he will deploy these legs:

Sell 22,050 CE at Rs 315
Sell 22,050 PE at Rs 237.25

In a perfect scenario, the maximum profit one can make from this short straddle is limited to the total premium received from selling the call and put options. This is because the options expire worthless if the price stays precisely at the strike price (Rs 22,050) at expiry.

> Maximum profit = Call option premium + Put option premium

Maximum profit   = Rs 315 + Rs 237.25 for 2 lots (1 lot of CE and 1 lot of PE).
                     = Rs 552.25
552.25 × 25 (quantity) = Rs 13,805

Nifty current market price – Rs 22,055, so nearest ATM strike is Rs 22,050

Strikes	21800	21900	22000	22050	22100	22200	22300
Calls	476	408	347	**315**	288	238	190
Puts	147	181	218.35	**237.25**	260	310	364

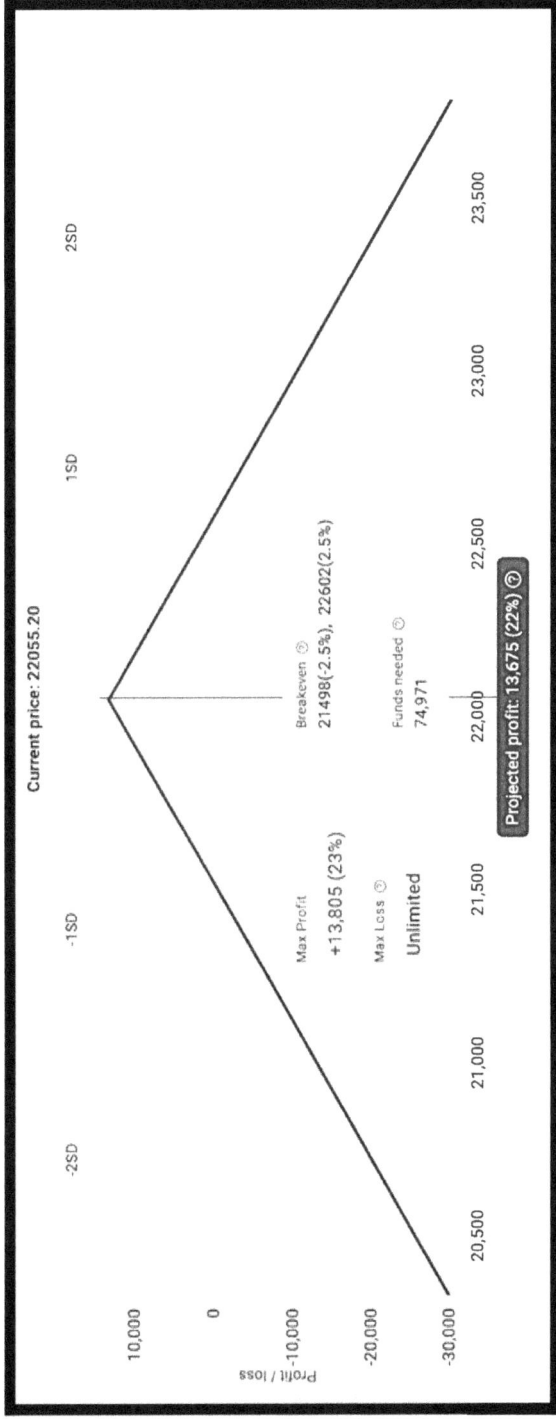

Image 8.10: Payout graph of Nifty short straddle

Unlike the limited profit potential, the short straddle has unlimited potential losses on both sides (up and down) beyond the strike price. The reasons are explained with examples below.

Scenario 1: Stock price increases significantly (call assigned)

If the Nifty price significantly increases above Rs 22,600 by expiry, you start to make losses.

> Maximum loss (price increase)
> = (Market price at expiry – strike price) – premium collected
> from call option

Scenario 2: Stock price decreases significantly (put assigned

If the Nifty price significantly decreases below Rs 21,500 by expiry, you start to make a loss.

> Maximum loss (price decrease)
> = (Strike price – Market price at expiry) – Premium collected
> from put option

Case 2: Trade in Infosys

We will consider the same example of Infosys Ltd. It is very evident that this stock has been in a sideways zone since a few weeks (image 8.11). So there is a high possibility of a sideways move for the next few days. Hence, another trader deploys short straddle strategy for this stock to make profits from the time decay.

Current Market Price (CMP) of Infosys Ltd. is 1,424.9. Nearest STM strike is 1,420.
Sell Infosys Ltd. in May 2024 1,420 CE at Rs 32.9, and
Sell Infosys Ltd. in May 2024 1,420 PE at Rs 23.3
Capital required to deploy this strategy is Rs 1,23,000.
Maximum profit is Rs 22,460 which comes when it expires at 1,420 (image 8.12).
This strategy starts to make loss whenever the price trades above 1,476.2 or below 1,363.8.

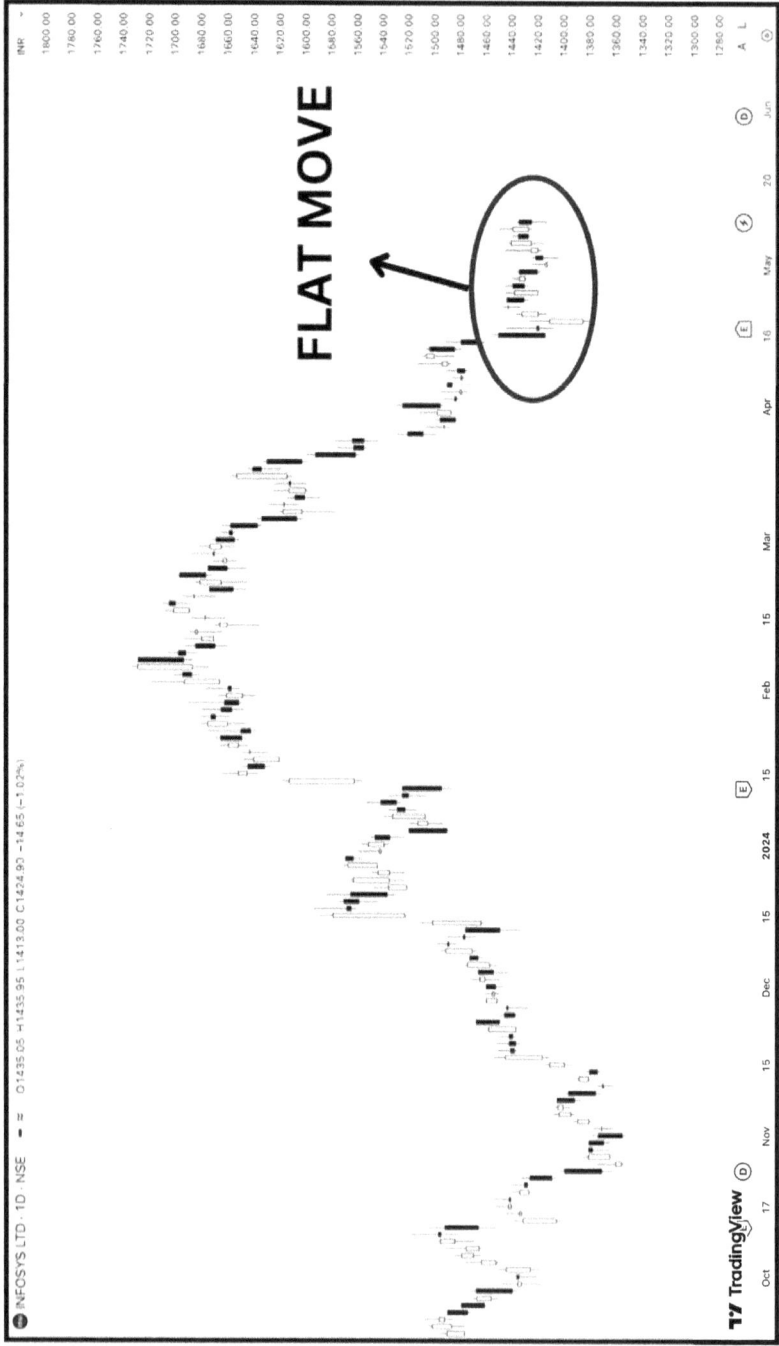

Image 8.11: Daily chart of Infosys Ltd. showing flat move for short straddle strategy

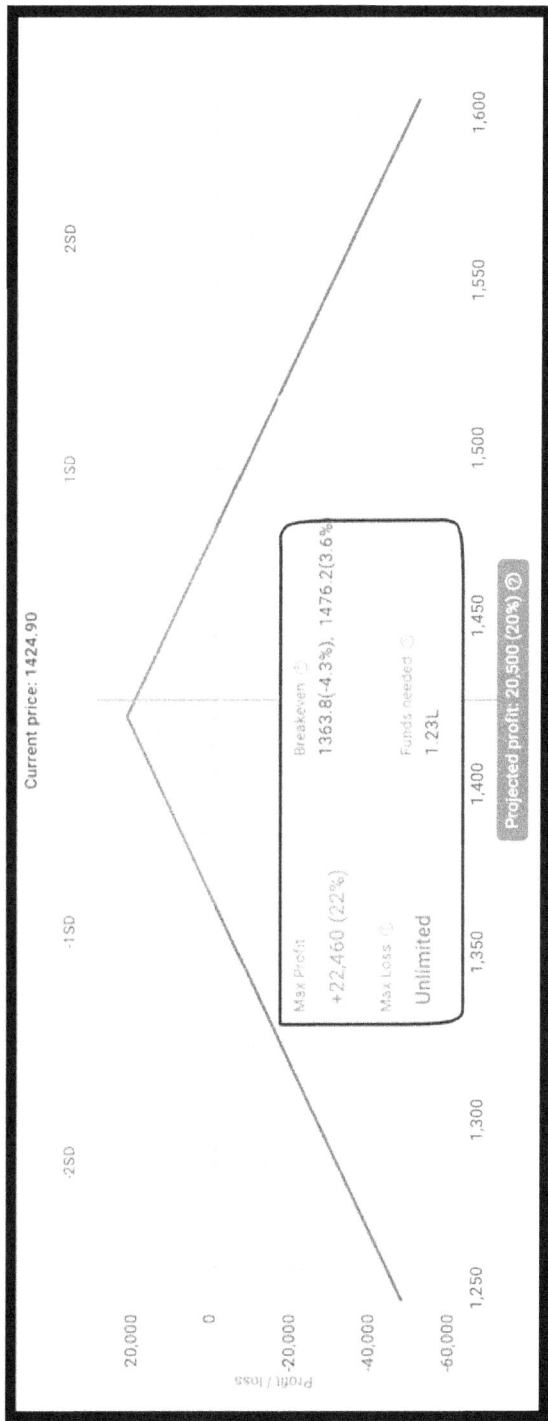

Image 8.12: Payout graph of Infosys Ltd. showing short straddle strategy

IRON CONDOR STRATEGY

An iron condor is a popular options trading strategy used when traders expect an underlying asset's price to remain within a specific range. It involves simultaneously selling an out-of-the-money call and put option while also buying a further out-of-the-money call and put option with the same expiry date. This creates a profit zone between the sold strike prices where the investor makes a profit. To follow this strategy,

i. **Identify range:** First, select a range within which you believe the underlying asset's price will remain relatively stable until expiry.

ii. **Sell OTM call spread:** You sell one out-of-the-money call option (higher strike) while simultaneously buying another call option with a higher strike price. This creates a bear call spread. The premium you receive from selling the call spread is your maximum profit potential.

iii. **Sell OTM put spread:** You sell one out-of-the-money put option (lower strike) while simultaneously buying another put option with a lower strike price. This creates a bull put spread. The premium you receive from selling the put spread increases your maximum profit potential. Now, it will be a combination of premium received from call spread and put spread.

Points to remember when you use iron condor

i. **Limited risk:** The difference between the strike prices of the sell leg and the buy leg will determine the maximum possible loss. This loss occurs if the price of the underlying asset moves beyond either of the buy strike prices by expiry.

ii. **Profit zone:** Your profit is maximised if the underlying asset's price remains within the range defined by the strike prices of the options sold.

iii. **Expiry:** If the price of the underlying asset expires between the two strike prices you sold, both the call and put options become worthless, and you get to keep the premiums you earned from selling both.

Let us take a simple example. Suppose stock XYZ is currently trading at Rs 50 per share, and you believe it will trade within a range of Rs 45 to Rs 55 over the next month. To implement an iron condor strategy, you could:

1. Sell a call option with a strike price of Rs 55 for a Re 1 premium per share.
2. Sell a put option with a strike price of Rs 45 for a Re 1 premium per share.
3. Buy a call option with a strike price of Rs 60 for a Re 0.50 premium per share.
4. Buy a put option with a strike price of Rs 40 for a Re 0.50 premium per share.

Here is a breakdown of the scenario:

i. You collect a Re 1 premium from selling each call and put option, which gives you a total premium of Rs 2.
ii. You pay a Re 0.50 premium for buying each call and put option, totalling Re 1.

So, your net credit for the trade is Rs 2 – Re 1 = Re 1 (since you received Rs 2 and paid Re 1)
This Re 1 is your maximum profit per share.

Now, let us look at the profit and loss scenarios:

i.   Suppose the stock price remains between Rs 45 and Rs 55 at expiry. In that case, all options expire worthless, and you keep the entire Re 1 premium as profit.

ii. If the stock price goes below Rs 45 or above Rs 55 at expiry, you start to incur losses. The maximum loss occurs if the stock price is below Rs 40 or above Rs 60, as your options would be exercised, and you would have to buy or sell shares at unfavourable prices. This maximum loss would be Rs 4 per share (the difference between the two strike prices minus the premium received).

iii. If the stock price is between Rs 40 and Rs 45 or between Rs 55 and Rs 60, you gradually incur losses as the stock price moves away from the short strikes.

Overall, the iron condor strategy allows you to profit from a sideways-moving market while limiting your potential losses if the stock moves significantly in either direction.

Let us take the same example of Nifty and see how this strategy works.

Nifty current market price – Rs 22,055

Strikes	21800	21900	22000	**22050**	22100	22200	22300
Calls	476	408	347	**315**	288	238	190
Puts	147	181	218.35	**237.25**	260	310	364

A trader thinks Nifty will display a flat move for the next few days and hence he will deploy these actions:

   i. Sell 22,300 CE at 190 and buy 22,450 CE at 134.35
  ii. Sell 21,800 PE at 147 and buy 21,650 PE at 111.6

The capital required to deploy this strategy is Rs 32,092 and the breakeven levels are 21,709 and 22,391. It means loss starts if the price starts to trade below 21,709 or above 22,391.

The maximum profit is Rs 2,276 when Nifty expires between 21,800 to 22,300 (image 8.13).

Please note that the iron condor options strategy involves higher execution costs. Be mindful of the multiple stages engaged in setting up this strategy, as each transaction incurs brokerage fees and taxes that can impact your overall profitability. Always consider transaction costs alongside potential gains and losses before implementing this strategy.

IRON BUTTERFLY STRATEGY

The iron butterfly is an options trading strategy used when traders expect the price of an underlying asset to remain stable within a specific range. It is essentially a combination of two different strategies—a short straddle and a long strangle. This strategy profits from low volatility and aims to generate income through the premiums received from selling options.

Here is how the iron butterfly works:

1. **Short straddle:** Traders simultaneously sell an at-the-money (ATM) call and an ATM put option with the same strike price and expiry date. This establishes your central profit zone.

2. **Long strangle:** To limit potential losses, traders buy an out-of-the-money (OTM) call option with a higher strike

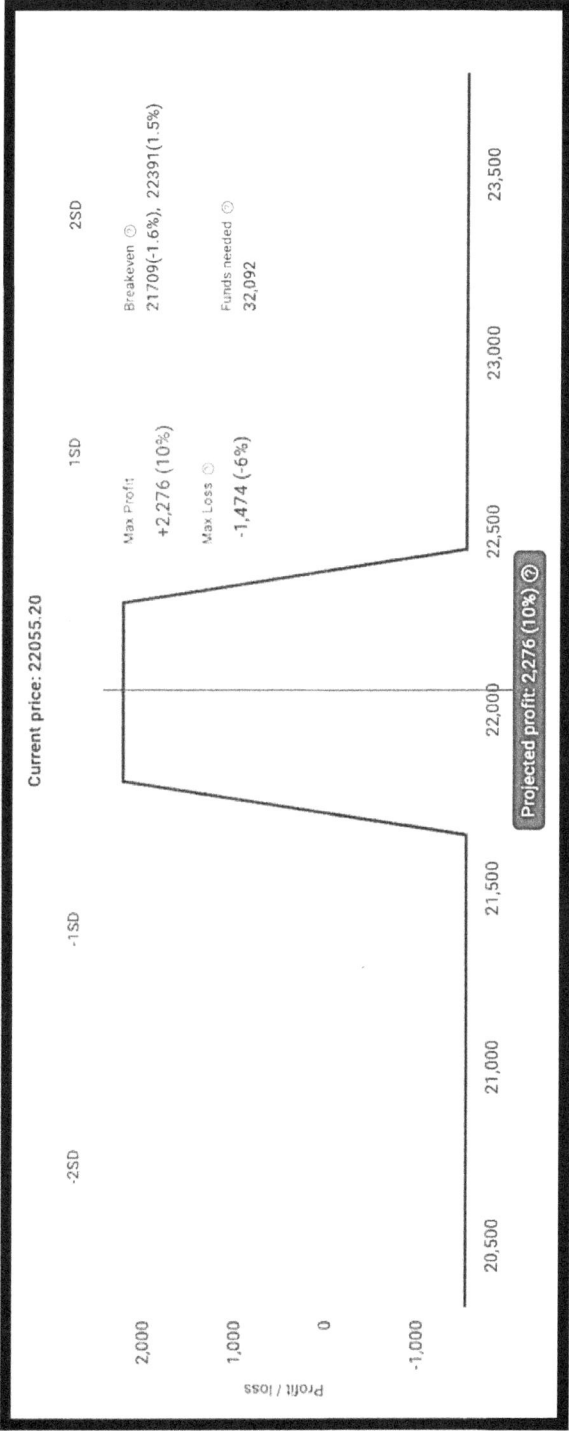

Image 8.13: Payout graph of Nifty showing iron condor strategy

price and an OTM put option with a lower strike price. This creates a wider range around the short straddle where losses are capped.

Let us break it down with an example. Suppose stock XYZ is currently trading at Rs 50 per share, and you believe it will remain relatively stable around this price over the next month. To implement an iron butterfly strategy, you could:

1. Sell an ATM call option with a strike price of Rs 50 for a Rs 2 premium per share.
2. Sell an ATM put option with a strike price of Rs 50 for a Rs 2 premium per share.
3. Buy an OTM call option with a strike price of Rs 55 for a Re 1 premium per share.
4. Buy an OTM put option with a strike price of Rs 45 for a Re 1 premium per share.

Here is the breakdown of the scenario:

i. You collect a Rs 2 premium from selling each call and put option, which gives you a total premium of Rs 4.
ii. You pay a Re 1 premium for buying each call and put option, totalling Rs 2.

So, your net credit for the trade is
Rs 4 – Rs 2 = Rs 2 (since you received Rs 4 and paid Rs 2).
This Rs 2 is your maximum profit per share.

Now, let us look at the profit and loss scenarios:

i. If the stock price remains around Rs 50 at expiry, all options expire worthless, and you keep the entire Rs 2 premium as profit.

ii. If the stock price moves away from Rs 50 in either direction, you start to incur losses. The maximum loss occurs if the stock price is below Rs 43 or above Rs 57, as your options would be exercised, and you would have to buy or sell shares at unfavourable prices. This maximum loss would be Rs 3 per share (the difference between the two strike prices minus the premium received).

iii. If the stock price is between Rs 43 and Rs 50, or between Rs 50 and Rs 57, you gradually incur losses as the stock price moves away from the short straddle.

Overall, the iron butterfly strategy allows you to profit from stable market conditions while limiting your potential losses if the stock moves significantly in either direction.

Let us take the same example of Nifty and see how this strategy works.

A trader thinks Nifty will display a flat move for the next few days and hence he will deploy the following:

i. Sell 22,050 CE at 315 and buy 22,300 CE at 190
ii. Sell 21,050 PE at 237.25 and buy 21,800 PE at 147

The capital required to deploy this strategy is Rs 37,127 and the breakeven levels are 21,835 and 22,265. It means loss starts if the price starts to trade below 21,835 or above 22,265.

Nifty current market price – 22,055

Strikes	21800	21900	22000	**22050**	22100	22200	22300
Calls	476	408	347	**315**	288	238	190
Puts	147	181	218.35	**237.25**	260	310	364

The maximum profit is Rs 5,380 when Nifty expires at 22,050 (image 8.14).

Please note, similar to iron condor strategy, this strategy also involves higher execution costs. Be mindful of the multiple stages engaged in setting up this strategy, as each transaction incurs brokerage fees and taxes that can impact your overall profitability. Always consider transaction costs alongside potential gains and losses before implementing this strategy.

It is also worth noting that both iron condor and iron butterfly need lesser margin to execute compared to short strangle and short straddle. This is because the loss is limited in iron condor and iron butterfly, whereas loss is unlimited in short strangle and short straddle.

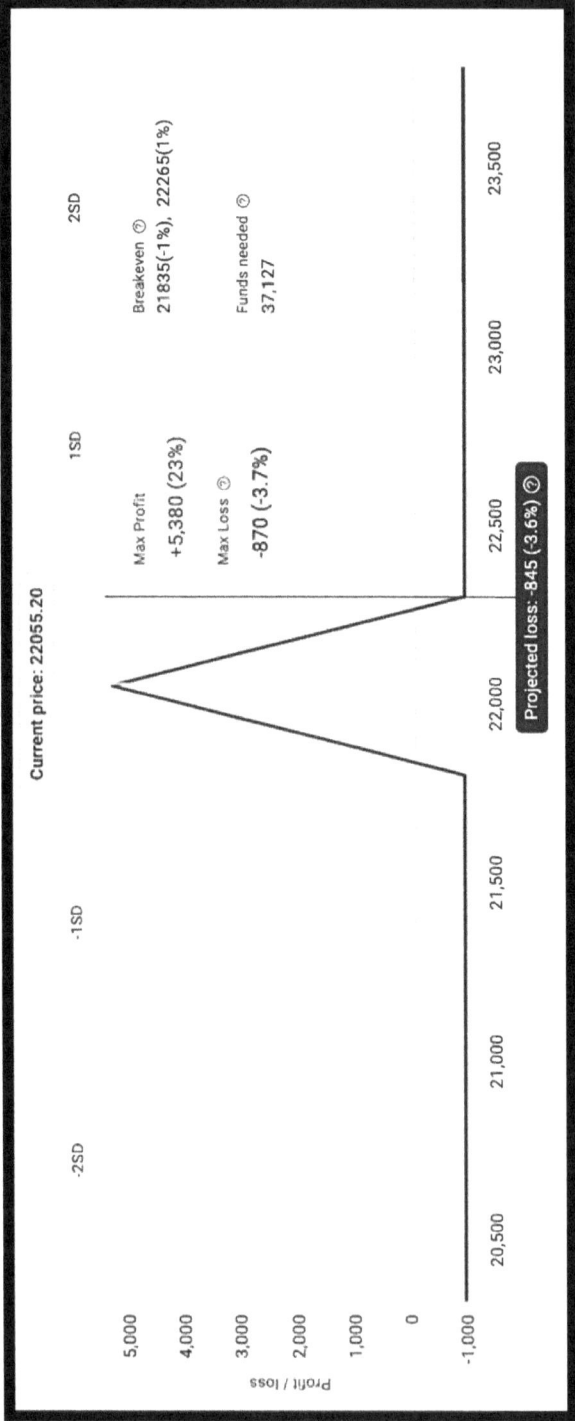

Image 8.14: Payout graph of Nifty in iron butterfly strategy

9

FIVE OPTIONS TRADING SYSTEMS

A few months after I quit the information technology industry and took up full-time trading as my career, an ex-colleague approached me to teach him trading. He was very helpful when I worked with him on a few projects. So I decided to meet him and discuss it. During our discussion, I realised that he did not know much about the markets, and he was having a tough time in the office because he recently got a new boss. So he also decided to take trading as a full-time career after a gap of two months!

I tried to explain to him that it was a daunting task to learn all the aspects of trading in just two months. Besides, quitting a well-paid job was not required. Unfortunately, he was not in a situation to understand all these things. So I explained a few simple concepts of trading and gave him some homework.

When I caught up with him again after a few days, he had a surprise for me. He told me that he had reduced my workload. When I checked with him, he told me he had bought a 90% accurate intraday trading system from someone by paying him Rs 50,000.

I did not know how to react to this. When my friend was learning all these things, he got a call from someone who explained and showed some proof that he had an intraday trading system with 90% accuracy. Without checking with me or using common sense, my friend bought the system by paying Rs 50,000. Somebody cheated my friend, because no such trading system exists in this world, and even if it exists, nobody will sell it for just Rs 50,000!

Before using any trading system, you must do your due diligence and thoroughly research the system.

Here are some factors to consider:

1. **Accuracy:** A trading system that claims 80-90% accuracy may sound impressive, but it is important to understand what that means. Does it mean the system has been backtested and produced profitable trades 90% of the time over a few years of historical data? Or does it mean the system has a success rate of 90% on trades taken in real-time? Keep in mind that past performance does not guarantee future results.

2. **Transparency:** Is the person sharing the trading system transparent about how it works and what indicators or strategies it uses? Are they willing to provide historical performance data to back up their claims? Be wary of anyone who promises a 'secret' system or is not forthcoming about how the system generates its trading signals.

3. **Cost:** Consider the cost of the trading system and whether it is worth the investment. Remember that even a highly accurate trading system can still incur losses, and it is essential to have realistic expectations about what the system can achieve.

4. **Compatibility:** Make sure the trading system matches your trading style and preferences. A system that works well for one trader may not be suitable for another.

SYSTEM 1: SHORT STRADDLE

The 9.20 short straddle system is a simple options trading strategy in India that involves selling both a call option (CE) and a put option (PE) with the same strike price and expiry date at 9.20 a.m. (5 minutes after the market opens). I have suggested a few tweaks to improve the results of both short straddle and short strangle in the next chapter.

The strategy is designed to generate income from the premiums collected from the sale of the options.

Key characteristics

1. **Same strike price and expiry date:** The call and put options sold have the same strike price and expiry date, so the trader hopes that the underlying asset's price will remain relatively stable or within a range until the end of the day.
2. **Stop-loss:** A stop-loss of 25-50% of the premium is placed on both sides. For example, if the call option is sold at Rs 100 and the put option is sold at Rs 110, then a stop-loss for the call option is placed at Rs 150, and a stop-loss for the put option is set at Rs 165 (assuming the 50% stop loss rule).
3. **Exit Rule:** If the stop loss does not hit both stages, traders can close both stages before the market closes. If the stop-loss hits for one stage, then trail the stop-loss for another portion to the entry price, hoping the price will move in the same direction.
4. **Limited profit and unlimited risk:** The maximum profit the trader can earn from the strategy is the total premium received from selling the call and put options. However, the unlimited loss scenario is covered by placing the stop-loss for both stages.

Overall, the 9.20 short straddle system is a simple options trading strategy that can generate constant income in stable markets.

I will take a simple example to explain this strategy.

On 27 March 2023, the price for Nifty Financial Services was at 17, 635 at 9.20 a.m. (image 9.1).

So we take the nearest strike price which is 17,650.

As per the short straddle strategy, we sell both 17,650 CE and 17,650 PE and place 50% stop-loss for both the stages (image 9.2).

Nifty Financial Services 17,650 CE sold at 98, stop loss placed at 147 (50% rule).

Nifty Financial Services 17,650 PE sold at 103, stop loss placed at 154.5 (50% rule).

Total premium collected is 201 points (98 + 103).

Nifty Financial Services displayed a sideways move on that day and hence stop-loss did not hit for both call option and put option stages.

Nifty Financial Services 17,650 CE closed at 39 and Nifty Financial Services 17,650 PE closed at 90.

Total premium at the close is 129 points (39 + 90).

Hence, total profit (201 – 129) = 72 points

When the markets are volatile, the price might show more fluctuations immediately after the open. In such scenarios, traders can plan to execute their trades at 9.30 or at later stages.

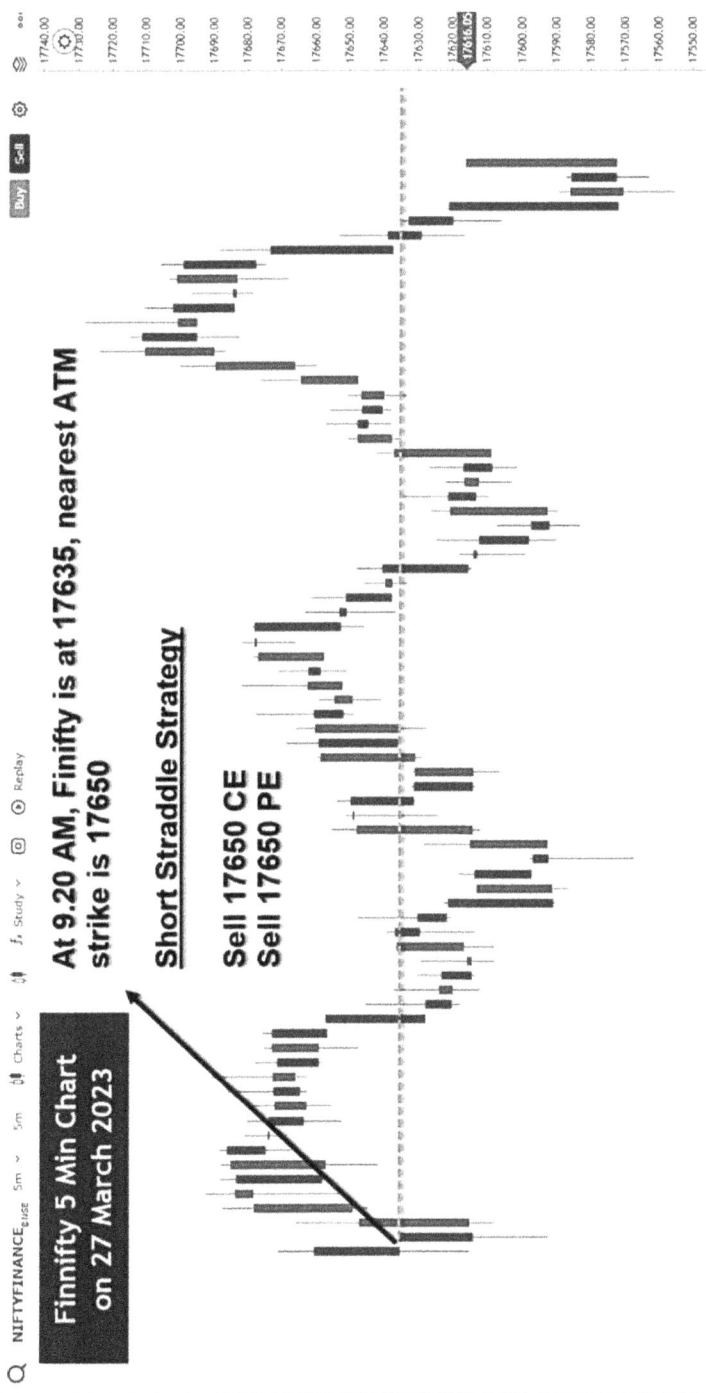

Image 9.1: 5-minute chart of Nifty Financial Services showing a short straddle

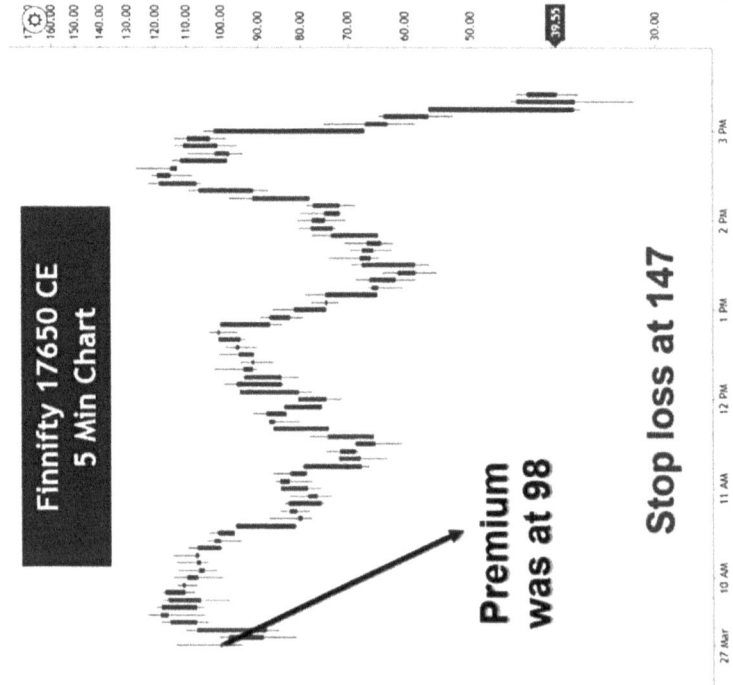

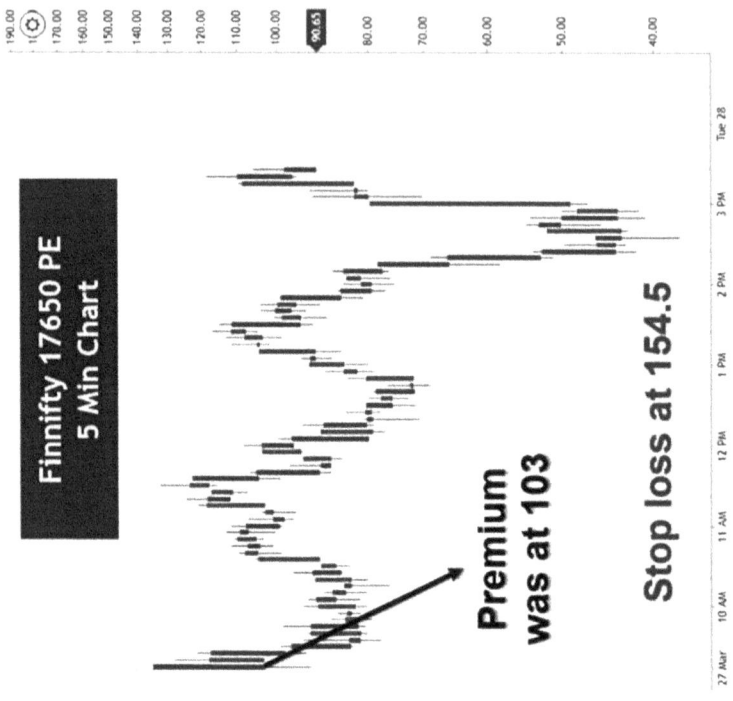

Image 9.2: Nifty Financial Services CE and PE short straddle trades

SYSTEM 2: COVERED CALL STRATEGY

A covered call options strategy is a way to generate extra income from the stocks you already own.

Let us break it down using an example of a stock. Assume you own 100 shares of Reliance Industries Ltd., currently trading at Rs 2,500 per share. You believe the stock price might not move significantly upside in the short term, but you do not prefer to sell as part of your investment strategy. So, you want to generate additional income using these shares.

Stages in a covered call strategy

1. **Own the stock:** You already have 100 Reliance shares valued at Rs 2,500 per share, totalling Rs 2,50,000.
2. **Sell a call option:** You decide to sell a call option with a strike price of Rs 2,600. This means you are giving someone the right to buy your 100 shares at Rs 2,600 each before a specific date, called the expiry date.
3. **Collect the premium:** You receive a premium, say Rs 50 per share, for selling this call option. Since you have 100 shares, you collect Rs 5,000 (Rs 50 × 100).

Possible Outcomes

1. **Stock stays below Rs 2,600:** If Reliance's share price stays below Rs 2,600 by the expiry date, the buyer will not exercise the option to buy your shares at Rs 2,600 because they can buy them cheaper on the market. You keep your 100 shares and the Rs 5,000 premium.
2. **Stock rises above Rs 2,600:** If the stock price goes above Rs 2,600, the buyer will likely exercise the option, buying your shares at Rs 2,600 each. You still keep the Rs 5,000 premium plus the profit from selling your shares at Rs 2,600 instead

of the initial Rs 2,500. So, you make loss of only Rs 50 per share (Rs 2,600 – Rs 2,500 – Rs 50 (premium captured)).

Let us look at another example.

TCS is trading near 4,404 levels and an investor of this stock thinks it will not go to 4,700 by end of next month (approximately 30 trading days are pending for the next month expiry) as shown in image 9.3. So he plans to make some returns by deploying a covered call strategy.

To make the calculation easy, let us assume he holds 175 shares of TCS which is equivalent to 1 lot size in futures and options (This can vary with time as exchanges keep changing it).

TCS 4,700 CE of next month is trading at Rs 32.95 (image 9.4). So the investor sells 1 lot of 4,700 CE and generates the revenue as shown below:

Revenue generated = 175 shares × Rs 32.95
                    = Rs 5,766

  i. If the TCS stock closes below 4,700, by the end of next month, then he will pocket the entire premium of Rs 5,766.
 ii. If the TCS stock moves above 4,700, then he will have to sell the shares of TCS to avoid the losses.
iii. Profit from stock appreciation: Assuming the investor bought or held the shares at Rs 4,404 and will sell them at Rs 4,700. Gain from the stock movement (Rs 4,700 – Rs 4,404) × 175 shares = Rs 51,800.

When TCS moves above 4,700 at expiry, the call option price will increase. In this case, the investor has to buy back the option at the new market price to close the position. The call option premium will increase based on many factors like delta, gamma, etc.

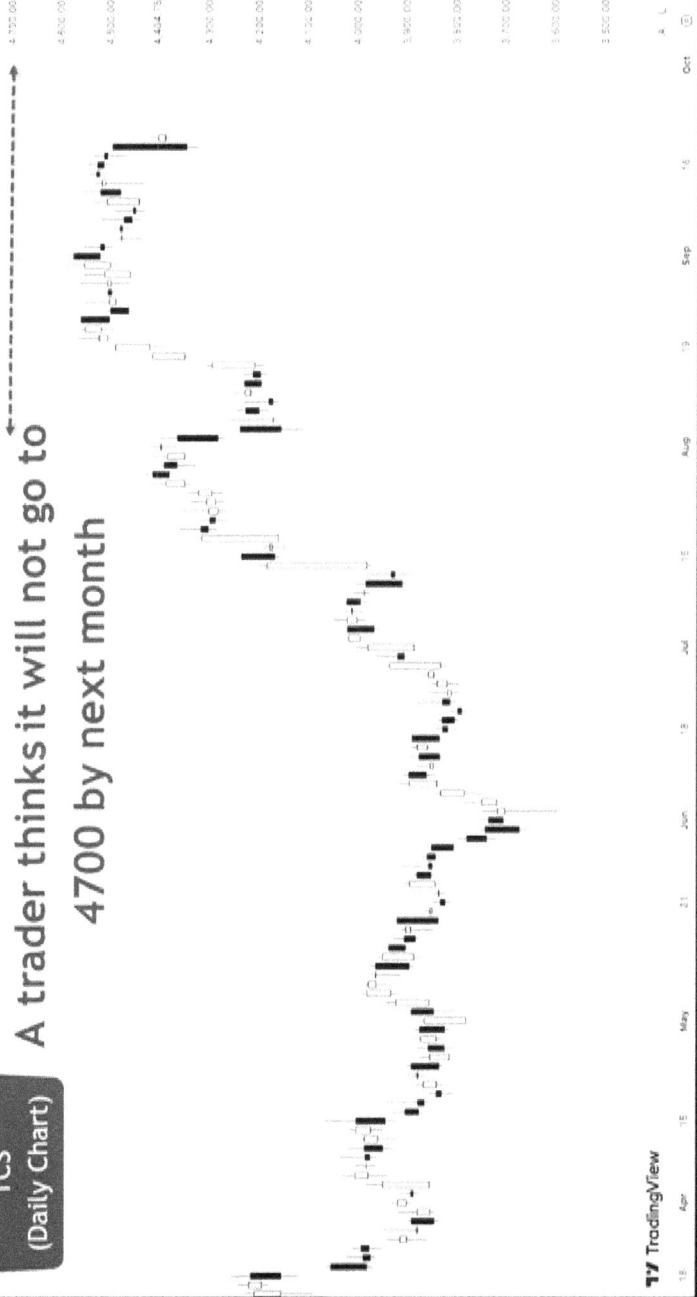

Image 9.3: Daily chart of TCS for covered call strategy

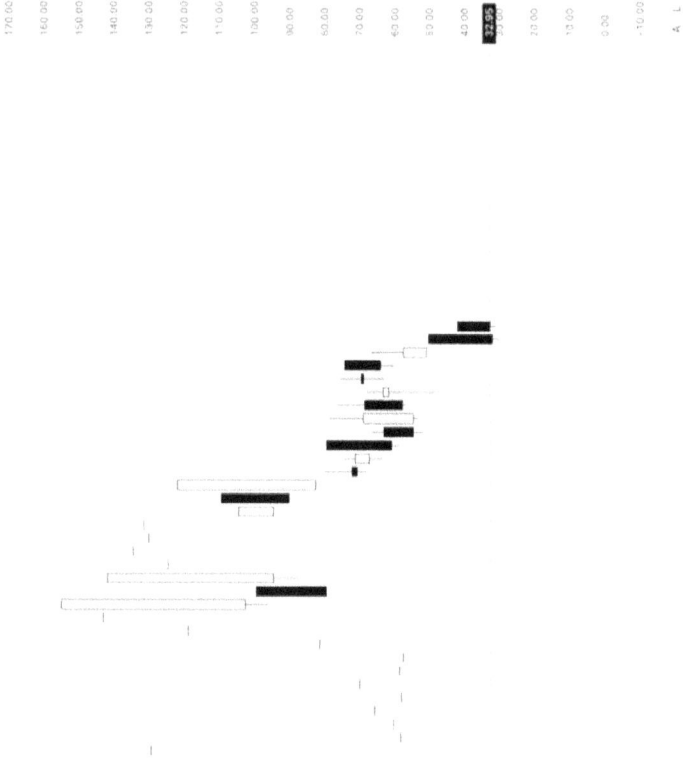

Image 9.4: Daily chart of TCS with 4,700 CE (next month)

If the investor does not want to sell the shares of TCS, then they can buy back the 4,700 CE option before it is exercised. However, since the stock price is now above Rs 4,700, the option's price (premium) would have increased.

This means this investor will likely incur a loss when buying back the option because he will pay a higher price than what he initially received.

SYSTEM 3: BULL CALL SPREAD

A bull call spread is an options trading strategy used when you expect a moderate rise in the price of a stock. It involves buying a call option at a lower strike price and selling a call option at a higher strike price. This strategy limits both your potential profit and risk.

Let us use Infosys Ltd. (INFY) as an example, trading at Rs 1,400.

Steps to create a bull call spread:

1. **Buy a call option (lower strike)**
   You buy a call option with a strike price of Rs 1,450 for a premium of Rs 30 per share. This option gives you the right to buy Infosys shares at Rs 1,450 before the expiry date.
   Total cost for buying this option (assuming 1 lot = 100 shares):
   Rs 30 × 100 = Rs 3,000.

2. **Sell a call option (higher strike)**
   Simultaneously, you sell a call option with a strike price of Rs 1,500 for a premium of Rs 10 per share. This option gives someone else the right to buy Infosys shares from you at Rs 1,500 before the expiry date.
   Total premium received from selling this option:
   Rs 10 × 100 = Rs 1,000.

Net Cost

The net cost of this strategy is the difference between the premiums
paid and received.

Net cost = Rs 3,000 (paid) – Rs 1,000 (received)
          = Rs 2,000.

Possible Outcomes

i.   Infosys Ltd. stays below Rs 1,450
ii. Both options expire worthless because the stock never
     reaches the strike prices.
     Loss = Net cost = Rs 2,000.
iii. Infosys Ltd. between Rs 1,450 and Rs 1,500

     • The option you bought (Rs 1,450 strike) gains value as
       the stock price rises.
     • The option you sold (Rs 1,500 strike) may not be
       exercised if the stock stays below Rs 1,500.
     • Maximum profit occurs if the stock price is exactly or
       above Rs 1,500 at expiry.
       Maximum profit
       = Difference between strike prices – Net cost
       = (Rs 1,500 – Rs 1,450) × 100 – Rs 2,000
       = Rs 3,000.

iv. Infosys Ltd. above Rs 1,500

     • Both options are exercised. You profit from the option
       you bought but lose on the option you sold.
     • Maximum profit is still capped at Rs 3,000, as explained
       above.
     • Even if Infosys goes much higher than Rs 1,500, your
       profit doesn't increase beyond this point.

SUMMARY

Risk: Limited to the net cost of Rs 2,000.
Reward: Capped at Rs 3,000.
Suitability: When you expect a moderate rise in Infosys Ltd.'s price but want to limit your risk.

By using a bull call spread, you reduce the upfront cost of buying a call option alone while still allowing for potential profit if the stock rises moderately.

Let us look at another example.

ICICI Bank stock is trading at 1,300 levels (image 9.5). A trader is moderately bullish on this stock. So, he decides to buy ICICI Bank 1,300 CE at 11.55 and sell ICICI Bank 1,350 CE at 1.25.

The payout graph shows the potential profit or loss for bull call spread option strategy on ICICI Bank (image 9.6). Here is a breakdown of the key points:

- Profit starts when the price starts to trade above 1,311
- Capital required to deploy this strategy is Rs 31,837.
- Maximum profit from this strategy is Rs 27,790.
- Maximum loss from this strategy is Rs 7,210.

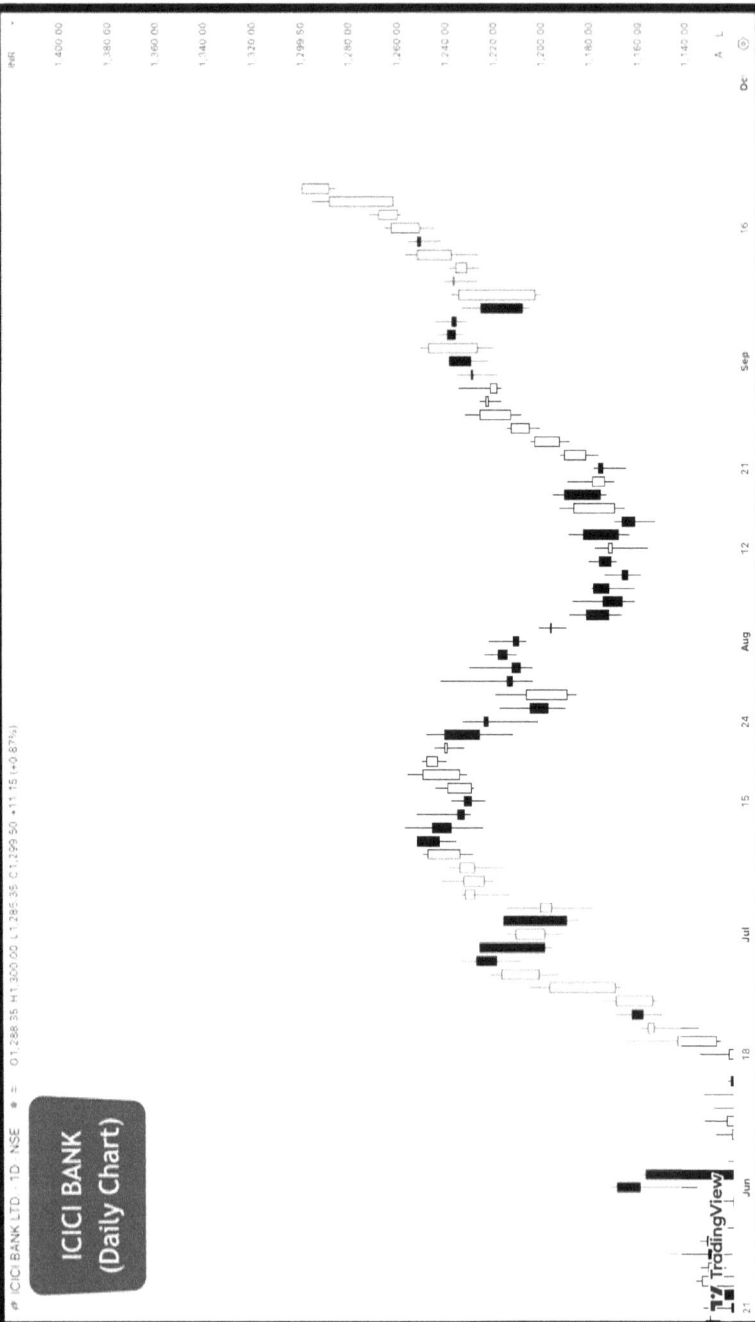

Image 9.5: Daily chart of ICICI Bank

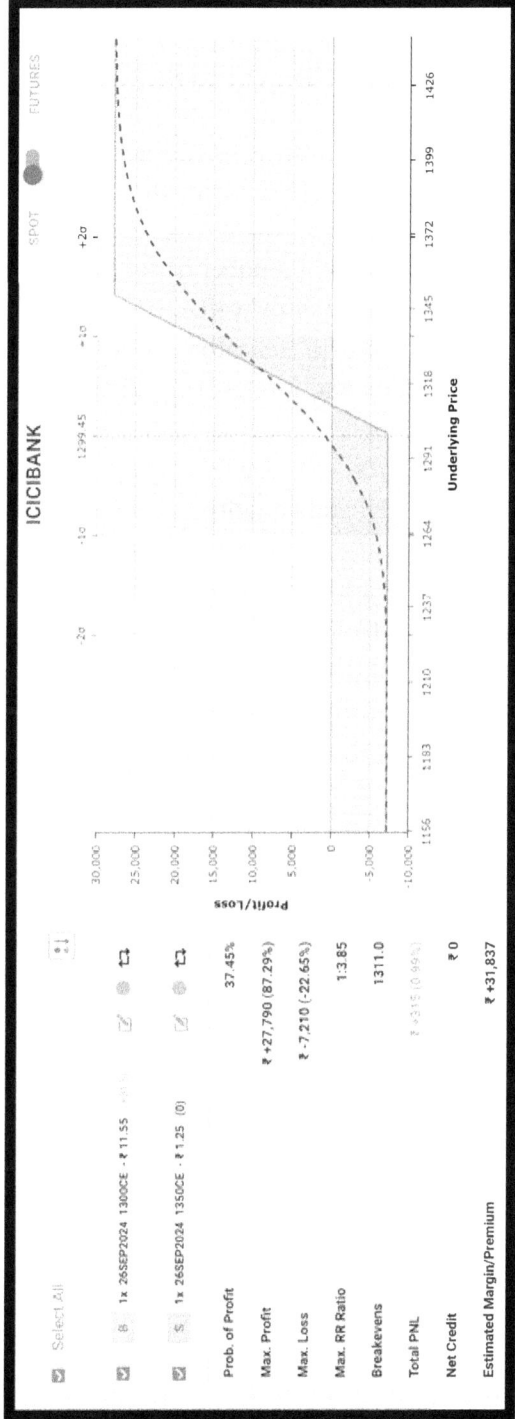

Image 9.6: Payout graph of bull call spread strategy for ICICI Bank

SYSTEM 4: OPEN INTEREST (OI) STRATEGY

The main essence of the trading system is open interest (OI). Open interest in trading refers to the total number of outstanding contracts or positions held by market participants at any given time. In simple words, OI is the total number of contracts or positions that have not yet been closed or delivered.

Open interest is an essential indicator in trading as it provides insights into the liquidity and interest in a particular market or asset. When the OI is high, it generally indicates a high level of trading activity and interest in a specific stock or index, which can lead to increased volatility and liquidity.

When the OI increases while the price is also increasing, it may suggest that more traders are entering the market and taking bullish positions. On the other hand, if the OI decreases while the price increases, it indicates that the market is becoming overbought, and a reversal could be imminent.

Note,

i. For *long trades* look for the stocks that showed *increase in price* along with increase in OI.
ii. For *short trades* look for the stocks that showed *decrease in price* along with increase in OI.

OI details for any stocks or index can be found in many sources like NSE option chain, Opstra Define Edge, Oi Pulse, Options Decoder, Stock Edge, etc.

18 Sep 2024

Major Stocks ×

Stock Name	Open Interest	Chg Since	Chg %
Oracle Financial Services Software Ltd OFSS	19,08,200	[illegible]	[illegible]
Mphasis Ltd MPHASIS	43,45,000	[illegible]	[illegible]

Image 9.7: Open interest scan results on 18 September 2024

As per an open interest scan, the stocks listed in image 9.7 received the highest open interest change on 18 September 2024.

After looking at futures charts for both OFSS Ltd. (image 9.8) and Mphasis Ltd. (image 9.9), it is evident that the price showed a bearish move with an increased open interest. Hence, there is a high possibility of price going further on the downside.

If you observe charts for both OFSS Ltd. (image 9.10) and Mphasis Ltd. (image 9.11), bears took control on the next trading day.

If a stock's future price rises and the open interest also increases significantly, it may signal that traders expect the price to continue rising. This can be an opportunity to buy call options with the expectation that the price will move higher by the next day, allowing for a profitable exit.

Similarly, if the stock's future price is falling and the open interest is increasing, this may indicate that traders are positioning for a continued downward move. In this case, buying put options could be a profitable buy today, sell tomorrow (BTST) trade. The logic is that the increase in OI suggests fresh buying or selling pressure, indicating that more traders are actively betting on the direction of the move.

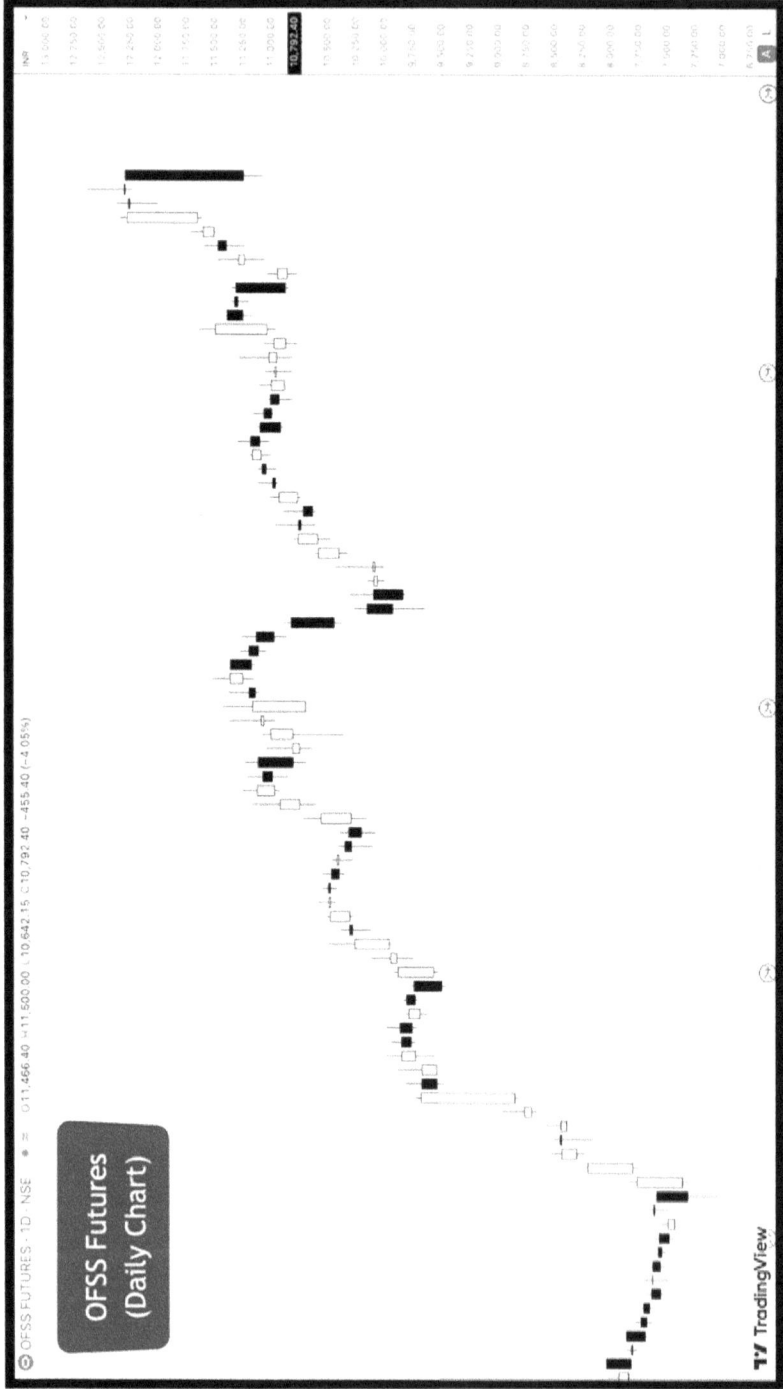

Image 9.8: Daily futures chart of Oracle Financial Services Software (OFSS) Ltd. on 18 September 2024

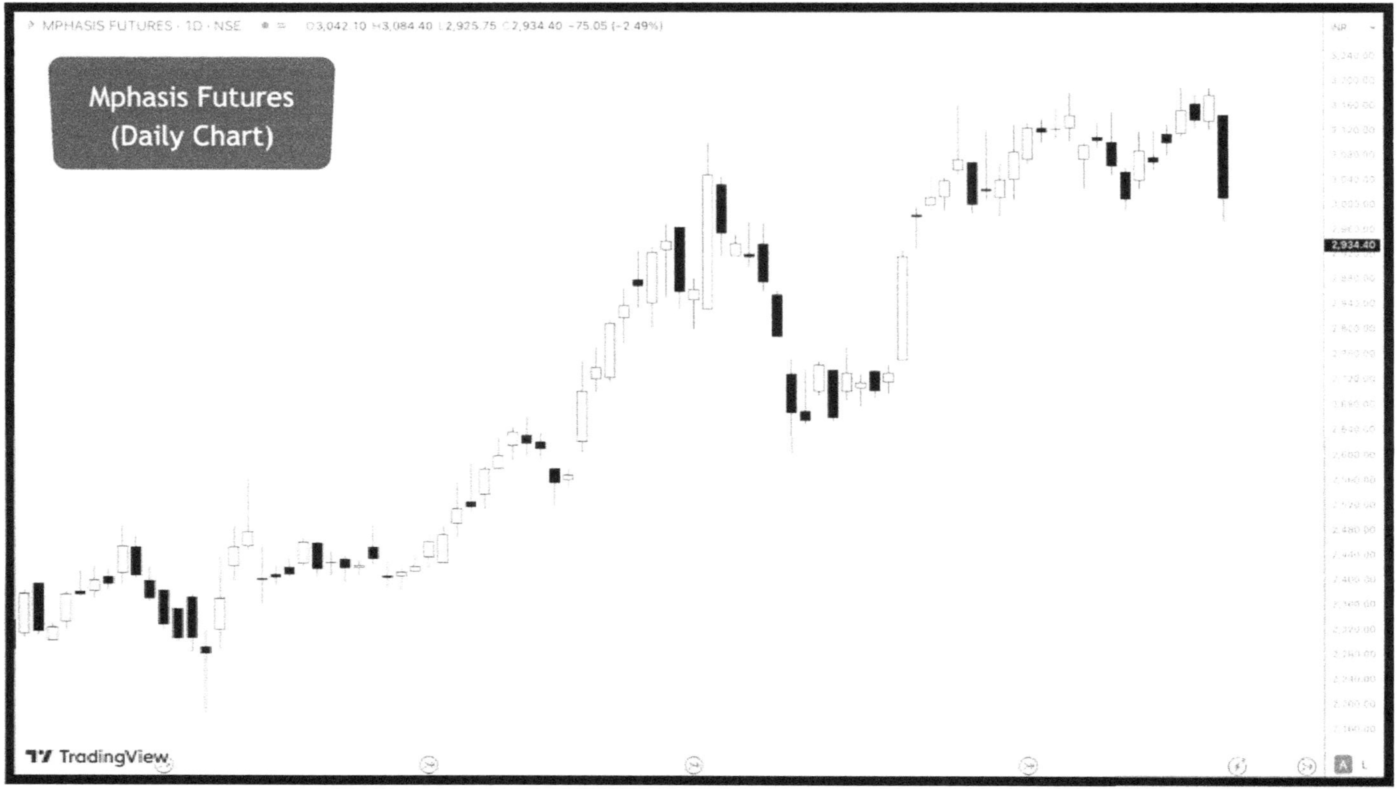

Image 9.9: Daily futures chart for Mphasis Ltd. on 18 September 2024

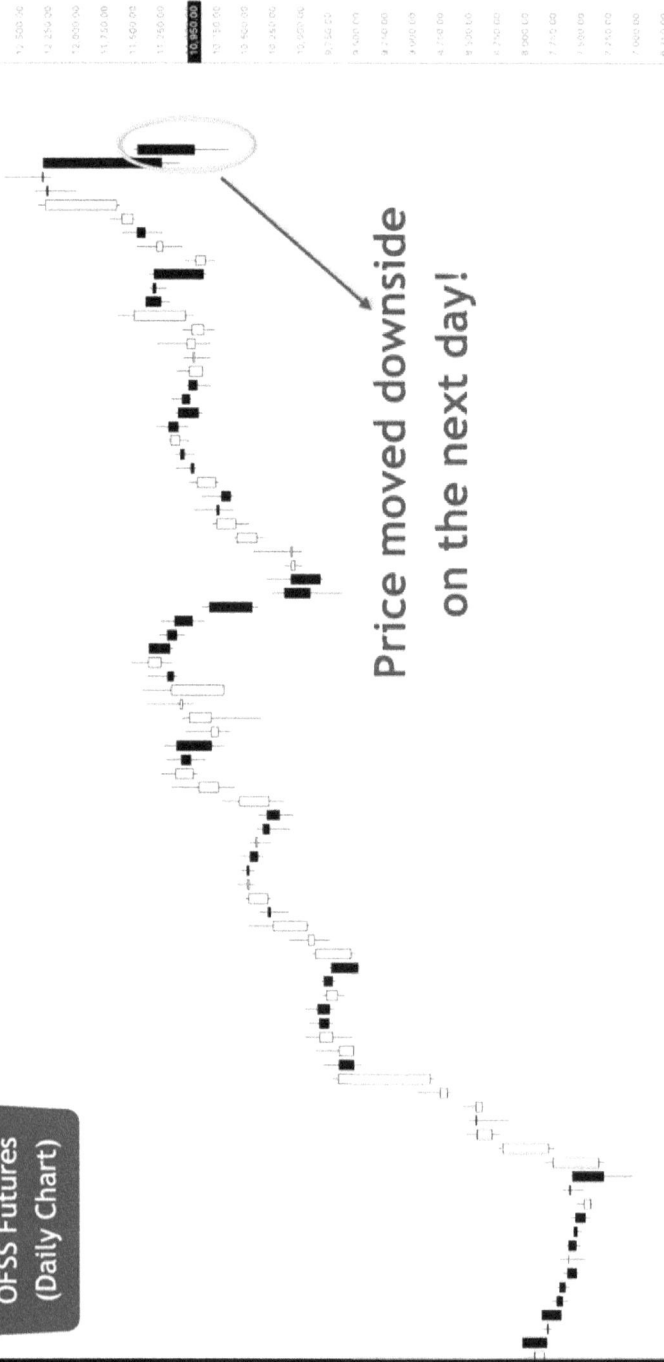

Image 9.10: Daily futures chart result for OFSS Ltd. on the next day

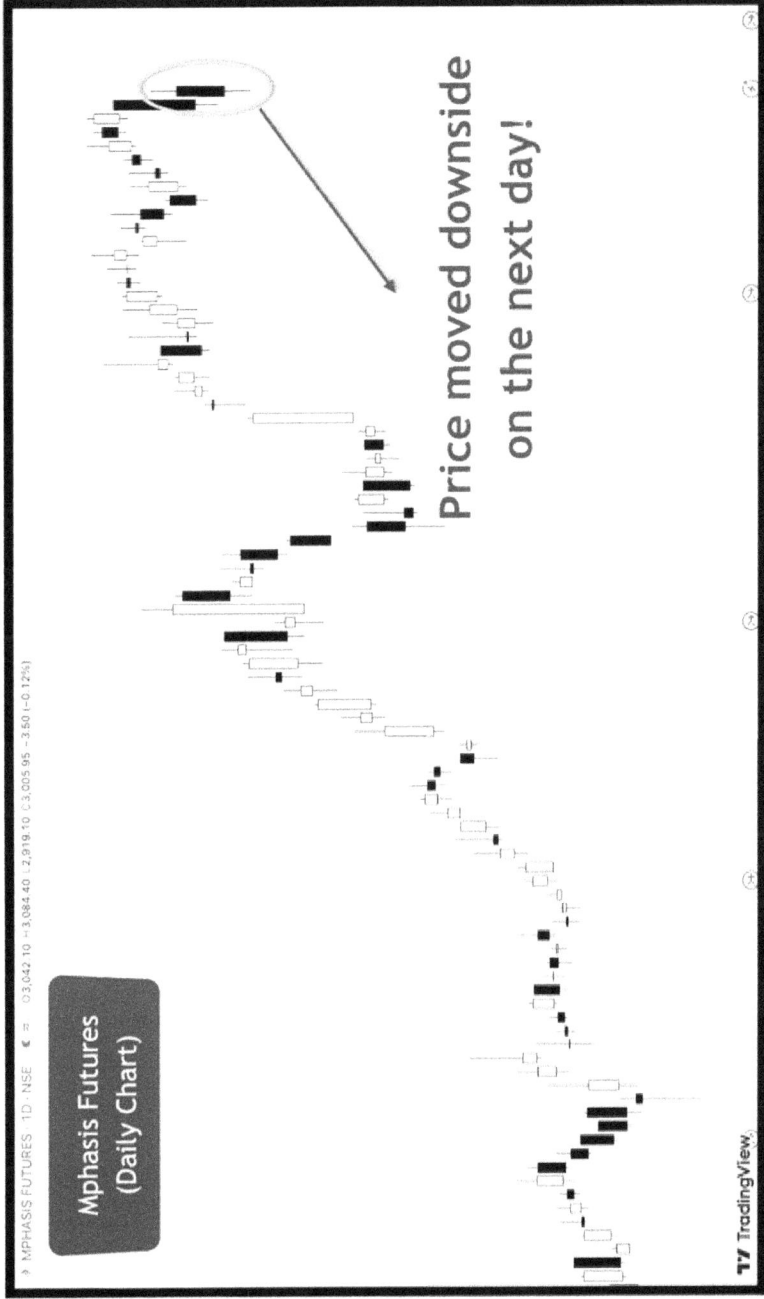

Image 9.11: Daily chart for futures result of Mphasis Ltd. on the next day

SYSTEM 5: IRON CONDOR STRATEGY

An iron condor is an options strategy that allows a trader to profit when they expect the stock to stay within a specific price range.

It is like setting up a net to catch a fish that swims pretty close.

Let us understand this with an example. Suppose Nifty 50 is currently trading at 18,000, and you believe it will stay between 17,800 and 18,200 over the next month.

Steps to set up an iron condor

1. **Sell an out-of-the-money call:** Sell a 18,200 strike call option. This means you earn a premium, but you might have to sell Nifty at 18,200 if it goes above this level.
2. **Buy a higher strike call:** Buy a 18,300 strike call option. This protects you in case Nifty goes way above 18,200. It limits your maximum loss if the market rises sharply.
3. **Sell an out-of-the-money put:** Sell a 17,800 strike put option. You earn a premium here too, but you might have to buy Nifty at 17,800 if it goes below this level.
4. **Buy a lower strike put:** Buy a 17,700 strike put option. This will protect you in case Nifty falls significantly below 17,800. It limits your maximum loss if the market drops sharply.

How this works

i. **If Nifty stays between 17,800 and 18,200:** You get to keep all the net premiums you received after selling the 18,200 call and the 17,800 put and buying the 18,300 call and 17,700 put. This is your profit.
ii. **If Nifty moves outside this range:** The bought call at 18,300 and the bought put at 17,700 limit your losses. You will not lose more than the difference between the sell and buy strikes minus the net premium you received.

Profit and Loss

Maximum profit occurs if Nifty stays between 17,800 and 18,200 until expiry. Your profit is the total premiums received from selling the 18,200 call and the 17,800 put minus the premiums paid for 18,300 CE and 17,700 PE.

Maximum loss occurs if Nifty moves significantly above 18,300 or below 17,700, your losses are limited to the difference between the sell and buy strike prices minus the net premium collected.

10

HOW TO IMPROVE SHORT STRADDLE AND STRANGLE OPTIONS STRATEGY

A few years ago, one of my friends messaged me on WhatsApp when I was trading as usual during market hours. He said that he came across an interesting options strategy and was making over 5% monthly returns without much effort.

Initially I was doubtful, but decided to check with him. It was true that he made around 8–10% returns every month for the last few months.

When I came across the strategy he used, I was very surprised.

He would sell both the at-the-money call option and put option for Nifty at 9.20 a.m. and keep a stop-loss of 2 times on both options.

For example, if he sold Nifty 20,000 CE at 30 and 20,000 PE at 30, he would keep a stop-loss at 60 for both options.

If the stop-loss hit for one side, he would trail the stop-loss of another stage to the entry price, that is, 30, and hold it for the rest of the day.

On days it went sideways, he would collect the premium for both the call and put options.

If the market trends in one direction, he will lose money on one option, but he would collect the same premium on the other options. So the trade would become breakeven.

Very rarely, the market would hit the stop-loss on both sides.

I was curious after learning this strategy and started experimenting with it.

Later, the same strategy became popular as '9.20 straddle' and '9.20 strangle', and many traders started to take similar trades.

SHORT STRANGLE

A short strangle involves selling a call option and a put option on the same underlying asset, with different strike prices but the same expiry date.

The strategy also profits from low volatility but has a broader range of acceptable price movements than a straddle.

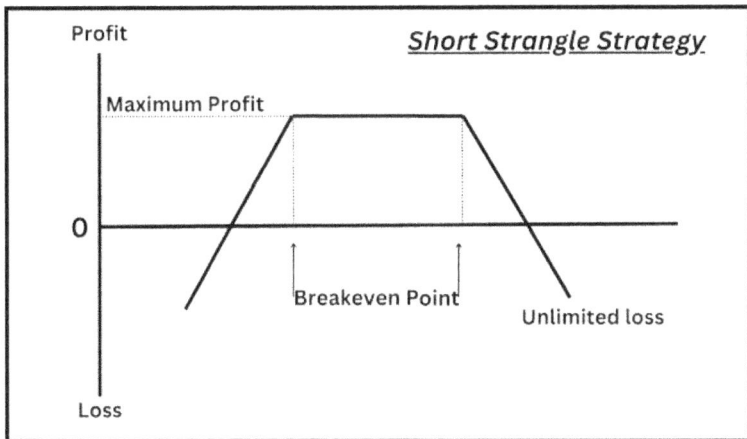

Image 10.1: Payout graph with short strangle strategy

How It Works

Profit: You collect premiums from both options. If the asset's price stays between the two strike prices, both options expire worthless, and you keep the premiums.

Risk: Like the straddle, significant price movements can lead to unlimited losses. Let us understand this with an example.

The underlying asset is stock XYZ, currently at $50.

Sell a $55 call option and a $45 put option.

You keep the premiums if XYZ stays between $45 and $55.

An example from Nifty is discussed below.

The current market price of Nifty is at Rs 24,951 (image 10.2).

There is one month to expiry in monthly options (20 trading days to be precise).

A trader thinks it will not move beyond 500 points in any direction. So he decides to sell 25,500 CE and 24,500 PE of the current month expiry (image 10.3).

Image 10.2: A short strangle on the daily chart of Nifty

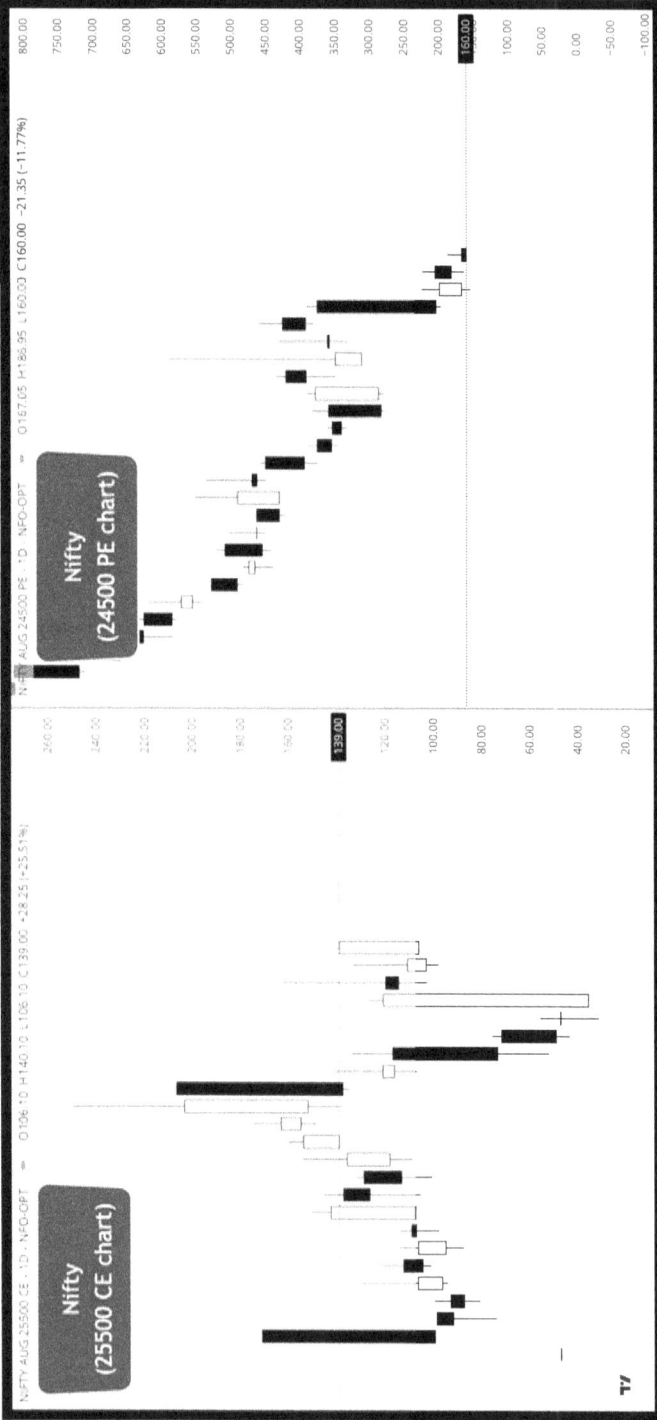

NIFTY AUG 25500 CE · 1D · NFO-OPT   ∞   O 106.10 H 140.10 L 106.10 C 139.00 +28.25 (+25.51%)

Nifty (25500 CE chart)

N-FTY AUG 24500 PE · 1D · NFO-OPT   ∞   O 167.05 H 186.95 L 160.00 C 160.00 −21.35 (−11.77%)

Nifty (24500 PE chart)

Image 10.3: Daily chart of Nifty showing a short strangle CE and PE

SHORT STRADDLE

A short straddle strategy involves selling (writing) a call option and a put option on the same underlying asset with the same strike price and expiry date.

The goal is to profit from low volatility. The trader expects the underlying asset's price to stay close to the strike price.

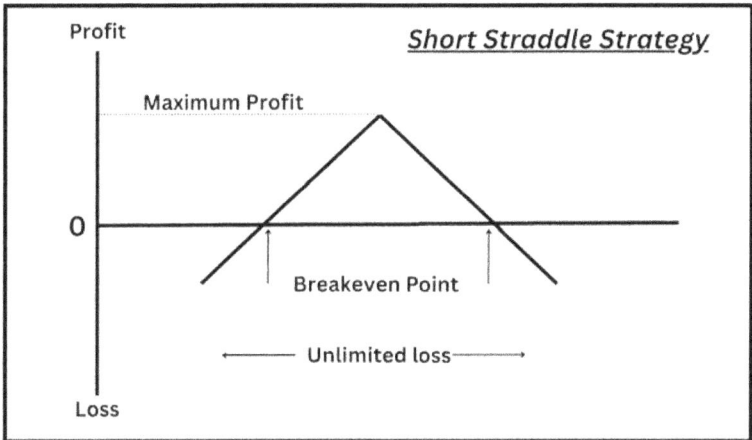

Image 10.4: Payout graph with short straddle strategy

How It Works

Profit: You earn a premium from selling both options. If the asset's price remains near the strike price at expiry, both options expire worthless, and you keep the premium.

Risk: You could face unlimited losses if the asset's price moves significantly up or down. If the price rises, the call option results in losses; if it falls, the put option results in losses.

Suppose the underlying asset, stock XYZ, is currently trading at $50. You sell a $50 call option and a $50 put option. If XYZ stays around $50, you keep the premium from both options.

USEFUL TIPS TO IMPROVE THE RESULTS OF SHORT STRADDLE OR SHORT STRANGLE

1. Delay the 'entry' timings from 9.20 a.m.

Changing the entry timing for a 9.20 straddle or strangle in the Indian markets to later, like after 9.30 or 9.45, can potentially improve the results.

The first 15–30 minutes after the market opens (from 9.15 to 9.30 or 9.45) are typically highly volatile. The processing of overnight news, global market reactions, and large institutional orders cause this volatility.

This initial volatility can lead to sudden price spikes or dips, causing higher premiums for options, which can quickly decay or move against the position. Early market volatility often results in false breakouts, where the price appears to move significantly in one direction only to reverse shortly after.

By waiting some time, we allow the market to settle and provide a more apparent trend or direction. The extreme movements and erratic price changes in the first 15–30 minutes are less likely to influence the premiums you pay.

Entering a straddle or strangle after the market has stabilised usually results in paying lower premiums for the options, as implied volatility decreases once the initial market frenzy calms down.

2. 0 to 1 DTE (Day to Expiry)

In options, 0 DTE stands for zero days to expiry. It refers to options contracts that are set to expire on the same day you are trading them.

Options traders use the short strangle strategy in 0 DTE weekly options to make some profits by taking advantage of the high time decay and the lack of significant moves expected in the price of the underlying asset.

Since these options expire on the same day, they have very little time value left. Their prices (premiums) are primarily driven by the expectation of how much the market may move before the end of the trading day. By selling these options, the trader collects the premiums upfront.

If the market stays within the expected range until the options expire, both the call and the put options will expire worthless, allowing the trader to keep the entire premium as profit. The rapid time decay, especially in the last few hours of trading, works in the trader's favour as the option prices decrease quickly.

Trading 1 DTE (one day to expiry) options instead of 0 DTE in a short strangle strategy can help to make profits by offering a slightly longer time horizon to capture premium decay while reducing the immediate volatility risk associated with 0 DTE options.

With 1 DTE options, you enter the trade a day before expiry, allowing you to collect higher premiums because the options still have a full day of time value left. This extra time value means the premiums are generally larger than what you would get on the expiry day.

Additionally, by trading the day before expiry, you are less exposed to the intense market fluctuations that often occur during the final trading hours on expiry day. This can lead to a more gradual and manageable decay of option premiums as the market stabilises overnight and into the next day.

Moreover, 1 DTE trading allows you to adjust the position if the market starts to move against you. Since you have an extra day, you can take steps like rolling the options to different strike prices or closing one leg of the strangle if a directional move seems likely. This flexibility can help mitigate potential losses that are harder to manage in the fast-paced environment of 0 DTE trading.

3. Use technical indicators to pick sideways market

When we use technical indicators to identify a sideways or range-bound market, it can significantly enhance the profitability of a short strangle options strategy, compared to mindlessly deploying it at 9.20 a.m. in the Indian markets.

Technical indicators, like Bollinger Bands, the Relative Strength Index (RSI), and the Average True Range (ATR), provide insights into market conditions and help traders gauge whether the market will likely remain within a specific range.

When these indicators suggest that the market is not trending strongly in either direction, it indicates a low-volatility environment, which is ideal for a short-strangle strategy. In such conditions, the underlying asset's price is more likely to stay within the predetermined range, allowing the sold options to expire worthless and the trader to keep the premium as profit.

On the other hand, deploying a short strangle mindlessly at the market open can be risky due to the high volatility and potential for unexpected price movements in the first few minutes of trading.

For example, when the RSI stays between 40–60 levels, we can expect a sideways market. Similarly, when stochastics stays between 20–80 levels, we can expect a sideways market. When average directional index (ADX) line stays below 20, it also indicates a sideways market.

4. Use balanced market situation

A balanced market refers to a simple market situation where buyers and sellers are in equilibrium, resulting in relatively stable price movements. In a balanced market smart money will be absent and there is no dominant force driving prices significantly higher or lower. The price displays movements within a narrow range (within the previous day's range at intraday level), indicating a state of agreement called 'fair value' between buyers and sellers.

Image 10.5 shows the example for a balanced market situation on the chart of Nifty. The price displayed the entire day's movement within the previous day range.

Whenever the price opens very close to the center of the previous day's range and makes one to two small candles in a 15-min timeframe or if it does not go near either the previous day's low or previous day's high, then there is a high possibility of a balanced market.

In image 10.6, the price opened exactly at the middle range of the previous day's range and displayed two small candles in the 15-min timeframe on the chart of ICICI Bank. Hence, there is a high possibility of sideways move for the rest of the day. So options traders can initiate a short straddle or strangle strategy using 0 DTE or 1 DTE.

Image 10.7 shows that the price displayed it's complete range within the previous day's range as per a balanced market situation on the chart for ICICI Bank.

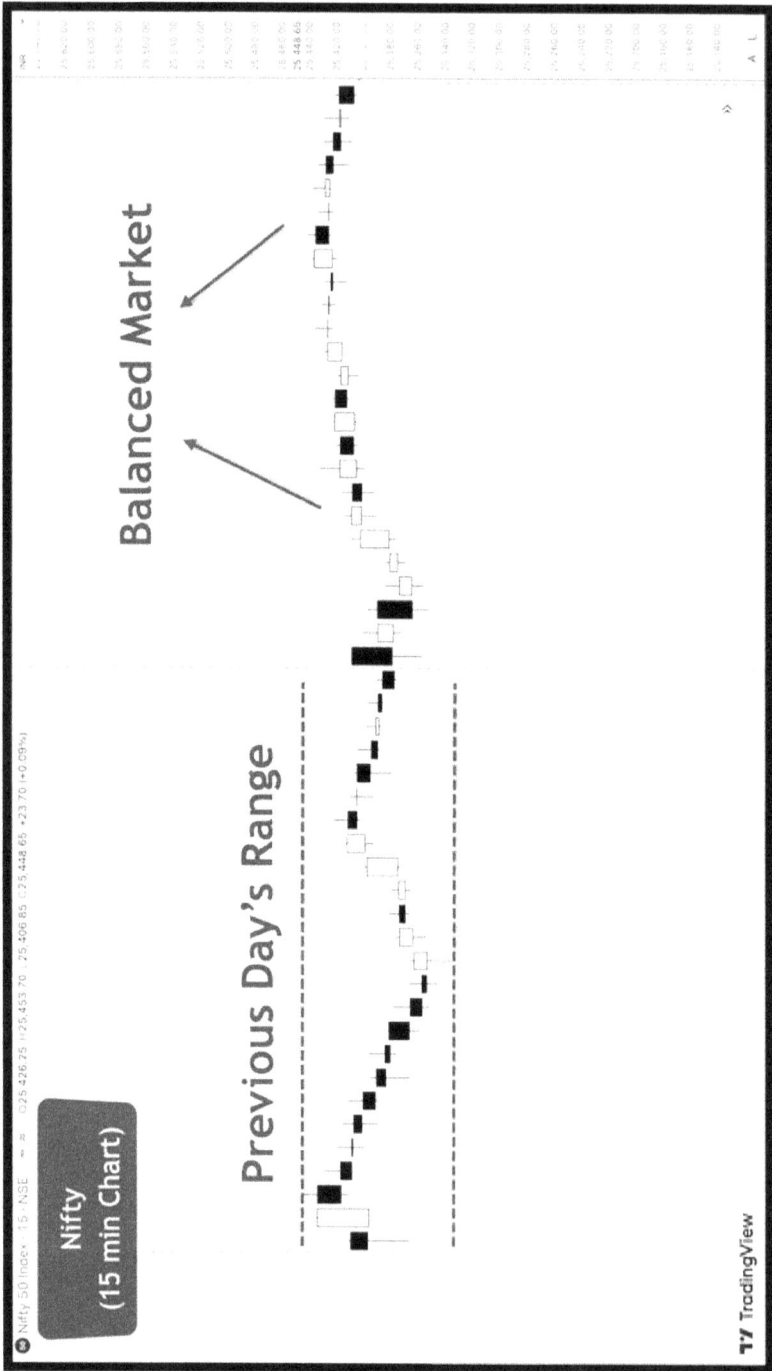

Image 10.5: 15-minute chart of Nifty showing a balanced market situation

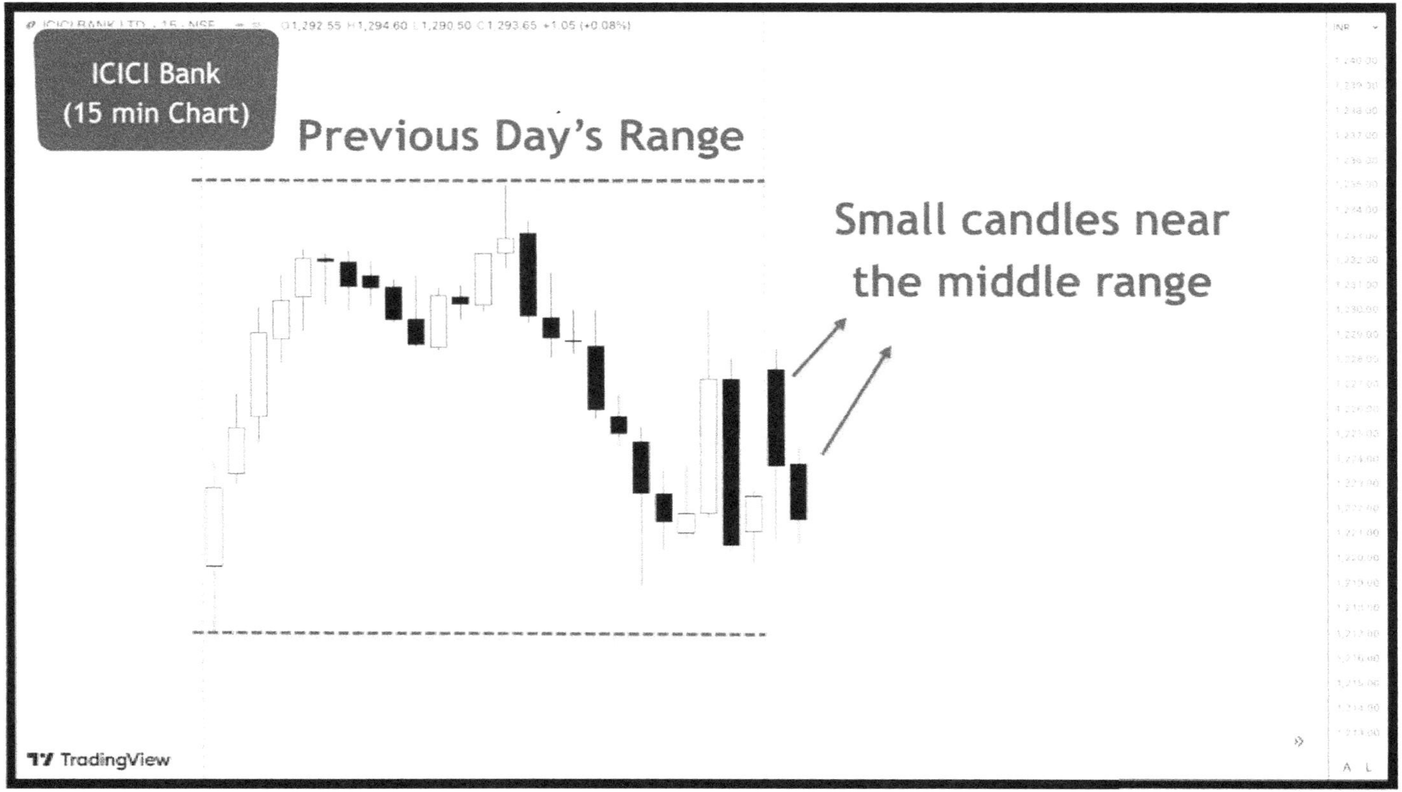

Image 10.6: Small candles on the 15-minute daily chart of ICICI Bank

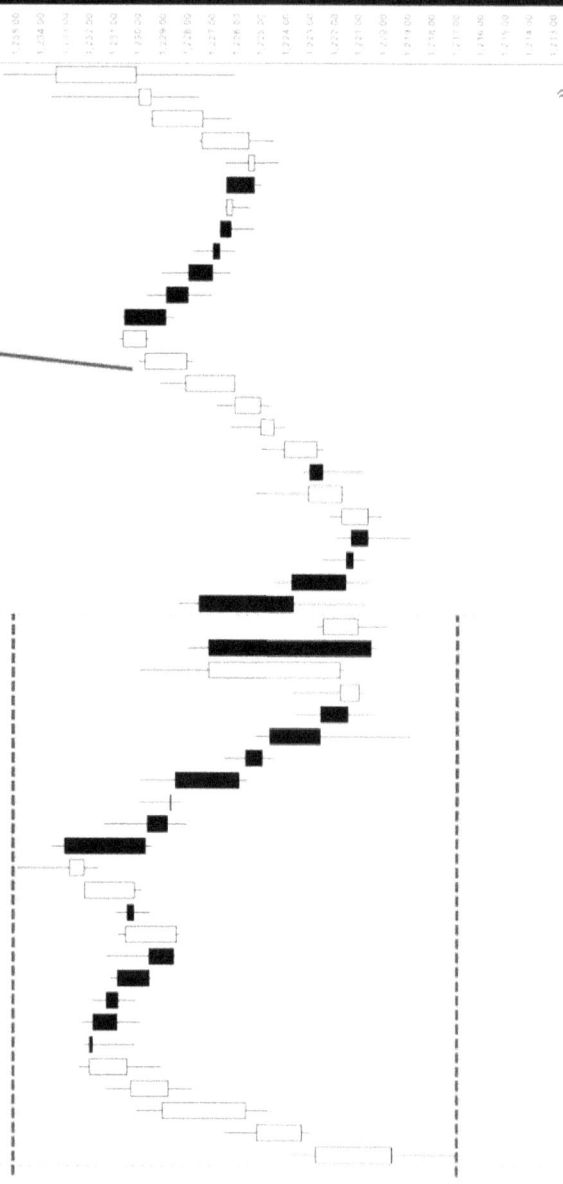

Image 10.7: Balanced market on the 15-minute daily chart of ICICI Bank

11

HOW TO AVOID COMMON PITFALLS OF OPTIONS TRADING

Options trading offers the potential for significant profits, but it also comes with a higher level of complexity and risk than other forms of trading. Many traders, especially beginners, can fall into common pitfalls that can erode their capital and negatively impact their trading results. Understanding and learning how to avoid these mistakes is crucial for long-term success in options trading.

Here is an in-depth look at these pitfalls and how to steer clear of them:

1. LACK OF UNDERSTANDING OF OPTIONS MECHANICS

Most traders jump into options trading without developing a proper understanding of how options work.

Compared to equity and futures, options have various other components like strike price and expiry date, and the greeks (delta, gamma, theta, vega, and rho) which affect their pricing and behaviour.

How to prevent losses

i.   Take the time to study the basics of options, including how they are priced and the factors influencing their value.
ii. Understand the greeks and how they impact options' prices and risk levels.
iii. Practise with paper trading or a simulation account to get comfortable with options trading mechanics before risking real money.

2. IGNORING THE IMPACT OF TIME DECAY (THETA)

Options premiums lose value as they approach expiry due to time decay, especially out-of-the-money options. Traders who hold options buying positions too long without considering this decay can see their positions lose value rapidly.

How to prevent losses

i.   Be mindful of the expiry date and the impact of time decay on your options positions.
ii. If you anticipate a sideways market, consider using strategies that benefit from time decay, such as selling options (for example, covered calls and iron condors).
iii. For long options positions, set a timeframe for the anticipated move and exit if the move does not occur within that period.

3. OVERLEVERAGING AND LACK OF RISK MANAGEMENT

Options offer leverage, which means you can control a prominent position with a relatively small capital. However, this leverage can lead to significant losses if not managed properly. Overleveraging, or taking on too large a position relative to your account size, can quickly wipe out your trading capital.

How to prevent losses

    i. Use proper position sizing and only risk a small percentage of your capital on any single trade, typically no more than 1–2%.

    ii. Set stop-loss orders to limit losses.

    iii. Avoid the temptation to 'go all-in' on any trade, no matter how confident you are in the outcome.

4. NO CLEARLY DEFINED STRATEGY

Many traders enter the options market without a clearly defined strategy, making decisions based on emotions, market rumours, or gut feelings. This lack of a structured approach can lead to inconsistent results and losses.

How to prevent losses

    i. Develop a trading plan with precise entry and exit criteria, risk management rules, and position sizing guidelines.

    ii. Choose an options strategy that aligns with your market outlook, risk tolerance, and trading goals.

    iii. Stick to your strategy and avoid making impulsive decisions based on short-term market movements or emotional reactions.

5. IGNORING VOLATILITY AND ITS EFFECTS

Volatility plays a crucial role in options pricing. Implied volatility (IV) represents the market's expectations of future price movements in an option. Higher implied volatility means larger expected price swings, while lower volatility implies smaller movements. Many traders overlook the impact of implied volatility on options premiums

For example, buying options during periods of high implied volatility can lead to paying a premium that is too high, which can result in losses even if the underlying asset moves in the desired direction.

How to prevent losses

   i. Always keep an eye on implied volatility levels and understand how it affects options prices.
  ii. Consider strategies that benefit from high or low volatility environments. For instance, options selling strategies are better during high volatility to capture higher premiums.
 iii. Use volatility indicators and tools to gauge market conditions and adjust your strategies accordingly.

6. HOLDING POSITIONS UNTIL EXPIRY

Holding options positions until expiry can be risky, especially if they are in-the-money. Unexpected assignments or exercises can result in unwanted stock positions or additional margin requirements.

How to prevent losses

   i. Have a clear plan for when to close your positions, ideally well before expiry.

ii. Monitor your positions as they approach expiry and be prepared to exit or roll them over to a later expiry if necessary.

iii. Understand the potential outcomes of holding options through expiry, including assignment and the impact on your portfolio.

7. OVERTRADING AND CHASING LOSSES

Overtrading occurs when traders take too many trades quickly, often trying to recover from previous losses. This behaviour can lead to poor decision-making, higher transaction costs, and increased risk exposure.

How to prevent losses

i. Set limits on the number of trades you take within a specific timeframe (for example, 2–3 trades in a day).

ii. Stick to your trading plan and avoid revenge trading to make up for losses.

iii. Focus on quality over quantity, seeking high-probability setups rather than taking trades out of boredom or frustration.

8. LACK OF DIVERSIFICATION

Concentrating too much on a single stock, sector, or strategy increases the risk if that particular market segment moves against you. This lack of diversification can lead to significant losses.

How to prevent losses

i. Diversify your options trades across different underlying assets, sectors, and strategies to spread risk.

   ii. Avoid putting a large portion of your capital into a single trade or market.

  iii. Balance your portfolio with different types of options strategies, such as a mix of directional and non-directional trades.

9. OVERLOOKING THE IMPACT OF FEES AND COMMISSIONS

Options trading involves brokerage fees and government taxes, which can add up quickly, especially for active traders. Ignoring these costs can erode profits and affect overall returns.

How to prevent losses

    i. Be aware of the commission structure and fees associated with your brokerage.

   ii. Factor in these costs when calculating potential profits and losses.

  iii. Consider using strategies that require fewer transactions or look for brokers with competitive commission rates.

10. NOT STAYING INFORMED AND EDUCATED

The markets constantly evolve, and what works today may not work tomorrow. Moreover, regulatory bodies keep changing the rules to accommodate current market conditions.

Traders who fail to stay informed about market developments, changes in options trading regulations, and new strategies may be at a disadvantage.

How to prevent losses

   i. Continuously educate yourself about options trading through books, courses, webinars, and market analysis.

  ii. Stay updated on market news and developments that could impact your trades.

 iii. Join trading communities or forums to exchange ideas and learn from other experienced traders.

12

MARKET PHASES

A few years ago, a close friend approached me and shared her desire to learn trading.

She wanted to learn trading within one year and earn an amount equal to her current salary.

She spent four years getting an engineering degree and worked for a decade in IT to earn that salary. But now she wanted to invest only one year and earn the same amount from trading. I told her that achieving that goal within one year was almost impossible. She was still adamant about learning to trade and making some profits from it.

So I met her one day and explained a positional trading system based on the RSI indicator. I discussed all the entry, exit, and money management rules required for the system in detail. This system was designed to take only long trades (as it was a positional system), and market cycles are critical to grasp it fully. As fate would have it, the market was in a bull run during that time, and whichever stocks she invested in showed good results.

Whenever we discussed the outcomes of the trades, she was pleased and said she could always quit her IT job if she got a similar return. I warned her many times that a person has to go through different phases of the market to get a complete grip of the trading system and control their emotions through each of them. I also told her that we were in a bull run so all her investments were making big profits. But whenever a bear market starts, stop-loss orders would automatically be hit for all trades, and you need to be quick to execute them. Besides, you also do not get long trades during a bear market.

But what I said did not make much sense to her, as most of her trades were profitable. She deployed all her life savings in the markets and started thinking about quitting her job. I tried to discourage her from doing this. So my friend stopped taking my advice and said she could manage trading independently.

After a few weeks, a bear trend started in the market and she was not tracking market trends due to her overconfidence. When she noticed this after a week, most of her profits had already vanished. But she decided to hold on to them, ignoring all the stop-loss rules of the system, hoping they would return to their uptrend. However, within 1–2 weeks, she also lost 40–50% of her capital, and then she needed my help to recover the lost money!

Most people who taste success in the beginning usually experience this. One particular market cycle instills tremendous confidence in them, and they assume the market will behave the same forever. They take more risks only to lose their hard-earned savings.

WHY IS THIS EXPERIENCE NEEDED?

One must experience different market phases, such as uptrend, downtrend, sideways trend, and volatile markets. Each phase offers unique insights about how the price fluctuates differently, the results vary, and different emotional triggers.

A few years ago, I taught a simple breakout trading system to a group of people. That system was designed to take only positional long trades in Indian equity markets.

When people started taking trades, the market was in an uptrend. They were getting many trades daily, and most of them made good returns. After some time, the market started to move in a sideways zone, and they were not getting enough trades. Still, they made decent returns, but many were unhappy with their results, mainly because they were comparing the current results with the past ones in an uptrend. After some time, the market started to move in a downtrend. These people were not getting enough trades, and 50% of their trades started to hit the stop-losses. However, on a monthly basis, they were at breakeven (meaning no loss, no profit).

But they all felt miserable because they did not get enough trades (excitement was missing), and many trades hit their stop-losses. The strange thing is they were not losing money, but most of them lacked the vision that this downtrend would not last forever and that they could start making money once the market started moving in an uptrend.

This emotional journey is essential for developing the discipline required for lasting success. As traders face both favourable and challenging market conditions, they enhance their ability to adapt, fine-tune their strategies, and improve their decision-making skills, no matter the circumstances.

13

DARK SECRETS OF THE MARKET

Stock market trading has spread worldwide. It has become popular among working professionals and business people (primarily men). But there is one thing that makes me immensely sad about how people approach the stock market and trading. Most people need complete clarity before they jump into the trading arena.

1. THE STOCK MARKET IS LIKE A TOUGH BOXING MATCH

Stock market trading is similar to a fierce fight—you vs. Mike Tyson, Muhammad Ali, Rocky Marciano, Manny Pacquiao, etc.—simultaneously. At least in boxing, you will see who is punching and the direction from which the punches are coming. But in trading, you do not see these punches from experts. It is because trading is designed in such a manner.

Anyone can enter and participate in the game. When you can take a trade, always remember you are fighting with many people who have spent decades in this business.

In a boxing match, any boxer who only throws punches without knowing the art of defending himself will quickly get knocked out. Defence blocking, dodging, and countering are just as important as attacking. Similarly, protecting your capital is crucial in trading. Like setting stop-loss orders, a sound risk management strategy is akin to keeping your guard up in a fight.

2. EXCEPT GOD AND A LIAR NOBODY CAN GET 90% ACCURACY

Every social media platform displays advertisements about traders who miraculously get 90% accuracy in their trading. Most of them have these kinds of advertisements to trigger some emotions in your mind about not losing money and to make you buy their products (a software product or a course, etc.). There is no such thing as 80–90% accuracy without compromising the profit factor. People who claim 80–90% accuracy are either god or fake.

For example, I can say, "Buy Nifty at 25,000, target 25,100, and stop-loss 24,000." With these calls, I can easily achieve 90% accuracy.

But do you think it will bring profits?

3. MANY PEOPLE CANNOT MAKE PROFITS EVEN AFTER KNOWING A PROFITABLE TRADING SYSTEM

Even if I share an excellent, profitable trading system, most people will not be able to profit from it because they are not convinced of its logic or results. The only way to get rid of the different thought process in their mind is by backtesting the system with historical data. However, most people are too lazy to do the work, so they may not be able to take trades following the same system.

Some people have the same ideas, similar to the system. However, they may have watched a few other methods on YouTube or read about some strategies in a book. These people face a tough time shortlisting the systems. They will not be able to follow and take trades as per the system.

Very few people understand the importance and work behind a system, and they are determined to implement it as it is. These people will be rewarded in the long run.

4. DO NOT THINK ABOUT TRADING AS A FULL-TIME CAREER UNTIL YOU SATISFY THESE CRITERIA

In the current market conditions, there is no need to pursue trading as a full-time career. One can easily manage positional trades or long-term investments alongside their day job or business. Even if a person is interested only in intraday trading, they can opt for algorithmic trading or semi-algo platforms, which help them take trades at the intraday level.

But if a person is still keen to try full-time trading, they should fulfil these conditions on the checklist before quitting their job.

1. No debt or loan

It is essential to have a cushion in case of unexpected hardships. Make sure you have no debt or loans outstanding. If you have an EMI to pay every month, it brings unnecessary pressure to generate profits every trading day. However, opportunities in the market only last a few trading days. So, it is better to have a free mind without any EMI.

2. Savings to run the family for two years

Please remember that trading should be treated as a business and that success takes time and hard work. Hence, you should have enough savings to cover your expenses and your family expenses for at least two years. This will reduce the stress of having to find another job if trading does not work out. Your family should not suffer because of your crazy ideas!

3. Consecutive six months of profit in trading

Trading in the market is always a roller-coaster ride. One should not think that they have become a successful trader just after one month of success. Make profits for at least six consecutive months before jumping into full-time trading.

4. Trading capital

It would help if you have enough trading capital to sustain yourself. This means having enough money to live on for at least a year without withdrawing from your trading account.

Suppose you generate a 5% profit every month and your monthly expense is Rs 25,000, you should have Rs 5,00,000 (5 Lakh) as your trading capital.

5. A passive income source

It is imperative to have at least one passive income source. This could be from a side business, rental property, or some other source of income that is not directly related to trading. Having this will help you weather any market downturns and keep you afloat financially.

5. REVENGE TRADING

I have seen hundreds of people losing crores of rupees in 1–2 trading days. However, I have not seen a single person yet who lost his entire capital (small or big) over 100 trades!

What does it indicate?

It shows that if we avoid the compulsive trades we take after experiencing a few failed trades, we can easily sustain ourselves in this business.

The Pareto principle or the 80-20 rule states that 80% of

outcomes come from 20% of causes. In trading, this means that 80% of your losses may come from only 20% of your trades. One of the critical reasons for this is revenge trading. It is a natural, quick, and emotional response when a trader suffers a decent loss. It is an attempt by the trader to prove his view or analysis is right.

Whenever a trader opts for a trade, it can only have any of the 5 outcomes mentioned below:

1. breakeven
2. small profit
3. small loss
4. big profit
5. **big loss**

Except the last one, all other outcomes will allow you to survive in the day trading business. However, a big loss on any trade is unacceptable in day trading. So, by avoiding revenge trading, a trader eliminates the big loss scenario. He will stay in the game either with small losses or small profits or as a breakeven trader.

6. TECHNICAL ANALYSIS IS NOT ENOUGH TO MAKE MONEY IN STOCK MARKETS

About ten years ago, when I was struggling to make profits in trading, I met a well-known trader and investment advisor in India. During our conversation, he said, "Over 90% people lose money in stock markets!" This was hard for me to hear because I wanted to become a successful trader.

This experience made me reflect.

After thinking about it for a while, I realised that many people, especially those who have lost money in trading, thought that only technical analysis was sufficient to get success in the stock market. But the reality is entirely different.

4 Steps for Success in Trading

Many people think only technical analysis is sufficient to get success in the stock market. But the reality is entirely different.

Four steps are crucial for achieving success with trading.

Technical analysis

Technical Analysis is a method used to predict the future price movement of a stock by analyzing historical data in different ways.

Money management

Money Management is a set of rules for allocating the required position size, reducing risk, and aiming for good returns in trading.

Psychology

The four primary emotions revolving around trading are greed, fear, regret, and hope.

Execution

Calmness in execution is the real Holy Grail in Trading.

Image 13.1: Four steps crucial for trading success

Four steps are crucial for achieving success with trading:

1. Technical analysis
2. Money management
3. Trading psychology
4. Execution

Step 1: Technical analysis

Technical analysis is a method used to predict the future price movement of a stock by analysing historical data in different ways. Technical traders believe current and past price action is the most reliable tool to predict future price movements. They do not use any fundamental information to make a trading decision.

Technical analysis is fun if you are on the right track. However, this alone is insufficient, and one must consider the steps below to make money in stock markets.

Step 2: Money management

"Even a poor trading system could make money with good money management"
— Jack D. Schwager

If a trader avoids big losses in his trading, he automatically survives in the game and starts to make money in the long run.

Money management is a set of rules for allocating the required position size, reducing risk, and aiming for good returns in trading. So, when a trade goes wrong, you do not lose more than 1–2% of your portfolio. Even if you get 10 successive failed trades, you do not lose more than 20% of your trading capital and stay in the game.

Step 3: Trading psychology

Trading psychology implies cognitive factors governing trading every day. The four primary emotions revolving around trading are greed, fear, regret, and hope. Please note that all these factors emerge due to a lack of, or, partial knowledge. Backtesting, meditation, and maintaining a trading journal help to achieve a better trading mindset.

Step 4: Execution

M.S. Dhoni won many trophies because of his calm and focused mindset. In high-pressure situations, he stayed composed and made clear decisions. Instead of reacting emotionally, Dhoni analysed the game and patiently executed his strategies. This allowed him to handle challenging situations without panicking. Similarly, calmness in execution is the real holy grail in trading. Suppose you have an excellent positive expectancy system and clear money management rules. In that case, you can make money in trading in the long run if you execute your plans in all market conditions.

7. PICK YOUR TIMEFRAME

A few years ago, one of my friends was trying hard to learn intraday trading. However, she had a successful business that consumed most of her time during market hours.

So she had a tough time managing her business, learning and executing intraday trades, and managing her family. I tried to convince her to focus on long-term trading, like swing or positional trading. Initially, she was adamant about continuing with day trading. After a few weeks, she could not do justice to all these areas and sought my help. When I asked her why she was so rigid about continuing with intraday trading, she told me that only intraday traders can make more profits than other traders, and hence, she wanted to continue only with intraday trading.

It was a pleasant surprise to me that, despite being well-educated with an MBA in Finance, she had this opinion of intraday trading. Finally, I managed to convince her that one can make money in any type of trading, whether intraday trading or swing trading, provided they follow the right basics.

Picking the correct time frame in trading is essential because it helps you balance trading with your work and family life. If you choose a time frame that fits your schedule, you can manage your trades without feeling any stress. For example, if you have a full-time job, shorter time frames like intraday trading or scalping might be too stressful because they require constant attention. A longer time frame, like swing or positional trading, allows you to focus on your career and family while still taking quality trades. It reduces the pressure of watching the market every minute and helps maintain a healthy work–life balance. This way, you can succeed in trading without sacrificing necessary personal or family time.

14

TECHNICAL ANALYSIS

When Indian cricketers visit Australia, South Africa or New Zealand for a cricket tour, what do they do? They spend many hours daily in net practice to get used to the pitch and environment. This practice provides a controlled setup for cricketers to adjust their skills to a new environment. It helps international cricketers develop muscle memory and quick decision-making skills that are crucial in a live cricket match.

However, some people underrate the importance of technical analysis in trading. They even claim that technical analysis is not necessary to succeed in trading, which is far from the truth.

Technical analysis allows traders to systematically study historical price movements, chart patterns, and market trends. By analysing historical data from different perspectives, traders gain insights into how markets behave over time, which helps them make better-informed decisions during live market hours.

Like cricketers who practise adapting to different playing conditions, traders must study technical analysis in-depth and adjust their strategies based on market conditions to achieve better long-term results.

TYPES OF MARKET TRENDS

Charles Dow wrote a series of Wall Street Journal editorials from 1900 until his death. According to him, all types of markets (equity, commodity, forex, etc.)—past, present, and even future—are discounted and reflected on the charts.

Many traders shared different versions of this theory from his editorials. However, you will find the most straightforward version in this chapter. As per Dow, market movements can be divided into four types. At any time, the price is a combination of these four types:

1. Uptrend
2. Downtrend
3. Sideways
4. Volatile

1. Uptrend

An uptrend consists of a series of higher highs (HH) and higher lows (HL), as shown in image 14.1. We can consider the price to be in an uptrend till it continues making higher highs and higher lows.

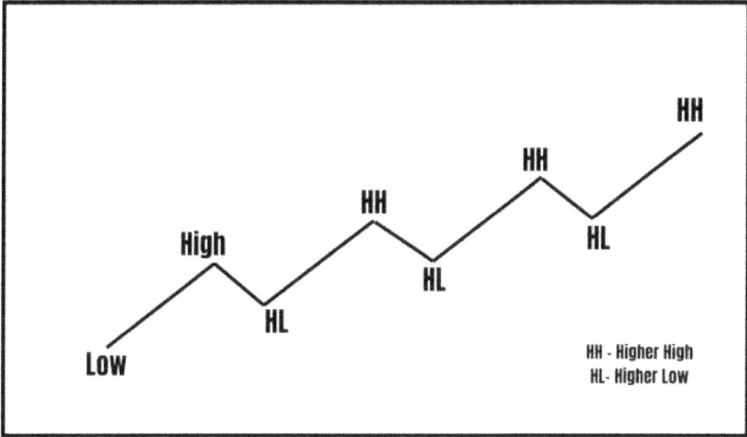

Image 14.1: Uptrend as per Dow Theory

Image 14.2 shows an example of uptrend in Nifty charts. The price continuously made higher highs and higher lows throughout the chart and hence we can easily say that the price is in a strong uptrend.

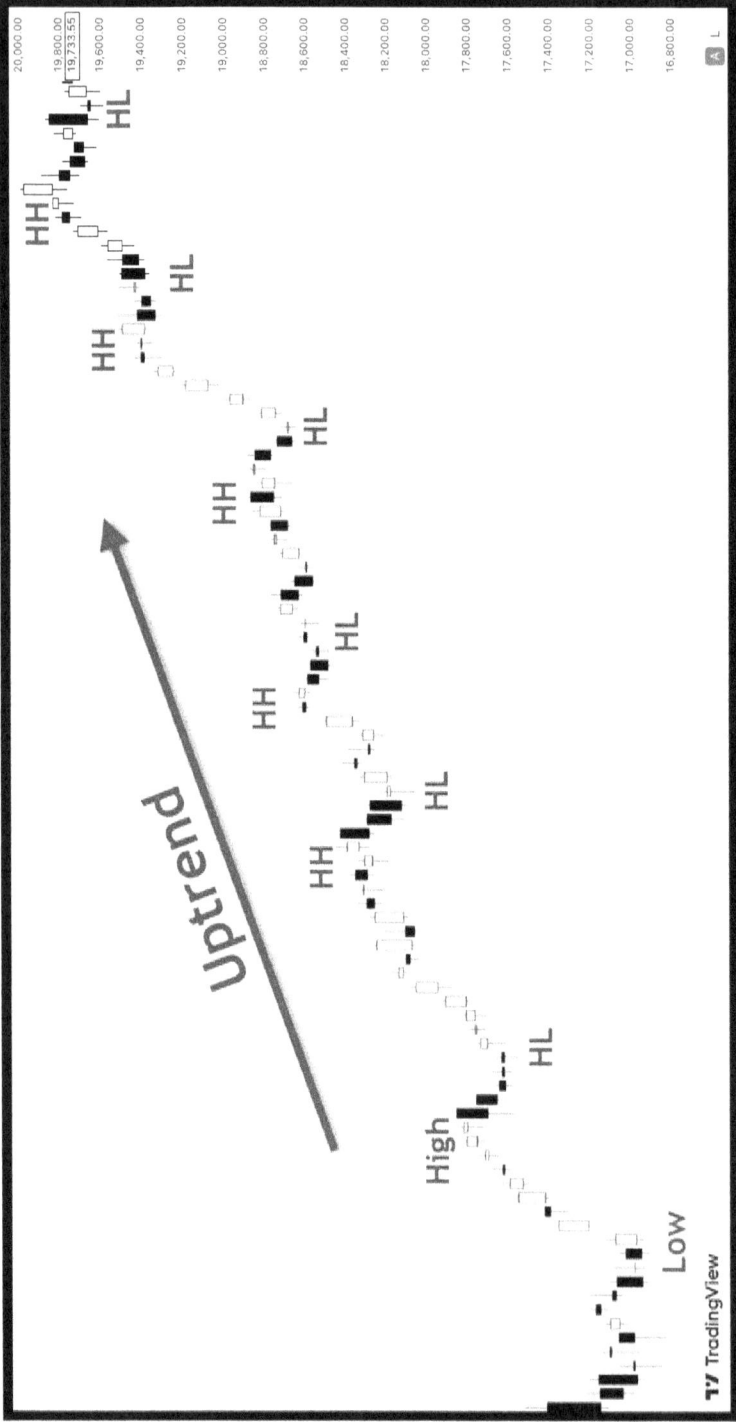

Image 14.2: Uptrend in Nifty

2. Downtrend

A downtrend consists of a series of lower highs (LH) and lower lows (LL), as shown in image 14.3. The price is in a downtrend making lower highs and lower lows.

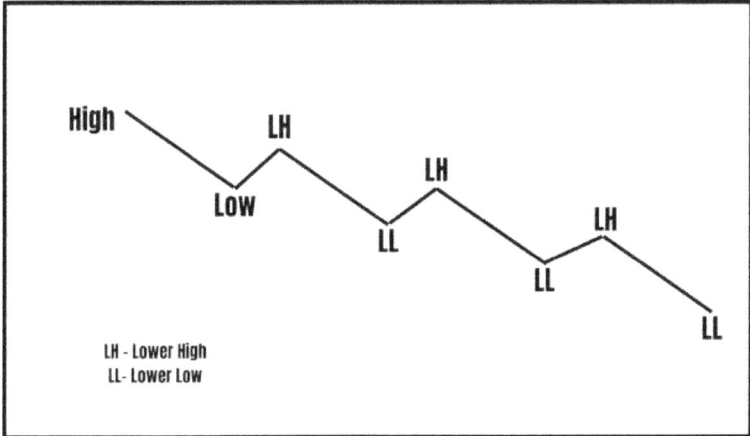

Image 14.3: Downtrend as per Dow Theory

Image 14.4 shows an example of a downtrend on the chart of Nifty Bank. The price continuously made lower highs and lower lows throughout the chart and hence we can easily say that the price is in a strong downtrend.

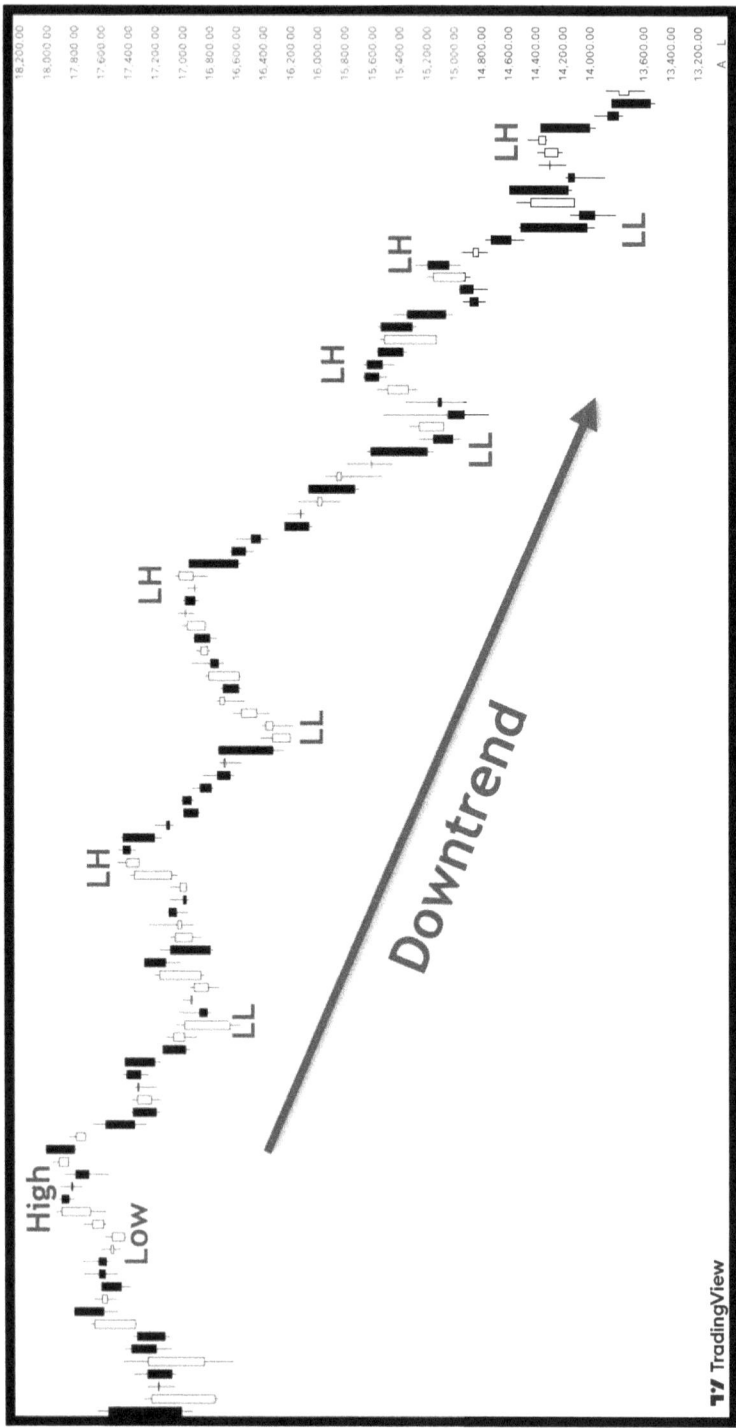

Image 14.4: Downtrend on the chart of Nifty Bank

3. Sideways trend

When the price has the same lows and highs, it can be recognised as a sideways trend (image 14.5). Please note that it need not be 100% the same level, and a slight deviation is acceptable.

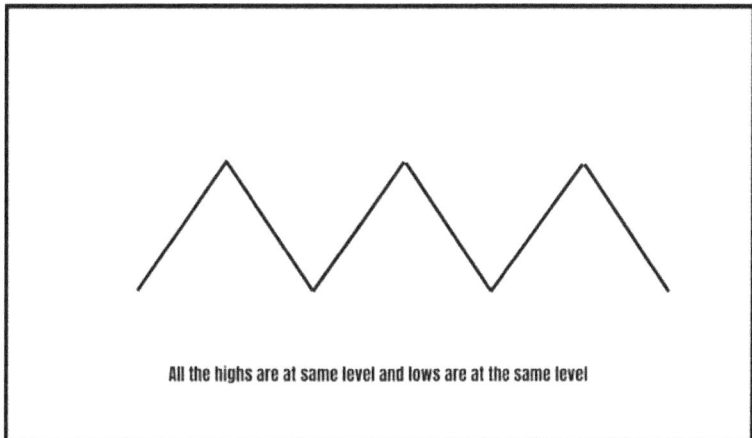

All the highs are at same level and lows are at the same level

Image 14.5: Sideways trend as per Dow Theory

Image 14.6 shows an example of a sideways trend on the Infosys charts. The price continuously made similar highs and similar lows throughout the chart. Hence we can easily say that the price is in a sideways trend.

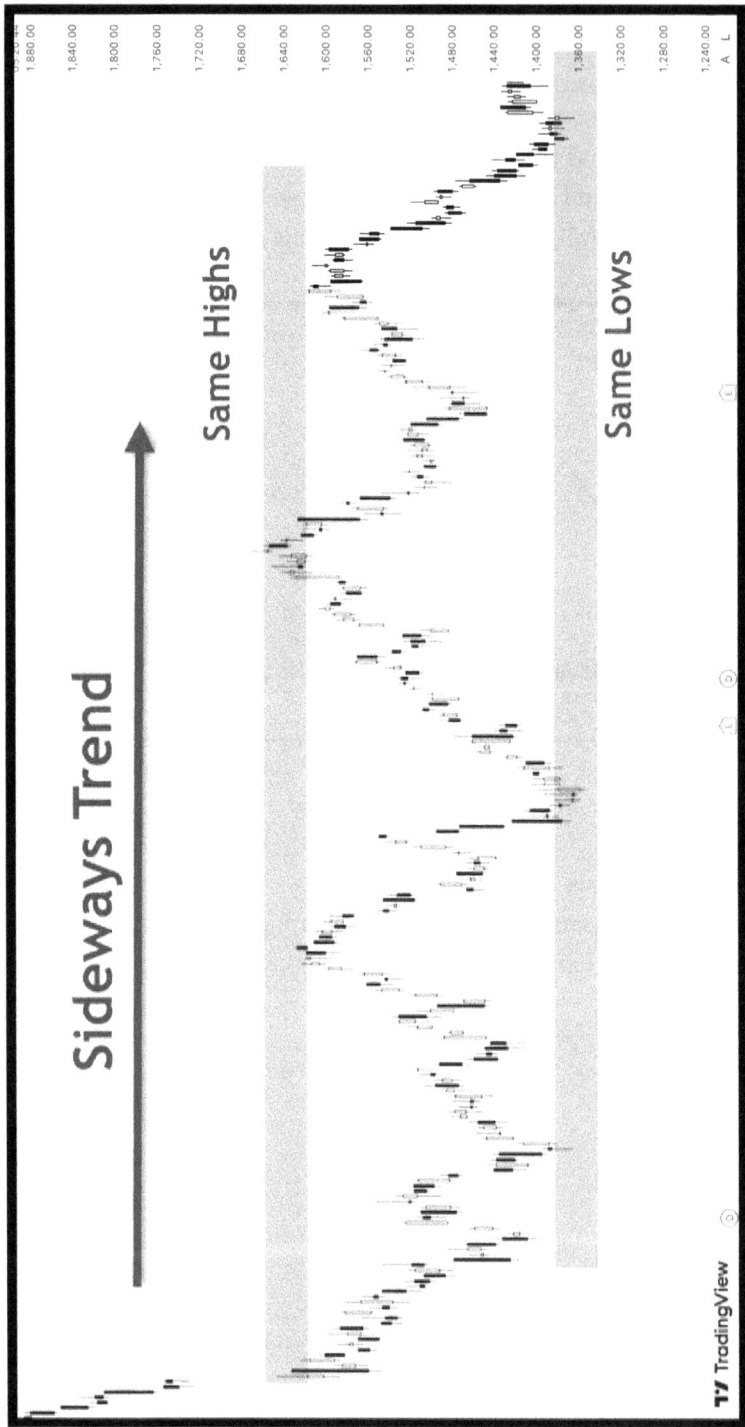

Image 14.6: Sideways trend on the chart of Infosys Ltd.

4. Random or Volatile Trend

Information on the volatile or random trend is not present in the original Dow Theory. However, after observing the market for a few years, I have added this type to the market trends.

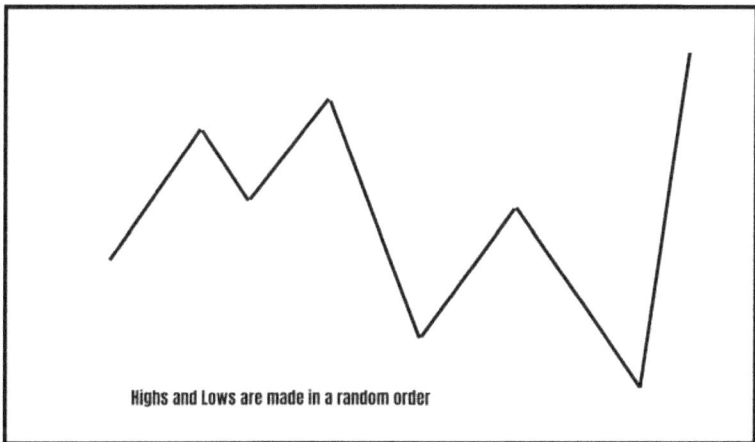

Image 14.7: Random or volatile trend

During volatile markets or when the market receives both good and bad news, one after the other, volatile moves could occur without giving much clarity about swing highs or swing lows, and traders must refrain from trading in this phase of the market.

In order to prepare accordingly, it is important to be able to identify the end of a trend.

HOW TO IDENTIFY THE END OF A DOWNTREND

Dow theory trend concepts work in all timeframes, whether a 5-minute, 15-minute, or daily timeframe. But whenever we get into a lower timeframe, there is a higher possibility of noise and frequent changes from uptrend to downtrend, downtrend to uptrend, etc.

So, one should keep these things in mind when they plan to take trades in lower timeframes.

To succeed with your trades, you have to enter at the beginning of the uptrend and exit at the start of the downtrend. However, it is always challenging to identify the beginning of the uptrend or the beginning of the downtrend. Dow theory helps us identify these market turns in a simple manner.

As shown in image 14.8, the price stops forming lower lows (LL) first and instead forms a higher low (point 1). Then, the price makes a higher high (point 2), and the break of point 2 can be considered the end of the downtrend or the beginning of a new uptrend.

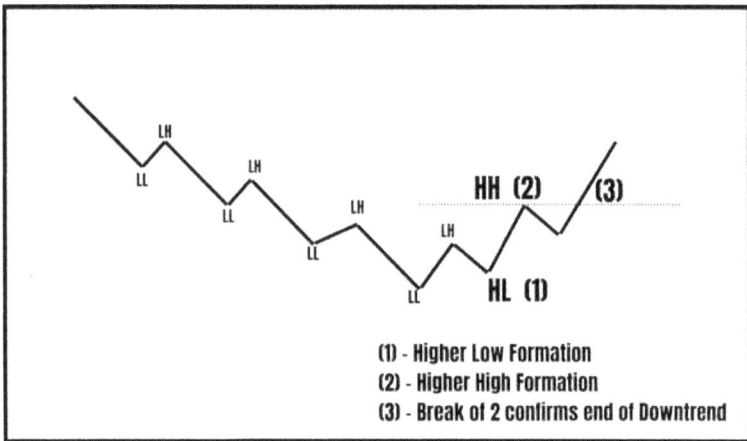

Image 14.8: End of a downtrend

In image 14.9 and 14.10, you can clearly see the end of a downtrend on the charts of Nifty and Reliance Industries Ltd.

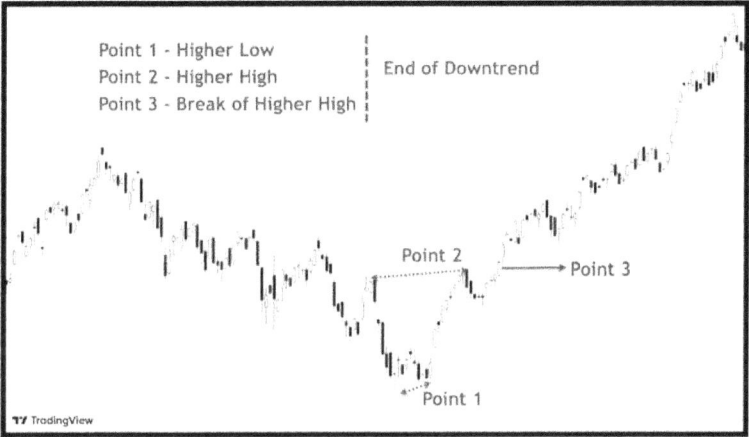

Image 14.9: End of a downtrend on the chart of Nifty

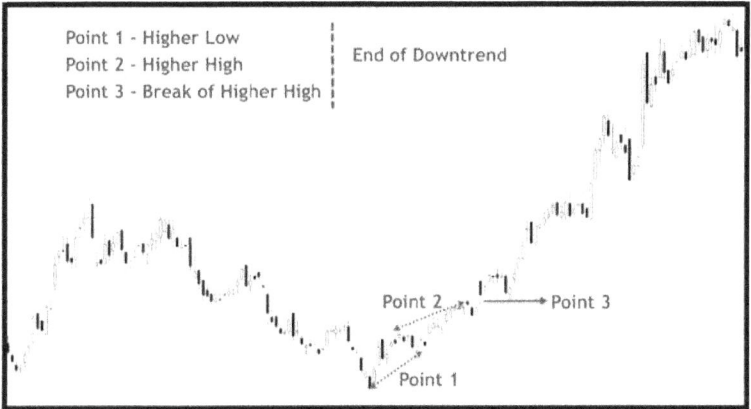

Image 14.10: End of a downtrend on the chart of Reliance Industries Ltd.

HOW TO IDENTIFY THE END OF AN UPTREND

As shown in image 14.11, the price stops forming higher highs (HH) first and instead forms a lower high (point 1). Then, the price makes a lower low (point 2), and the break of point 2 can be considered the end of the uptrend or the beginning of a new downtrend.

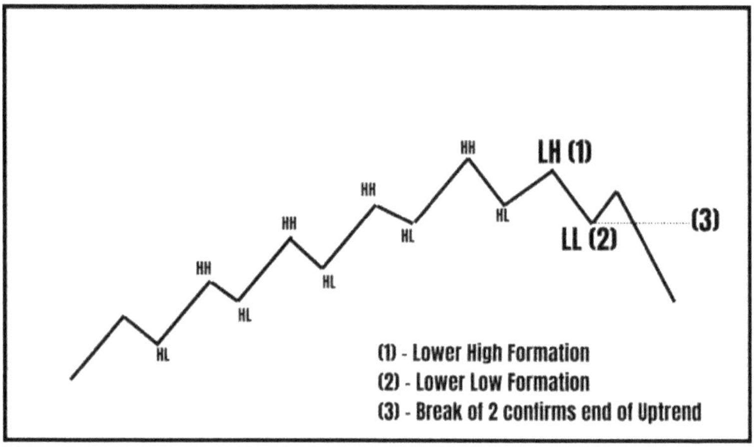

Image 14.11: End of the uptrend

Image 14.12 and image 14.13 show the end of an uptrend on the chart of Aurobindo Pharma Ltd. and Canara Bank, respectively.

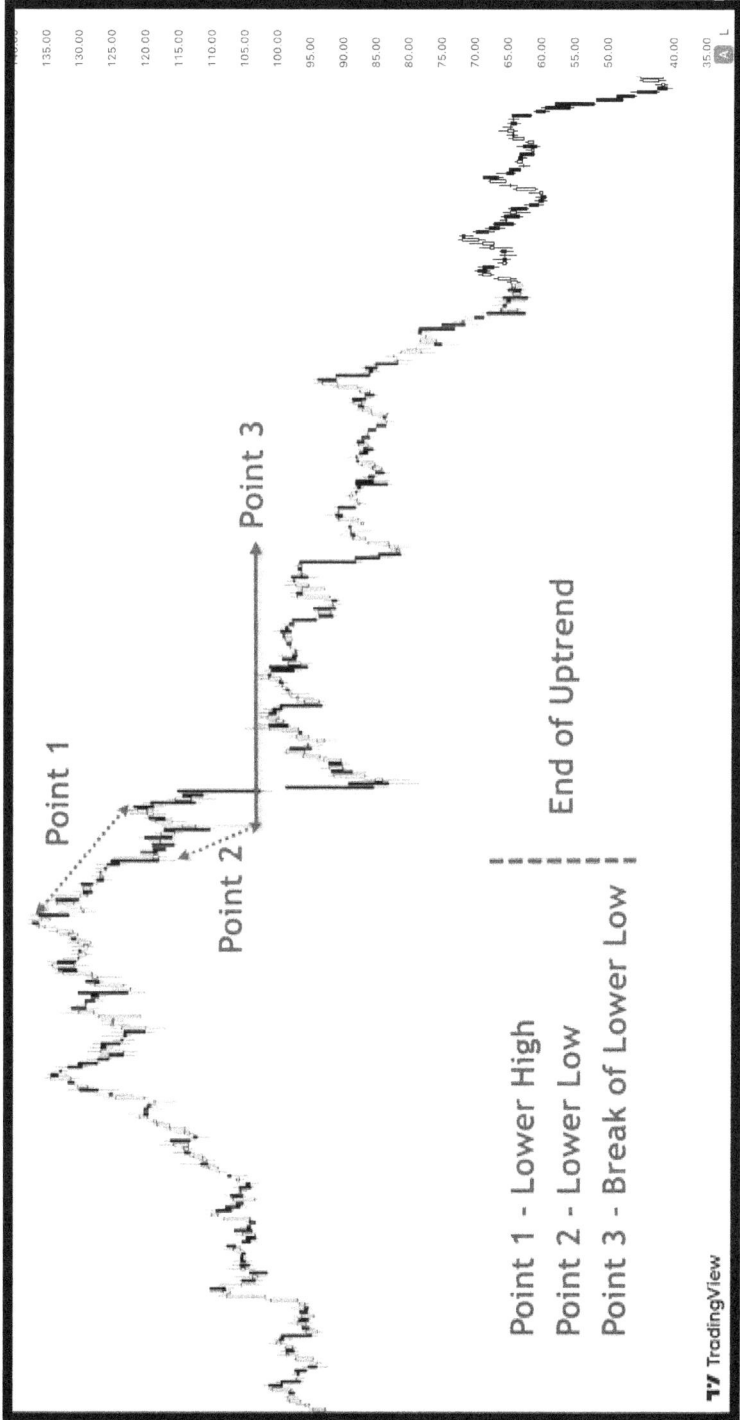

Point 1

Point 3

Point 2

Point 1 - Lower High
Point 2 - Lower Low
Point 3 - Break of Lower Low

End of Uptrend

TradingView

Image 14.12: End of an uptrend in Aurobindo Pharma Ltd.

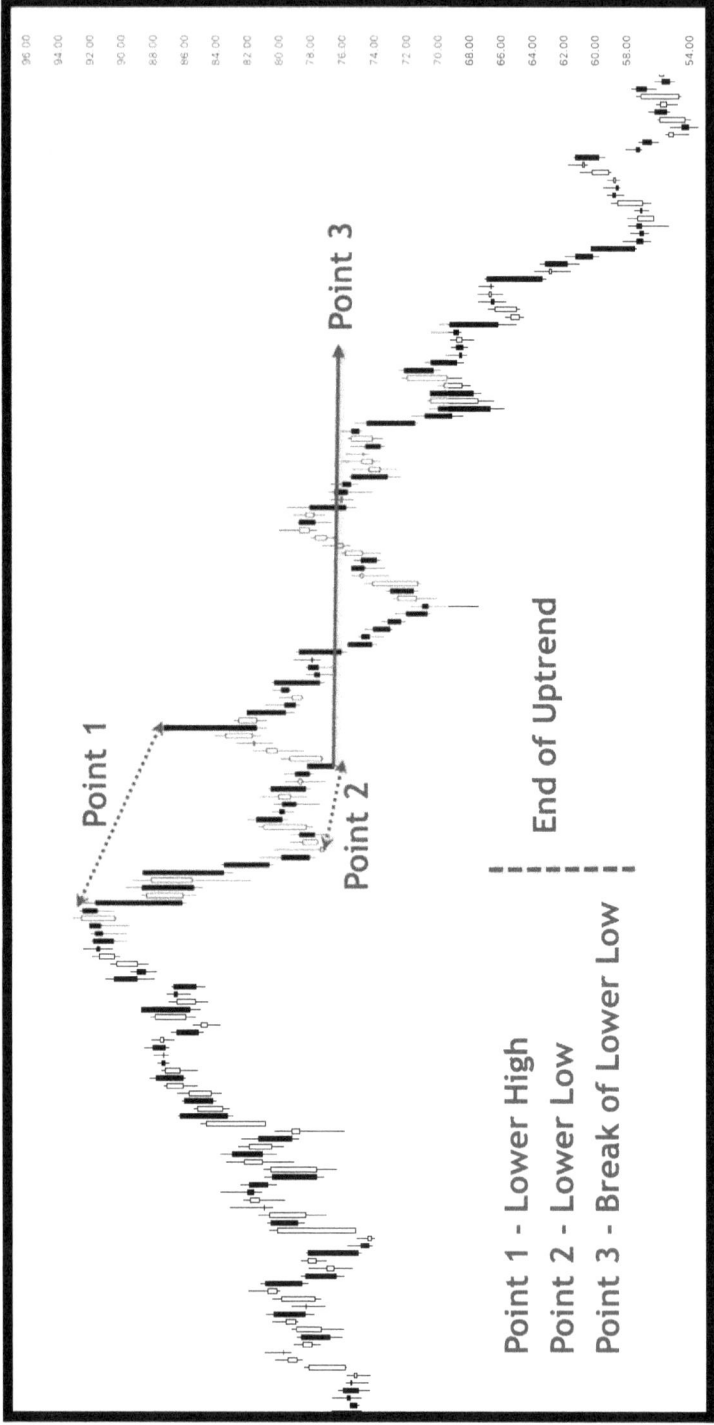

Image 14.13: End of uptrend on the chart of Canara Bank

TRENDLINES

Trendlines are an interesting concept in technical analysis because they not only help traders see the overall direction of a market but also help to identify potential entry and exit points for trades.

By connecting two or more price peaks (swing highs or swing lows) on a chart, trendlines show whether the price is moving up, down, or staying sideways. Whenever you connect more peaks, the impact or power of the trendlines increases (image 14.14).

Image 14.14: An example of a trendline

Image 14.15 shows an example of a simple trendline. Only three peaks are connected in this image, and hence this is a decent (but not powerful) trendline.

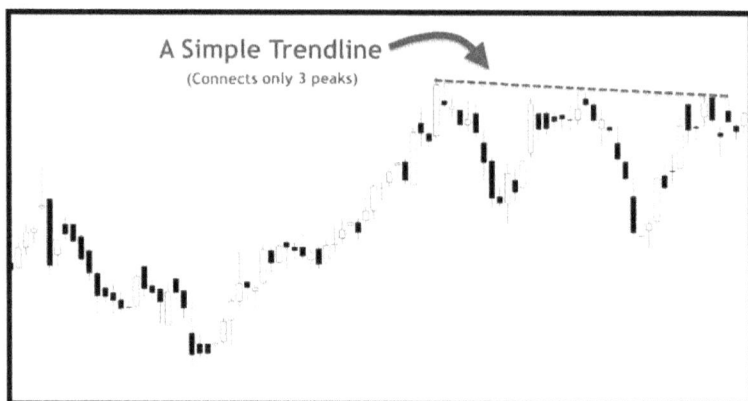

Image 14.15: A simple trendline

Image 14.16 shows an example of a powerful trendline. In the image, six peaks are connected making this is a powerful trendline.

You need to know the rules for drawing trendlines because trendlines also act as support and resistance in trading. If you draw trendlines incorrectly, you may take erratic and unnecessary trades. When you draw a trendline by connecting the swing lows in an uptrend, it acts as support. It means the price tends to bounce from this line instead of falling below it (high probability).

Image 14.16: A powerful trendline

Rule 1: Avoid charts with pathetic price action

Images 14.17 and 14.18 show examples of pathetic price action. It always makes sense to avoid such charts for drawing trendlines, which does not make sense. Besides, even if you can draw trendlines, there is a high possibility of triggering false entries, hitting your stop-loss and going in the expected direction, or slippage due to gap openings.

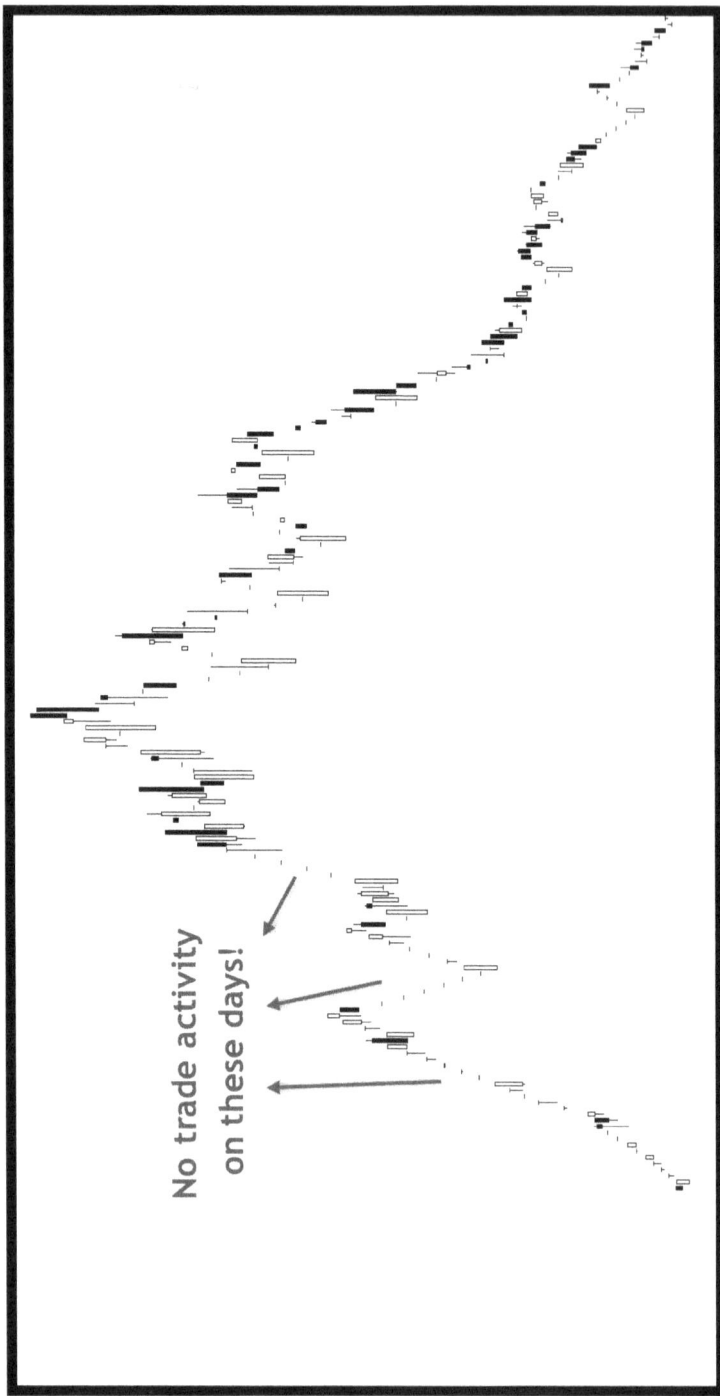

No trade activity on these days!

Image 14.17: Price action on this chart is pathetic

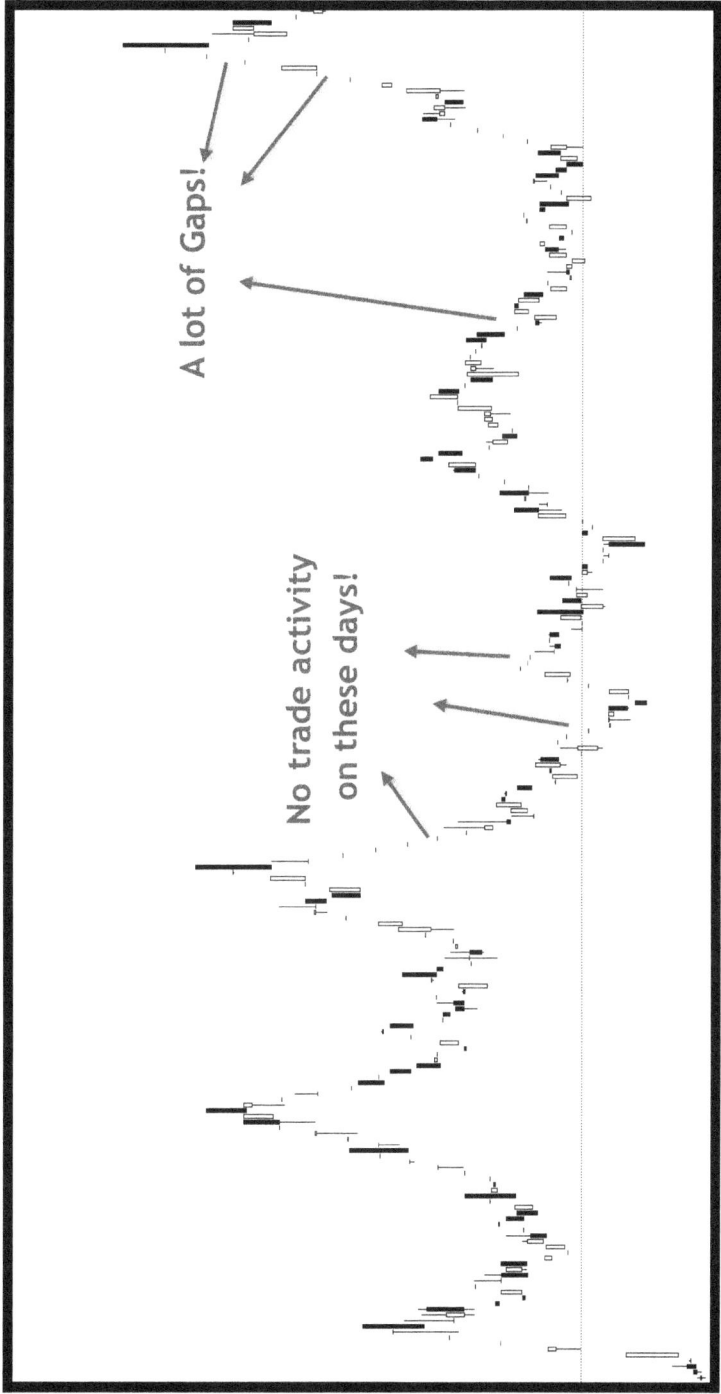

Image 14.18: Price action is pathetic

Rule 2: Try to connect more peaks

When drawing trendlines, it is vital to connect as many peaks as possible. This makes the trendline more reliable.

The more times a price touches or bounces off the trendline, the stronger that line becomes. It shows that many traders are reacting to that level, which means it is a key point of support or resistance.

One should connect a minimum of two peaks to consider it as a valid trendline. It is better if you can connect more peaks as shown in image 14.19.

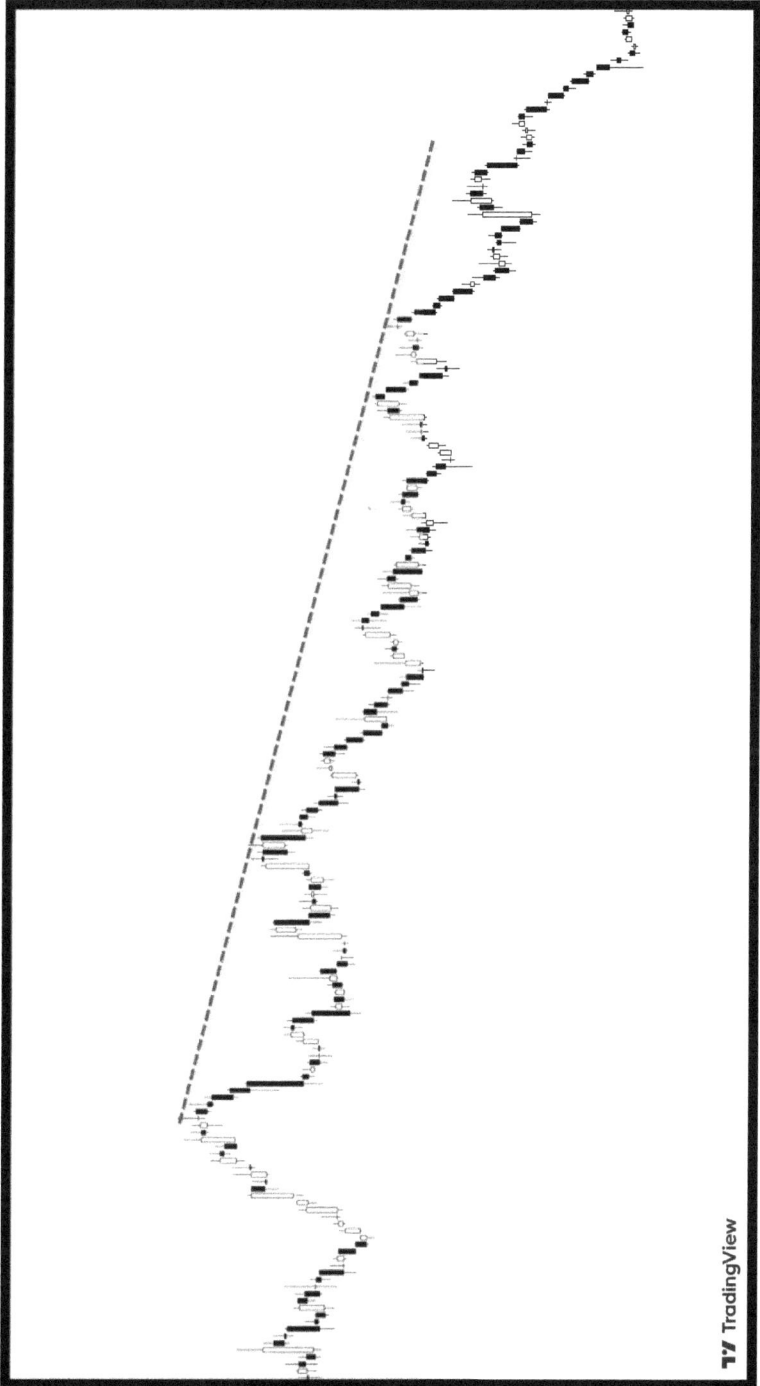

Image 14.19: Trendlines with more peaks

Rule 3: Trendlines with less slope

While drawing trendlines, ensure that the slope is less than 45 degrees, as this indicates a healthy trend.

If a trendline is too steep, it indicates that the price is rising or falling too quickly and often suggests that the trend might not last long. So always avoid drawing trendlines if the slope appears to be more than 45 degrees.

Image 14.20 shows a trendline depicting a healthy trend as the angle of the slope is less than 45 degrees.

On the other hand, image 14.21 shows a trendline depicting an unhealthy trend as the slope is steep.

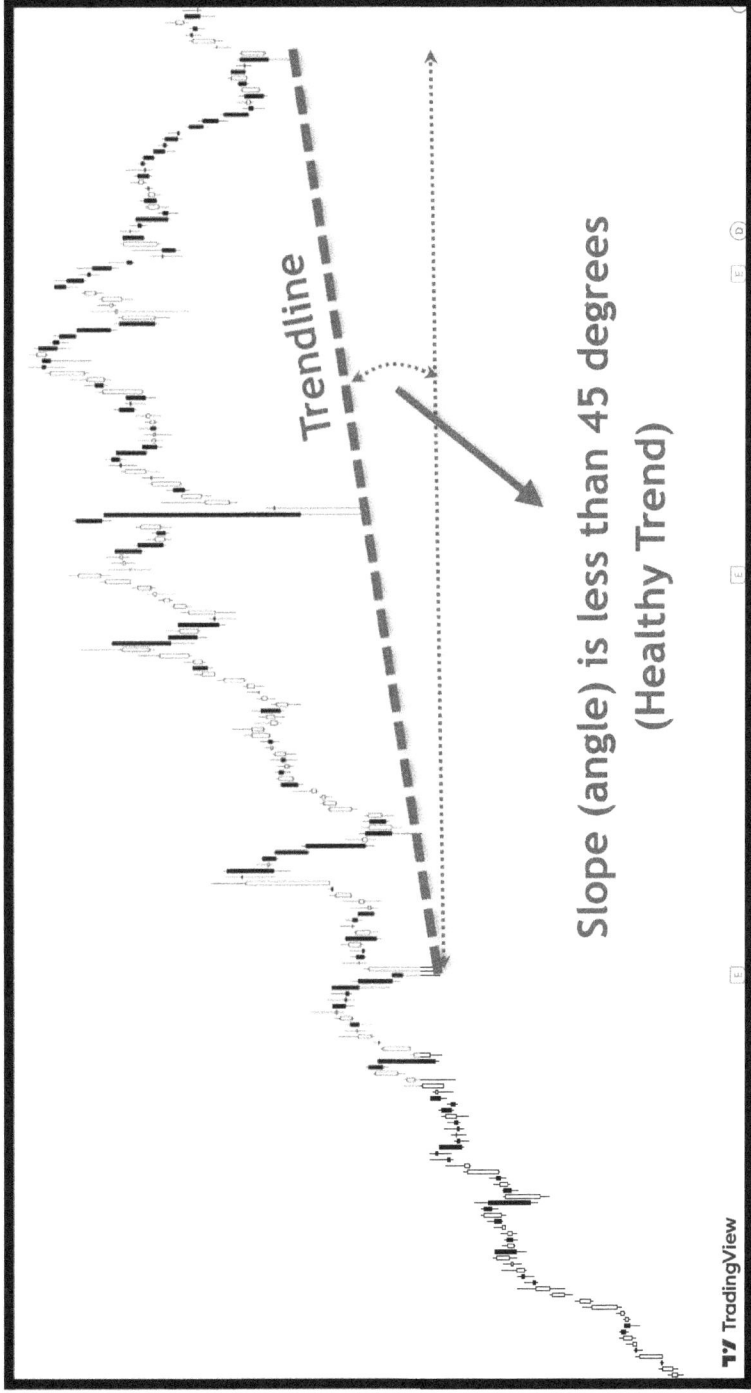

Image 14.20: Trendlines with less slope showing a healthy trend

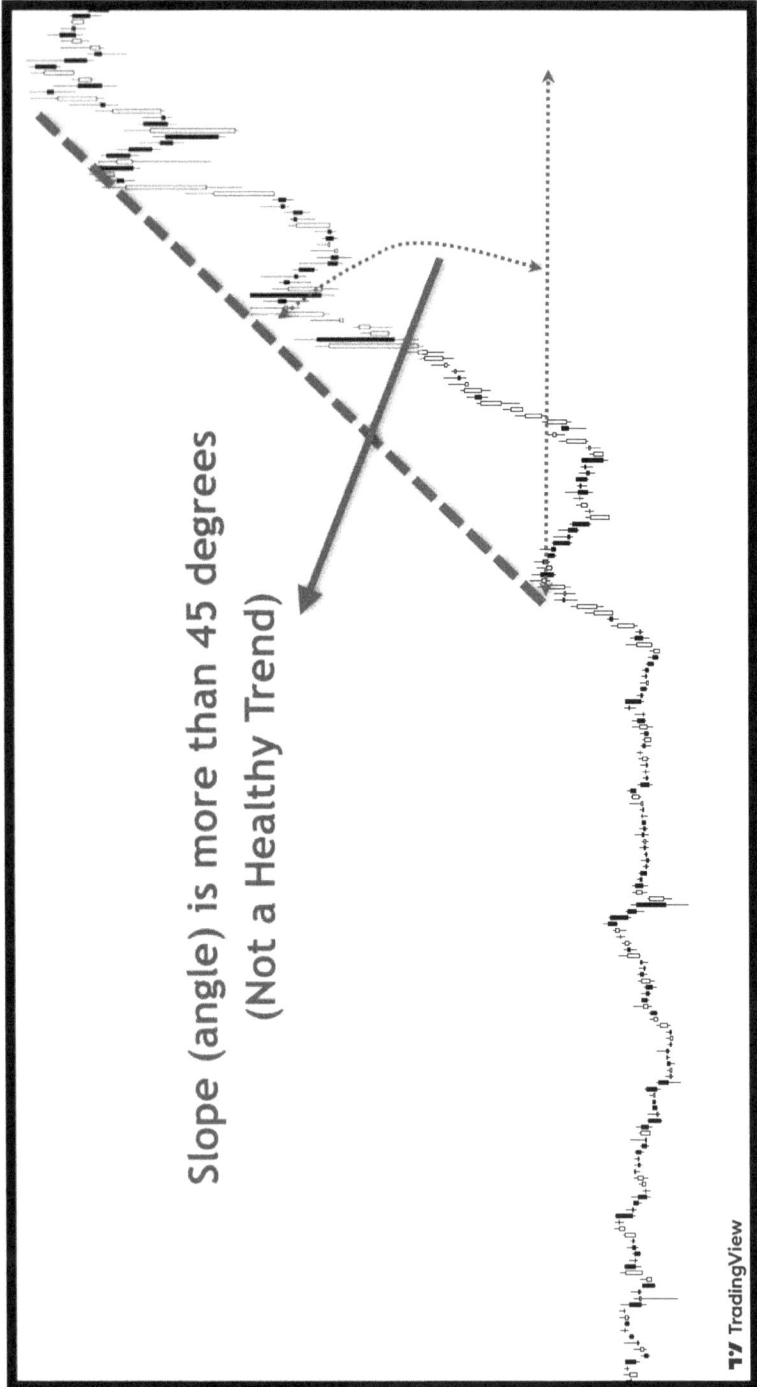

Image 14.21: Trendlines with a steep slope showing an unhealthy trend

Rule 4: Price respect

When you draw a trendline, the price should respect it with its peaks. Only then will it indicate that the trendline is impactful.

Suppose the price has not shown much respect to a trendline through its peaks. Then the trendline's impact automatically reduces.

In image 14.22, the price respects the trendline and adheres to the pattern it formed.

On the other hand, image 14.23 shows a chart where the price does not follow the pattern of the trendline, thereby disrespecting it.

If a trader correctly uses trendlines, they help him spot trends (uptrend, downtrend, and sideways) and make decisions based on them. For example, if a stock is in an uptrend, traders might look for opportunities to take long trades, expecting the price to keep rising. Similarly, if a stock is in a downtrend, they might avoid long trades and even consider opting for short trades. Trendlines also help traders to identify crucial areas of support and resistance, which are important for setting targets and managing risk.

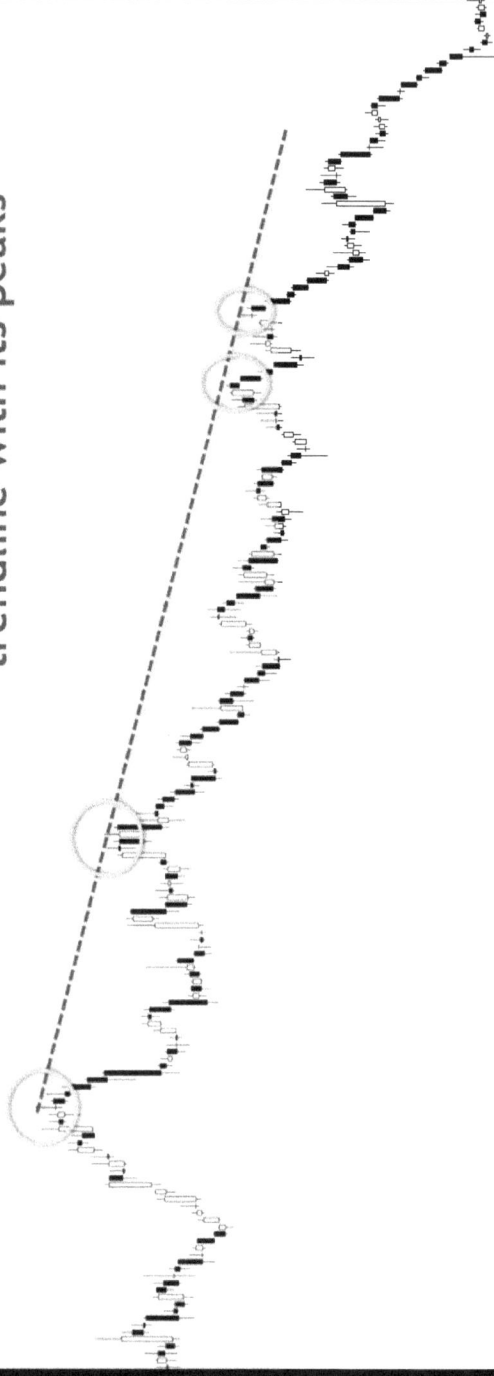

Image 14.22: Price respect for the trendline

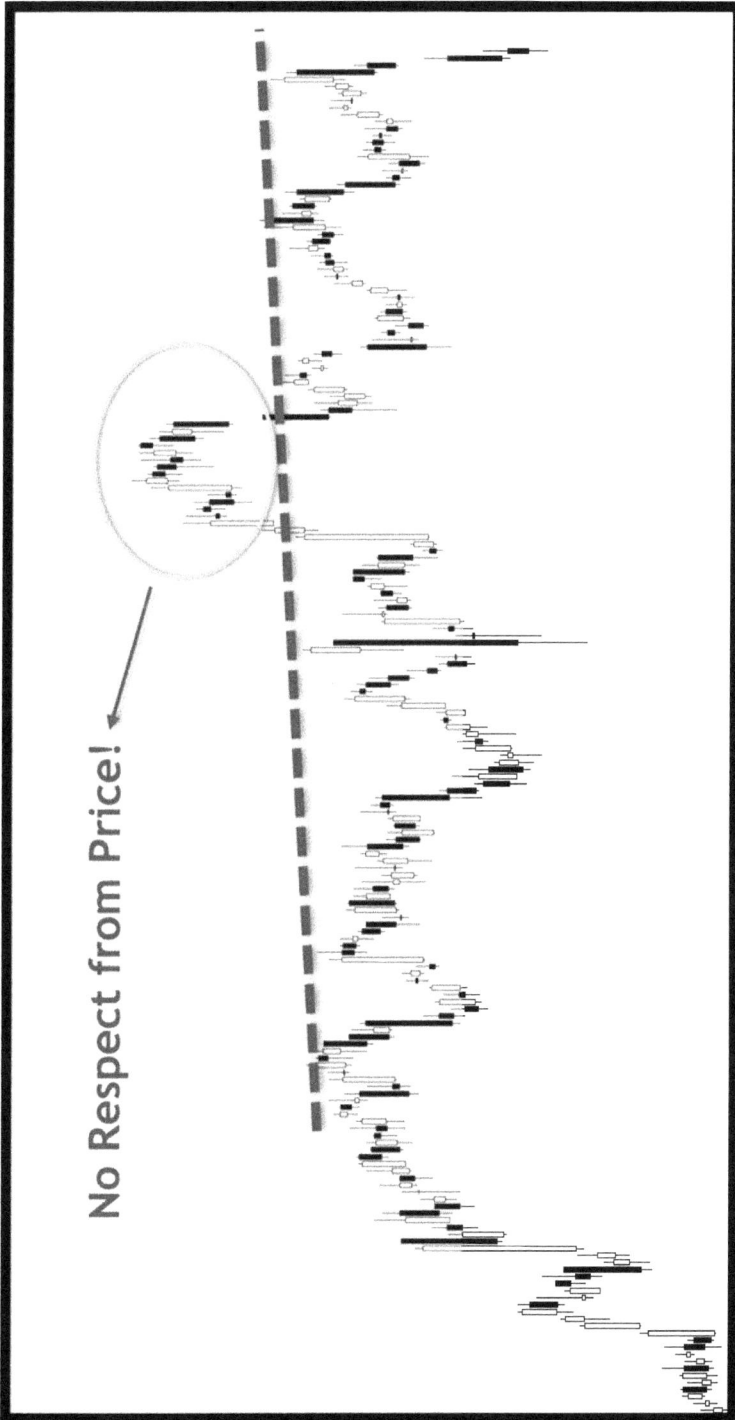

No Respect from Price!

Image 14.23: No respect from price for the trendline

SUPPORT AND RESISTANCE

There is an interesting insight over the last decade in India. Whenever the petrol or diesel price crosses Rs 100, people start protesting on the roads in India. After a few days, if the price goes back below 100 rupees, let us say Rs 97 or Rs 98, people call off their protests and continue with their business as usual.

It is just a matter of 2–3 rupees, yet people do not worry much if the price stays below 100. Can you think of any reason?

Visit any mall in any part of the world; you will see price tags like 99, 199, 999, or 4999, etc. These marketing experts are absolute geniuses. They keep prices like 99, 199, or 499, a common marketing trick known as "psychological pricing." Customers tend to focus on the first digit of the price, so when they see 499 instead of 500, it feels like a better deal, even though it is just one unit less.

Our brains naturally round down, so 499 seems closer to 400 than to 500, making the price feel cheaper. Due to this slight difference, people are more likely to buy because they feel like they are saving money, even if the actual difference is minimal.

Similarly, all these round numbers play a crucial role in most stocks as well. Unknowingly, people buy or sell whenever a stock reaches a round number like 100, 1000, 5000, etc.

In image 14.24, the price tried to cross 2,000 a few times, but it failed on multiple occasions. The simple reason is it is a round number and people sell their shares whenever the price reaches 2,000.

Along with these round numbers, some numbers related to stocks play a crucial role in their advances or declines. The only reason I can think of is a pool of people being constantly interested in a particular stock at a specific price level.

Either they made profits from this stock at that particular price level, or they would have lost money from this stock at that specific price level, or they would have lost a chance to make profits from

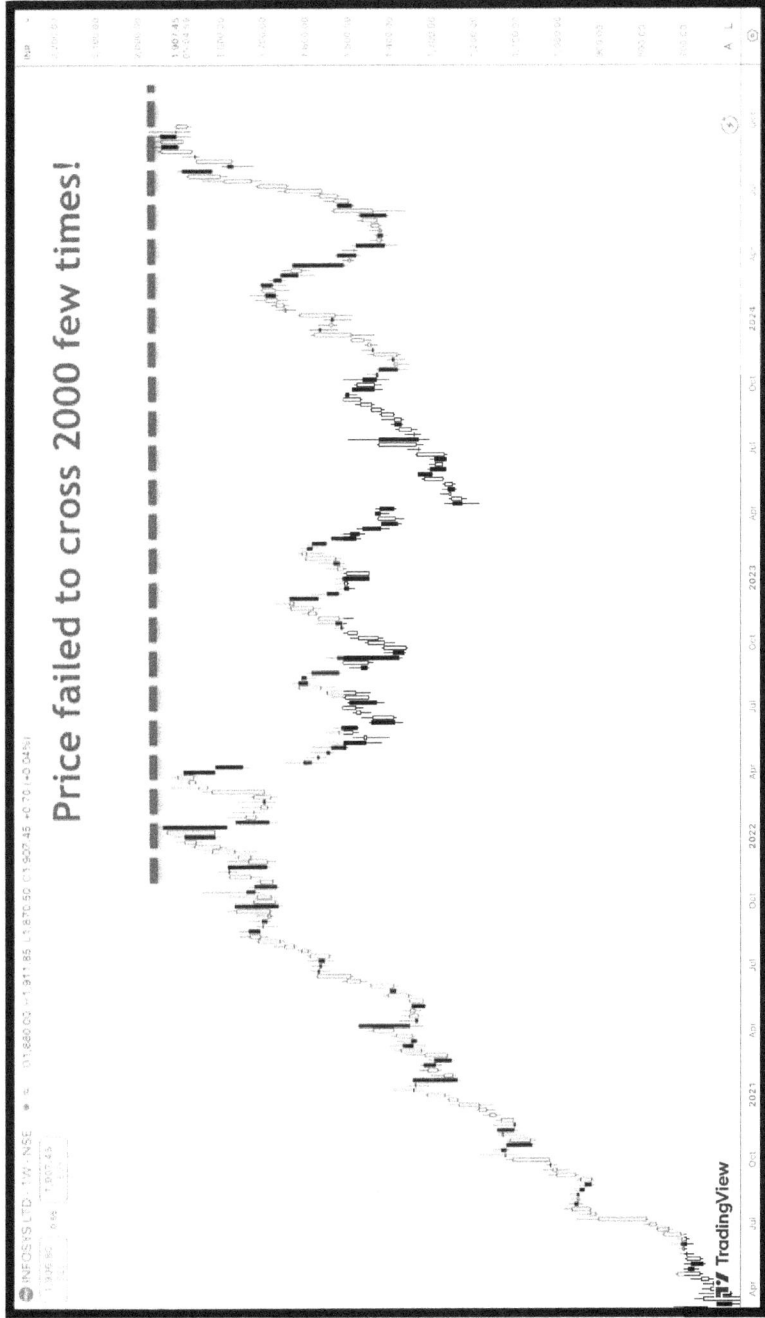

Image 14.24: Price failed to cross 2000 on the weekly chart of Infosys Ltd.

that stock at that particular price level. Hence, whenever that stock comes to that price level, it triggers some emotions in their mind, so they participate in the trade.

Image 14.25 is the weekly chart of TCS. Whenever the price reached Rs 2,300, people rushed only to sell their shares. This is called the resistance level.

Resistance is a price level at which a stock stops rising because many traders or investors start selling their shares at that point. It is like a ceiling that the price struggles to break through. This usually happens for a simple reason: when the price reaches a certain level, many investors believe it is an excellent time to make profits by booking their long positions (or opting for a short position), creating more supply than demand.

In image 14.26, whenever the price came back to 750, traders and investors participated in the game by buying the shares of Titan Company Ltd. as much as possible. Their participation prevented the price from falling below 750 many times. This can be called support.

Support refers to a price level where a stock tends to stop falling and often bounces back up. This happens because many traders/ investors see it as a good buying opportunity at the support price level, creating enough demand to prevent the price from dropping further. It is like a floor that helps hold the price up. If the price repeatedly bounces off this level, it strengthens the idea that support exists there.

We discussed only horizontal support and resistance levels in images 14.24 to 14.26. These support and resistance levels are drawn horizontally by connecting the available price peaks on the charts. They undoubtedly play a crucial role in trading.

However, traders also use inclined support and resistance levels, which are derived by drawing trendlines, where the price moves at an angle, either up or down. These lines show how the price trends over time, and they adjust as the stock moves.

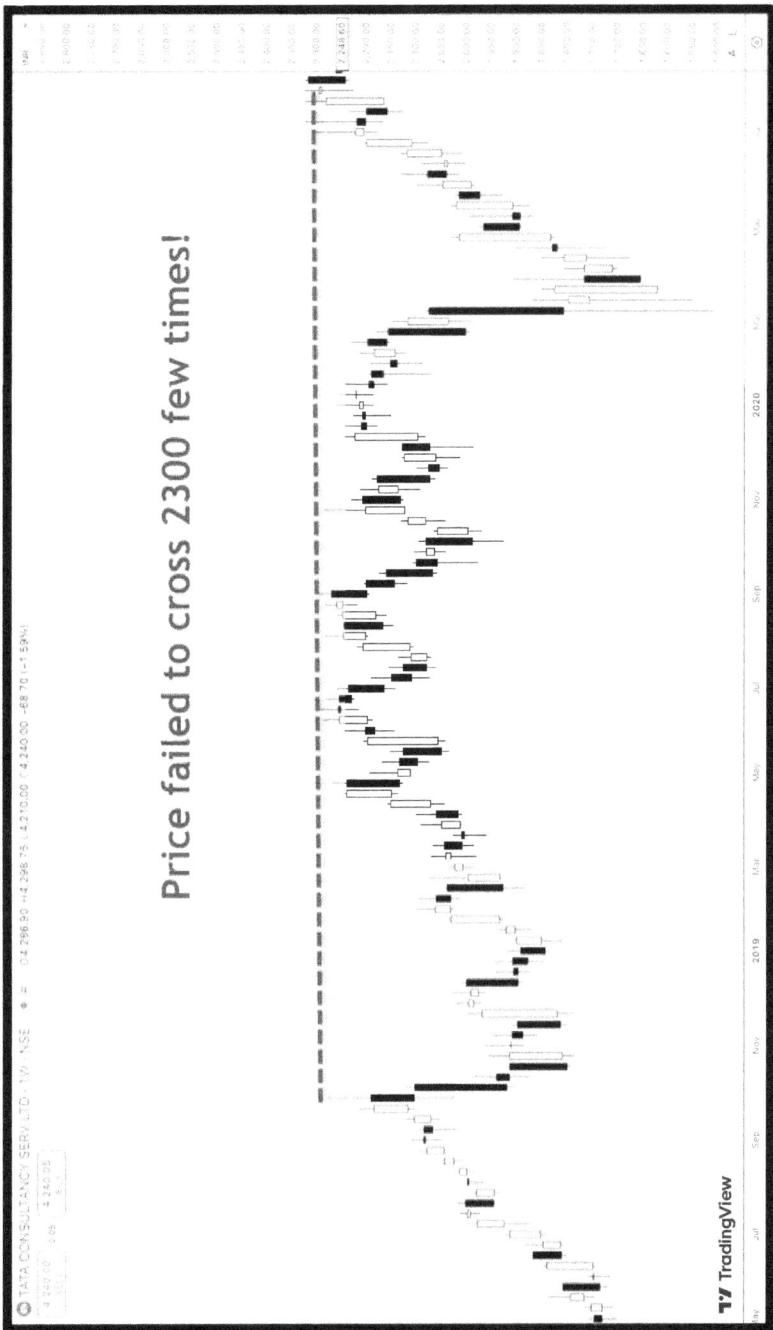

Image 14.25: Price failed to cross 2,300 on the weekly chart of TCS

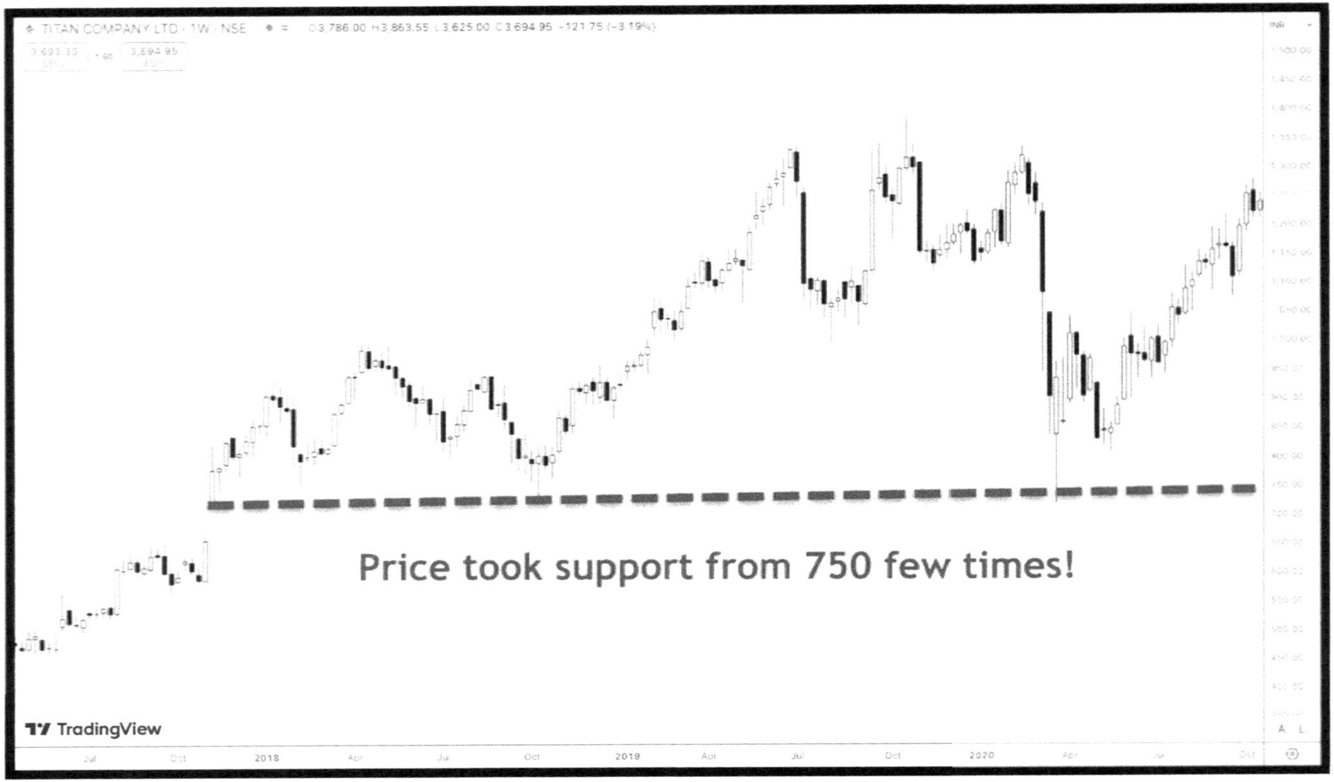

Image 14.26: Support on the weekly chart of Titan Company Ltd.

Image 14.27 shows an example of a resistance line by drawing a simple trendline with a small incline. This is completely acceptable and useful in trading. These inclined support and resistance levels are also helpful in trading because they help identify key areas where the price might reverse, allowing traders to plan their entries and exits.

FIVE BRILLIANT CANDLESTICK PATTERNS FOR SUCCESS

A few years ago, a trading group with people from different backgrounds practised only intraday trades. Everyone studied patterns, read books, and followed an independent approach to take their trades.

One person attended a trading workshop conducted by an expert and started taking trades based on that concept. After seeing success through these methods, many people started following the trading system. I turned curious and enquired with a group member. She was also following the same system as it gave good results. I asked her to explain the logic behind the system.

It was an interesting system comprising only one indicator on a 5-min chart. If the price is above the moving average (or crosses the moving average from down) and displays a bullish marubozu pattern, then go long above the bullish marubozu candle, keeping a stop-loss below the low of the marubozu candle. They need to have the trailing stop-loss below the low of each 5-min candle. They were taking a short trade on similar but opposite logic (price is below the moving average and bearish marubozu, explained later).

Initially, I could not believe that such a simple trading system could give good results. But after looking at many charts, I realised moving average is used in this system to identify the trend (so that beginners align to take trade only in one direction and bring discipline in them), and marubozu is a powerful candle pattern that is used as the entry criteria.

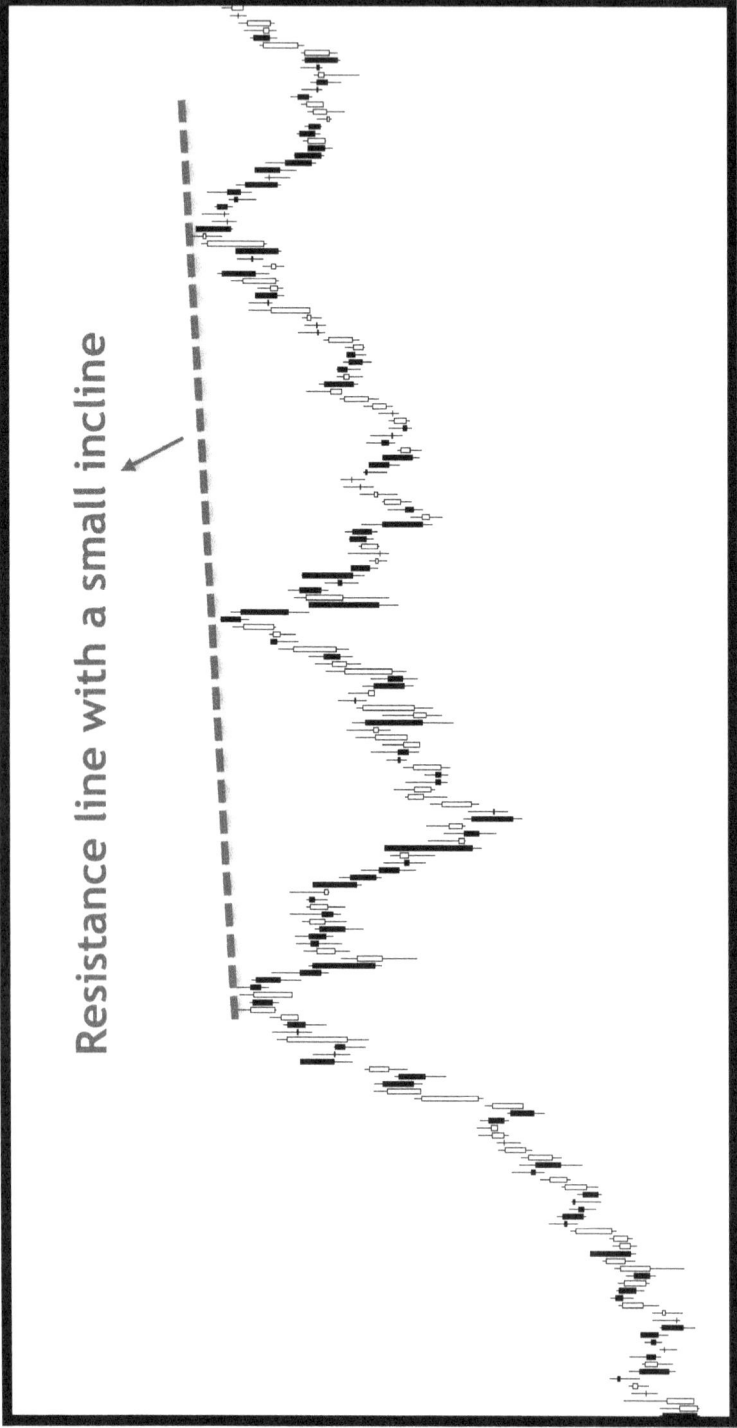

Image 14.27: Resistance line with a small incline

Candlestick patterns (explained later) should be used in conjunction with support and resistance levels to identify potential trading opportunities and increase the probability of a successful trade. Support and resistance levels are key levels where the price has previously bounced off or stalled in the past, indicating potential buying or selling pressure at these levels. When they are combined with candlestick patterns, traders can look for confirmation that the price may reverse or continue to move in the direction of the trend.

For example, let us say that the price is approaching a key support level, and a bullish reversal candlestick pattern forms at that level. This can be seen as a confirmation that the buying pressure is likely to increase, and the price may reverse from that level.

Similarly, suppose the price is approaching a key resistance level, and a bearish reversal candlestick pattern forms at that level. In that case, this can be seen as a confirmation that the selling pressure is likely to increase, and the price may reverse from that level.

Traders can also use candlestick patterns to confirm the support and resistance levels breakout. For instance, if the price has been consolidating between a support and resistance level for some time, and a bullish breakout occurs with a bullish candlestick pattern, this can be seen as confirmation that the bullish momentum is increasing, and the price is likely to continue moving higher.

Using candlestick patterns in combination with support and resistance levels can help traders identify potential trading opportunities with a higher probability of success.

BULLISH ENGULFING PATTERN

A bullish engulfing pattern is a candlestick pattern that indicates a potential reversal in a downtrend or from a downswing in an uptrend. This pattern consists of two candles, with the first candle being a bearish candle and the second, a bigger bullish candle that engulfs the previous bearish candle.

The bearish candle in the pattern shows that the sellers were in control in the earlier stages of trading (image 14.28). Still, the next bullish candle indicates buyers have taken over and pushed the price higher, engulfing the previous bearish candle. This shift in momentum from bearish to bullish is a strong indication that the trend may be reversing.

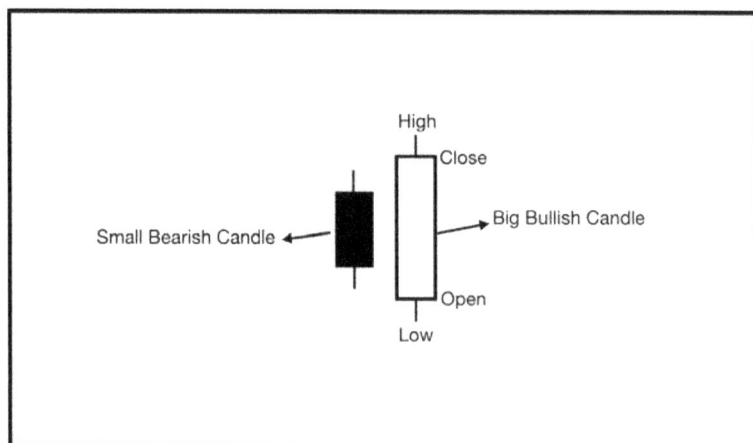

Image 14.28: Bullish engulfing pattern

Images 14.29 and 14.30 show examples of bullish engulfing pattern. In both cases, the previous trend was down, bullish engulfing pattern formed exactly at the important support zone and the price rallied on the upside from that point.

The strength of the bullish engulfing pattern depends on the size of the second candle relative to the first candle. A large bullish candle that completely engulfs the previous bearish candle is a stronger signal than a small bullish candle that only partially engulfs the last bearish candle. Traders can use the bullish engulfing pattern as a potential buying opportunity, indicating that the price may continue to increase.

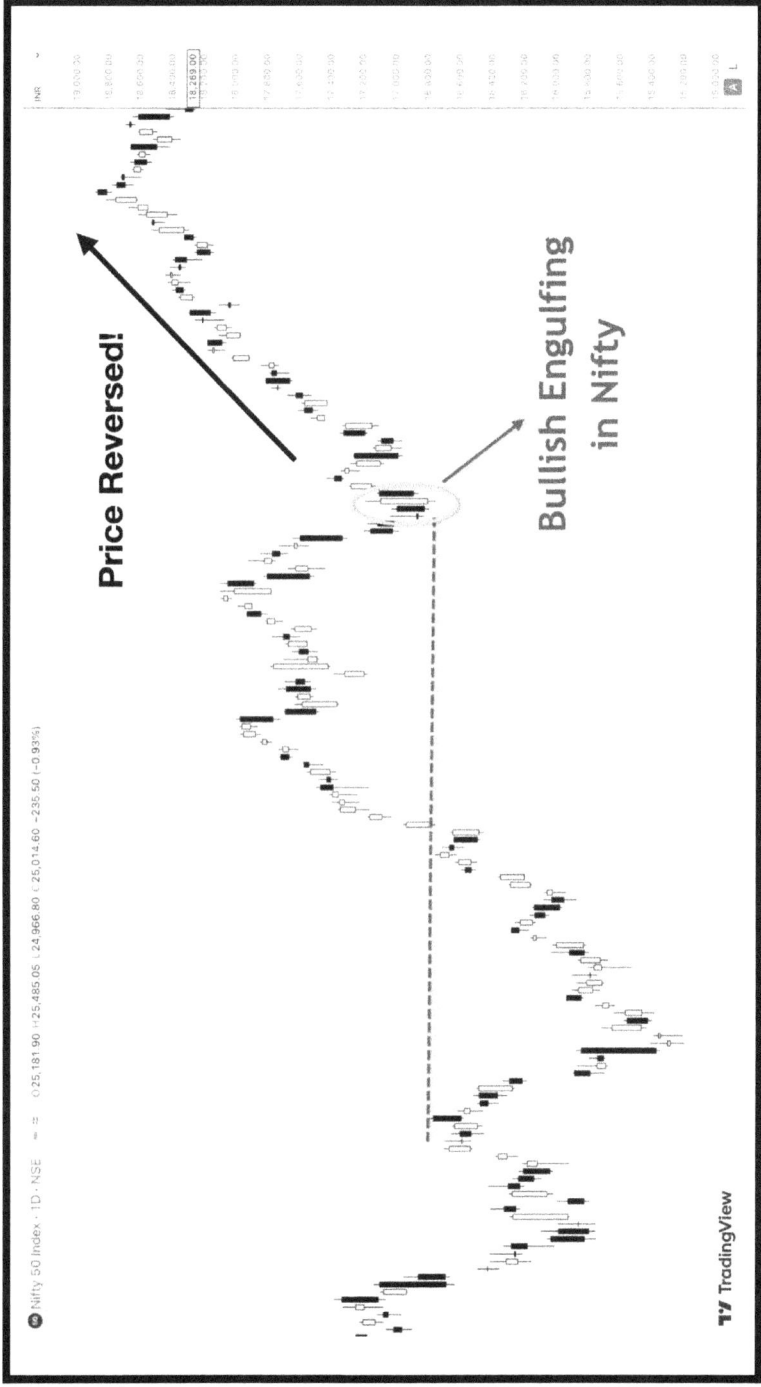

Image 14.29: Bullish engulfing candle on the daily chart of Nifty

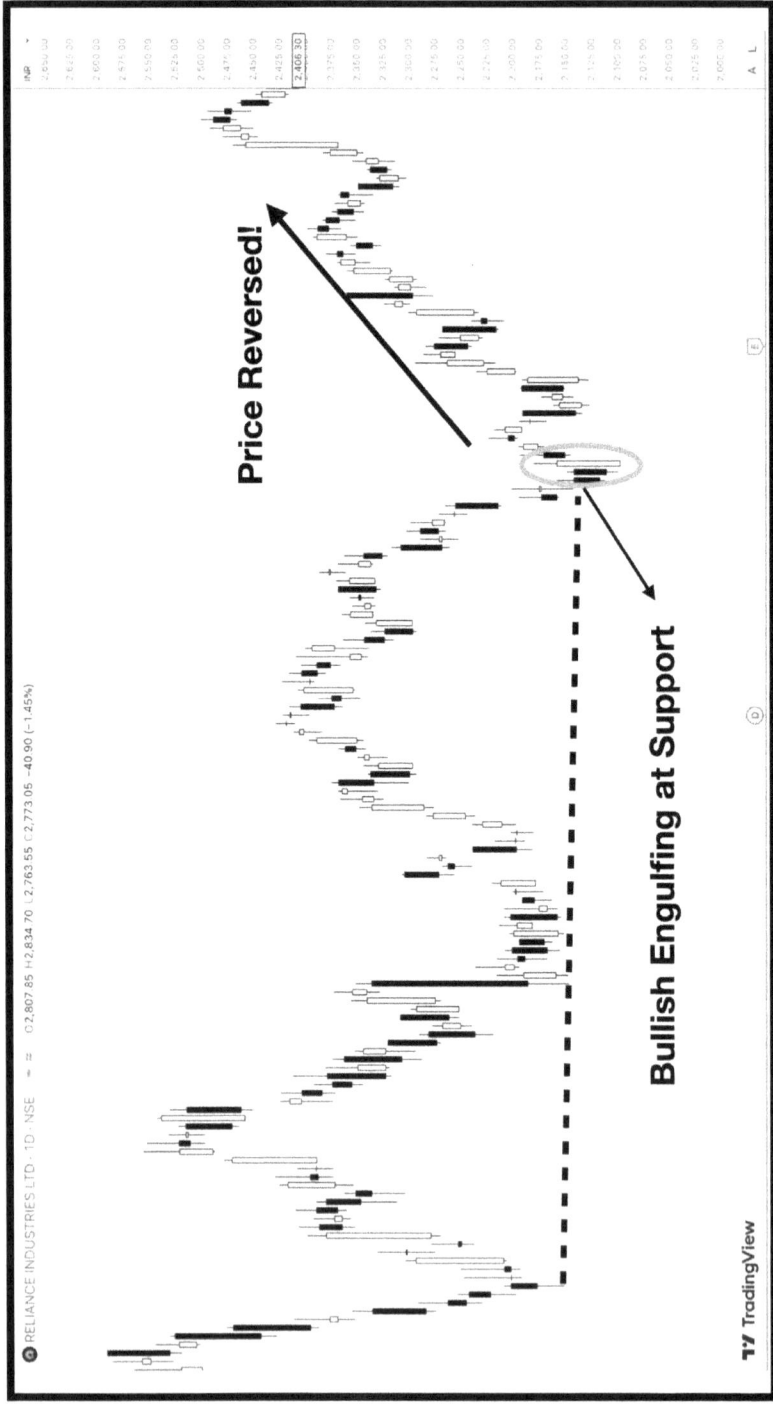

Image 14.30: Bullish engulfing candle on the daily chart of Reliance Industries Ltd.

BEARISH ENGULFING PATTERN

Bearish engulfing pattern is similar to bullish engulfing pattern, but it is the opposite of it. A bearish engulfing pattern consists of two candlesticks, one bullish and one bearish, that are situated next to each other on a price chart. The first candlestick in a bearish engulfing pattern is typically a bullish candle, that is, it has a higher closing price than the opening price. The second bearish candle has a lower opening price than the previous candlestick's closing price and closes below the previous candlestick's opening price. In other words, the bearish candlestick completely 'engulfs' the bullish candlestick, hence the name 'bearish engulfing' (image 14.31). This pattern suggests that the bears (sellers) have taken control of the market, overpowering the bulls (buyers), and that the price is ready to fall ahead.

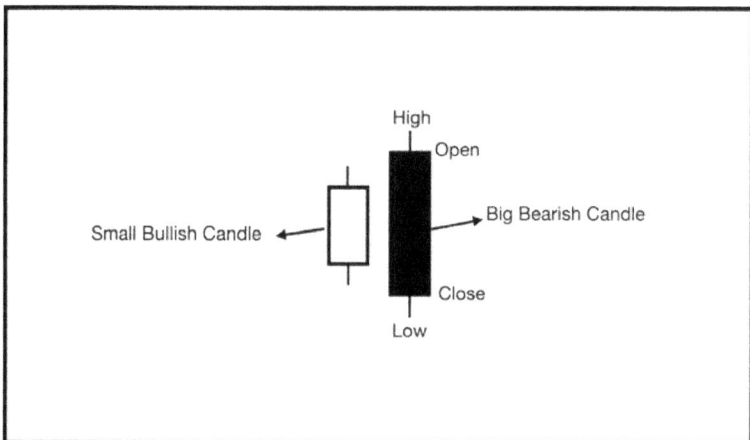

Image 14.31: Bearish engulfing pattern

Images 14.32 and 14.33 show some examples of bearish engulfing pattern. In both cases, the previous trend was up, the bearish engulfing pattern formed exactly at the important resistance zone and the price fell rapidly from that point.

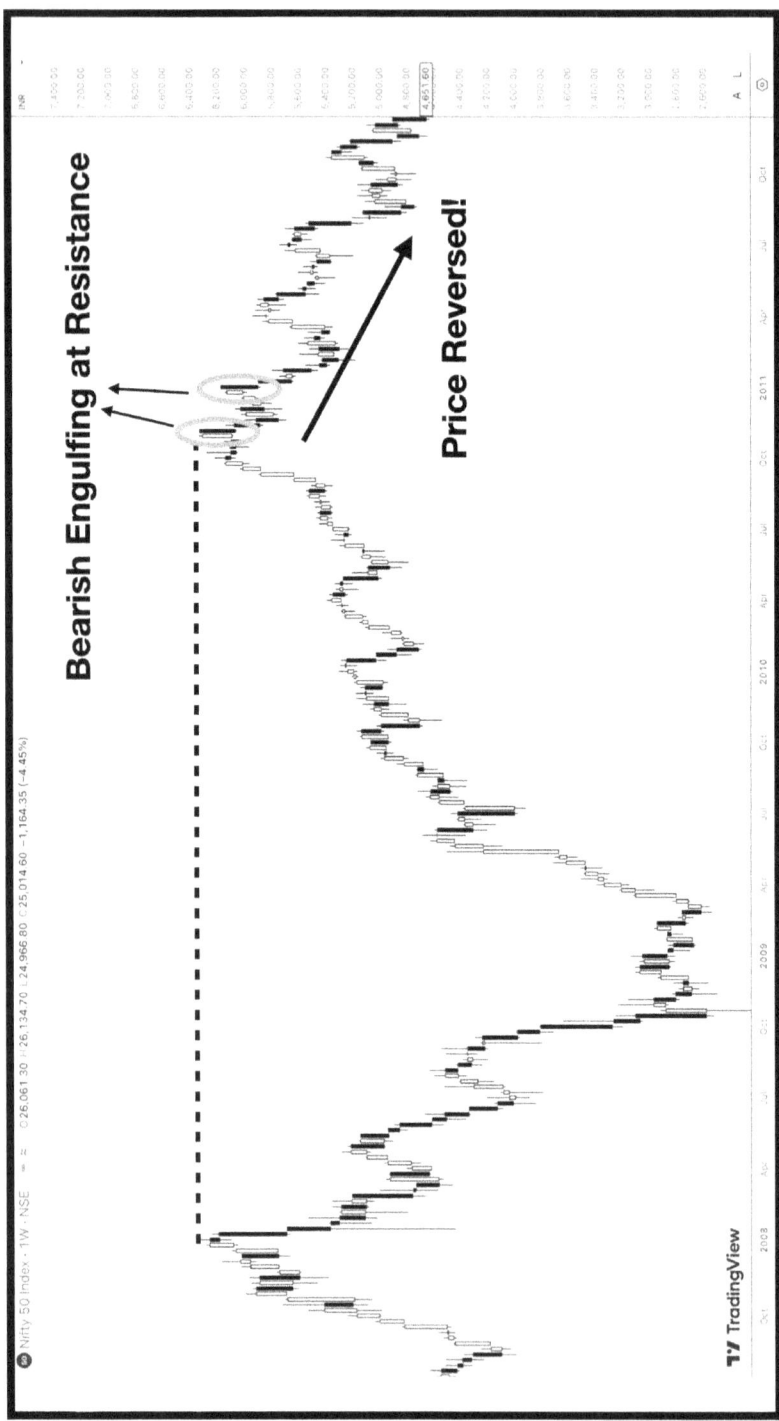

Image 14.32: Bearish engulfing pattern on the weekly chart of Nifty 50 Index

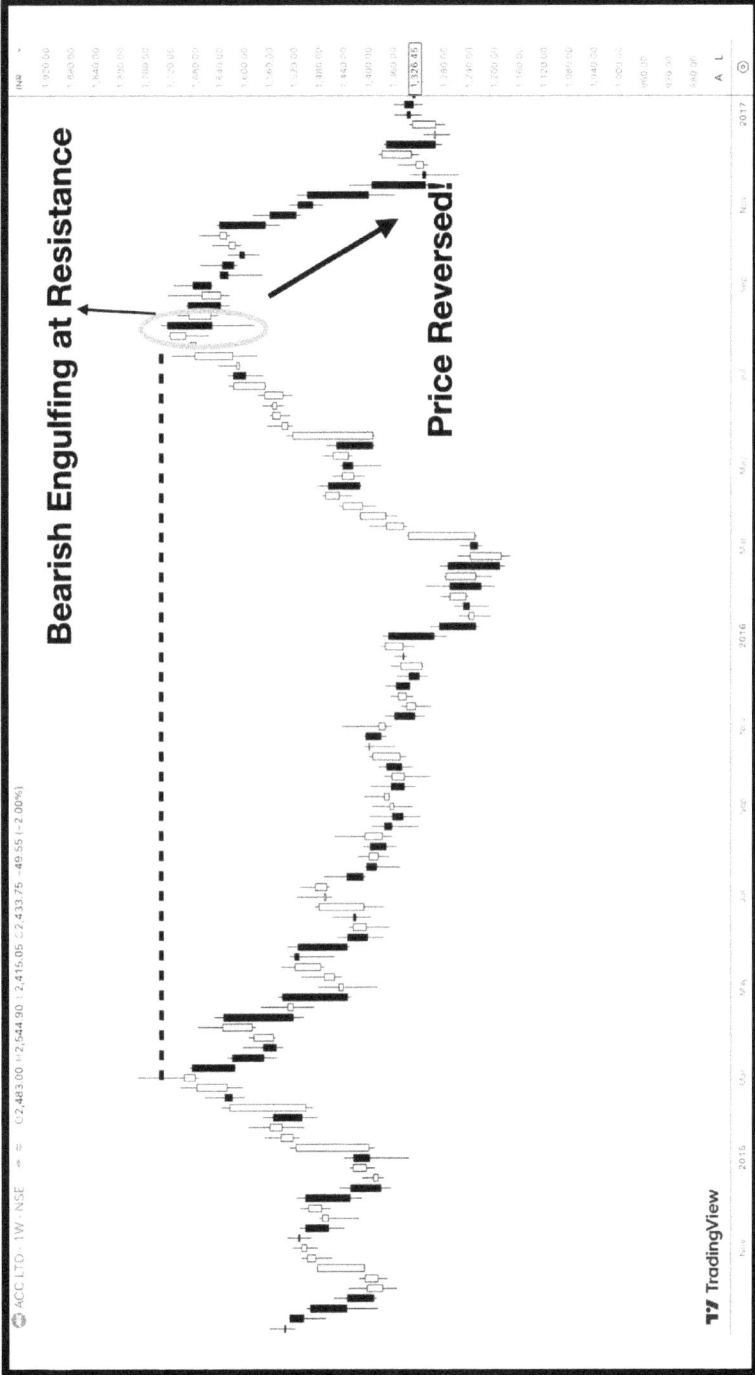

Image 14.33: Bearish engulfing pattern on the weekly chart of ACC Ltd.

Traders often look for bearish engulfing patterns as a signal to sell or take a short position in the asset, which indicates that the price trend is about to reverse and move lower.

BULLISH MARUBOZU PATTERN

A bullish marubozu candlestick pattern is one of the strong bullish signals among candlestick patterns (image 14.34).

Full Marubozu: This is the ideal bullish marubozu pattern that occurs when a single candlestick opens at or near the low of the period and closes at or near the high of the period, with little or no upper or lower shadow.

Marubozu Open: In marubozu open, open levels do not contain any wicks and swiftly rally on the opposite side. Compared to full marubozu, the closing price on the other side will have a slight wick.

Marubozu Close: In marubozu close, the open contains a small wick. The price swiftly rallies on the opposite side. However, the

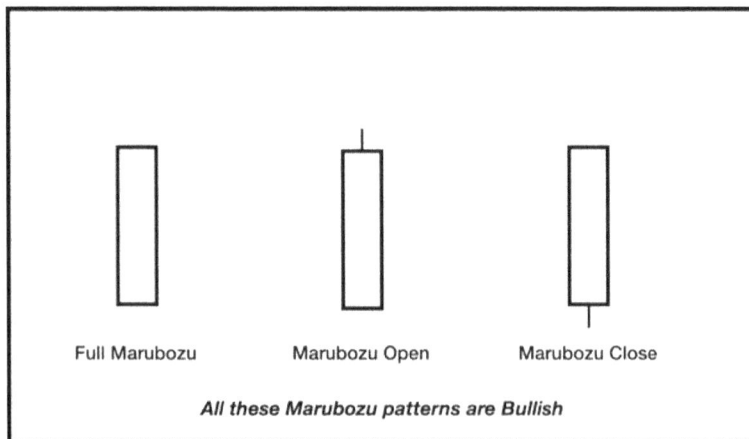

Image 14.34: Bullish marubozu candlestick pattern

closing price on the other side will not contain any wick. This pattern indicates that the buyers have complete control over the market and are pushing the price upward without any significant resistance from the sellers.

The name 'marubozu' comes from the Japanese word for 'shaved,' as the candlestick has no upper or lower shadows and is 'shaved' at both ends. The lack of shadows on the candlestick suggests that the price opened and closed at the same level, with no intra-period price movement.

In image 14.35, the price displayed a bullish marubozu pattern during the breakout of the resistance line and then it rallied swiftly on the upside on the Nifty Bank chart.

In image 14.36, the price displayed a bullish marubozu pattern at the support line and then it rallied swiftly on the upside on the chart of Nifty Financial Services..

Usually marubozu patterns occur in a lower time frame like 3-min, 5-min, and 15-min chart, and are highly beneficial for intraday traders and option buyers.

Full marubozu is more powerful compared to marubozu open and marubozu close. However, all these patterns can be used in short-term trading.

Traders use bullish marubozu pattern to initiate long positions or add to existing long positions in the asset.

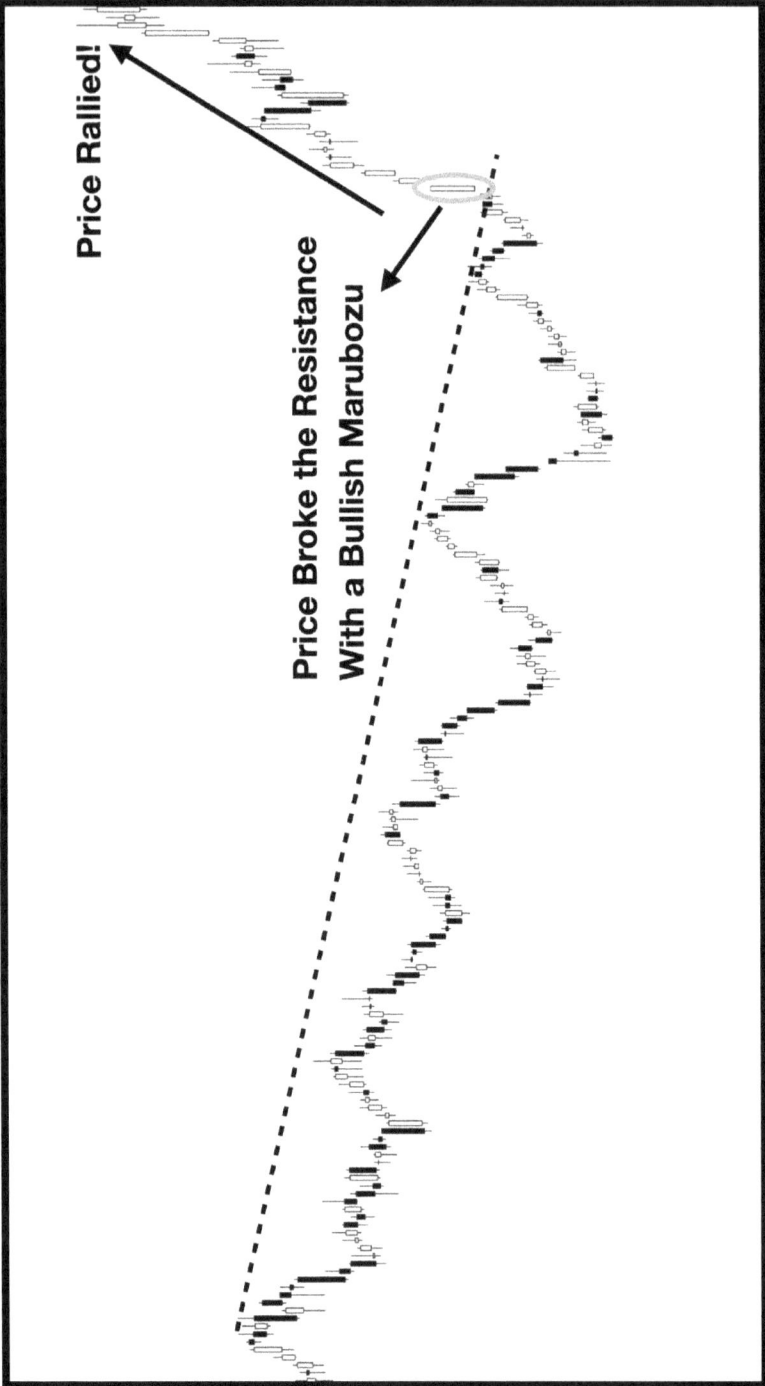

Image 14.35: Bullish marubozu on the chart of Nifty Bank

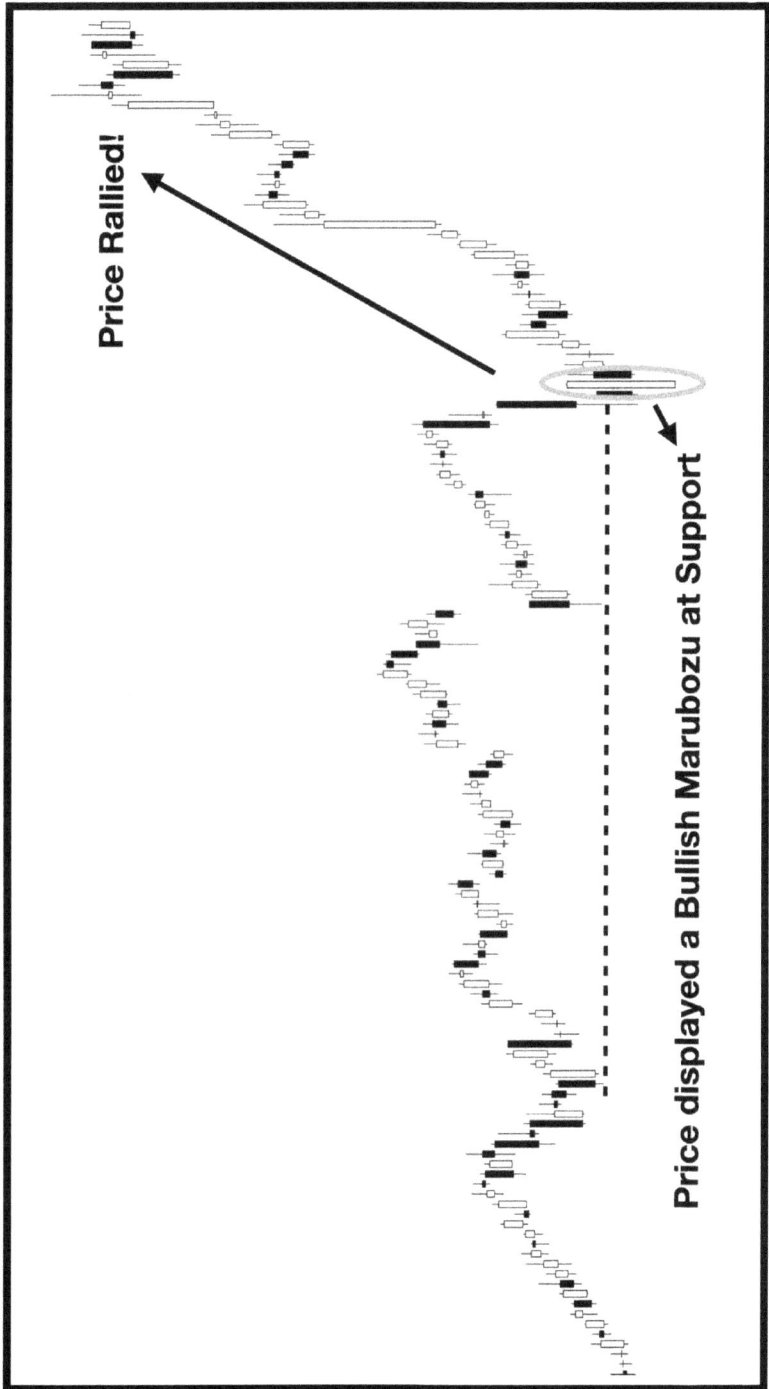

Image 14:36: Bullish marubozu on the chart of Nifty Financial Services Ltd.

BEARISH MARUBOZU PATTERN

A bearish marubozu candlestick pattern indicates intense selling pressure in the market. It is characterised by a long black (or red) candlestick with little or no upper shadow and no lower shadow (image 14.37).

The opening price of the period is usually the high of the period, and the closing price is typically the low of the period.

This pattern suggests that the sellers controlled the market throughout the trading period, causing the price to drop significantly. The lack of an upper shadow indicates that there was no buying pressure during the period, while the absence of a lower shadow implies that the selling pressure was continuous and substantial.

Traders often interpret the bearish marubozu candlestick pattern as a sign of a bearish trend continuation or reversal. If it appears after a long uptrend, it may suggest that the bulls (buyers) have lost their momentum and the bears are taking over. As a result, traders may consider selling their long positions or opening short positions.

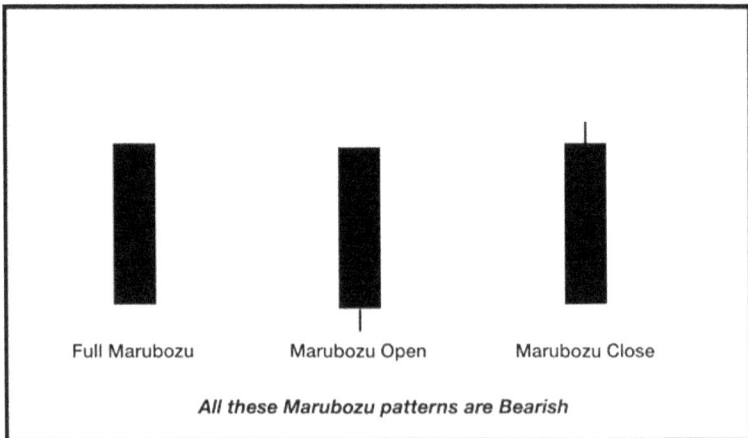

Full Marubozu   Marubozu Open   Marubozu Close

All these Marubozu patterns are Bearish

Image 14.37: Bearish marubozu candlestick pattern

Images 14.38 and 14.39 show examples of bearish marubozu pattern on the charts of Nifty and Nifty Bank, respectively. In both

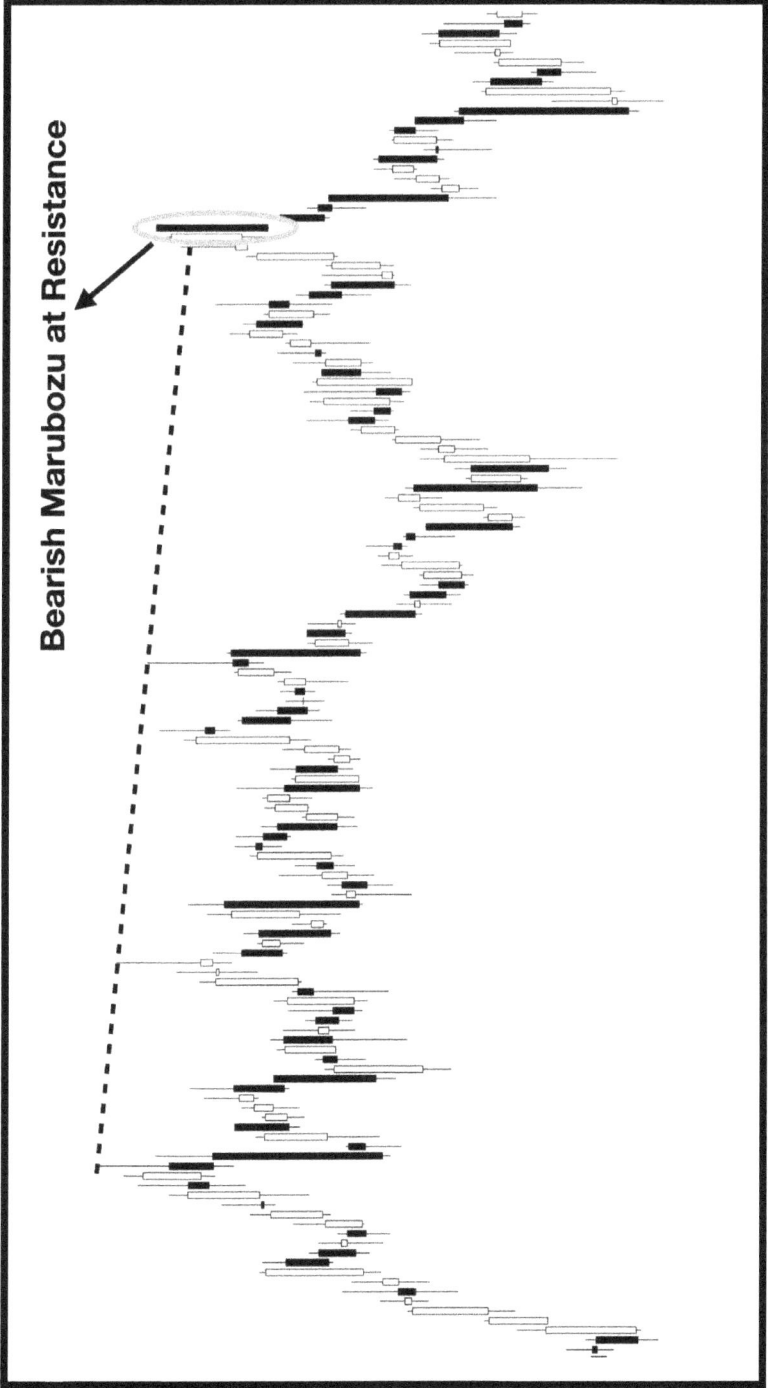

Image 14.38: Bearish marubozu on the chart of Nifty

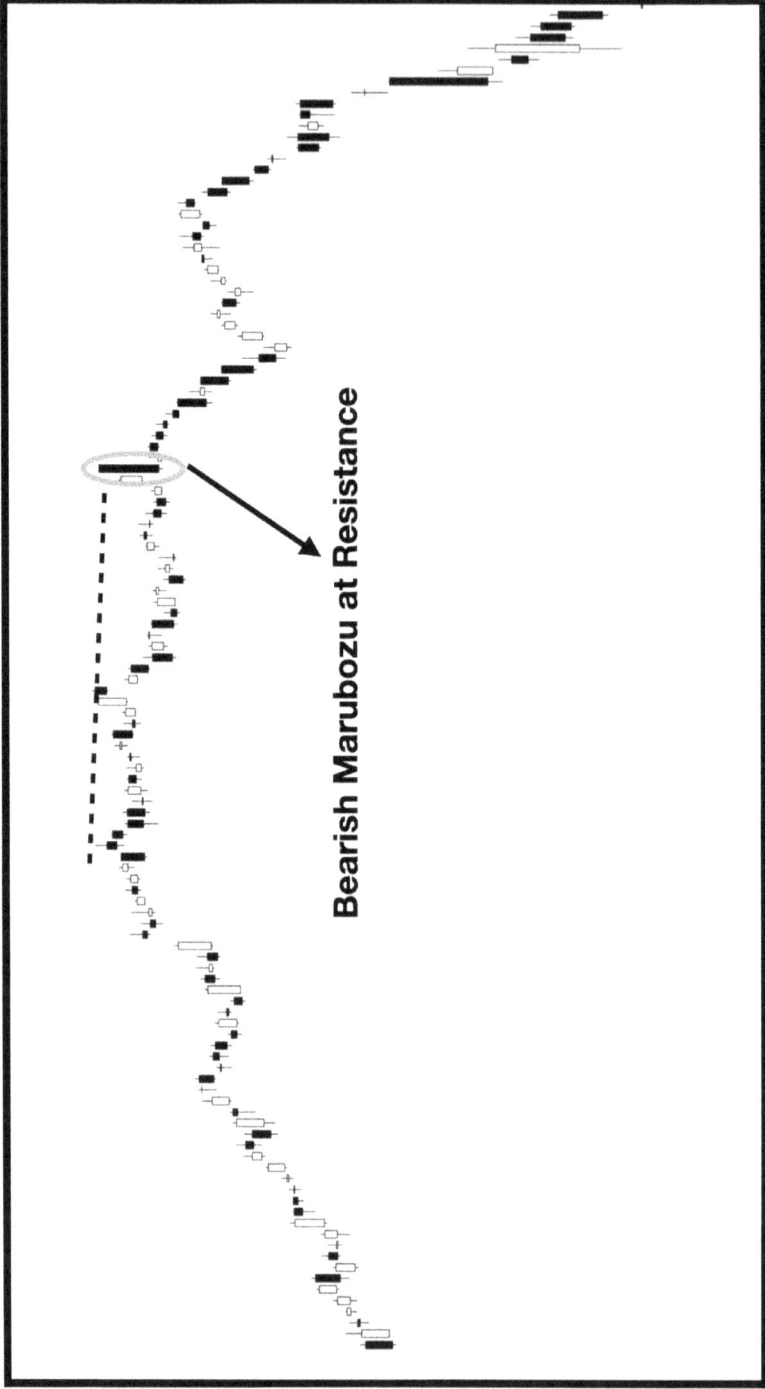

Bearish Marubozu at Resistance

Image 14.39: Bearish marubozu on the chart of Nifty Bank

the cases, bearish marubozu pattern formed at the important price levels and the price fell rapidly from that point.

PINBAR PATTERN

The pinbar candlestick pattern is a type of candlestick pattern that can provide traders with valuable information about potential trend reversals or price rejections.

A pinbar candlestick is characterised by a small body (or 'real body') and a long shadow, or 'wick,' on one side of the candlestick. The wick can either be above or below the body, and it should be at least two times the length of the body. The other side of the candlestick should have little to no shadow.

The pinbar pattern can be bullish or bearish, depending on the direction of the wick. If the wick is above the body, the pinbar is considered bearish, and if the wick is below the body, the pinbar is considered bullish (image 14.40).

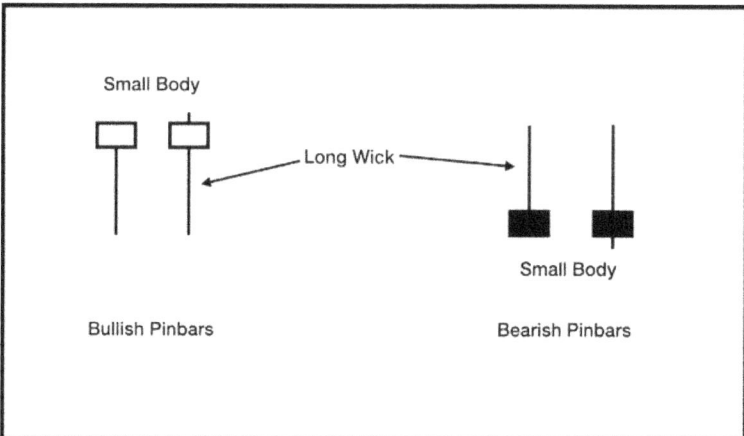

Image 14.40: Pinbar pattern

Traders often use pinbars as a signal that a price rejection has occurred, meaning that the price has attempted to move in one direction but was rejected and pulled back. This can indicate a potential reversal in the current trend.

Image 14.41 shows an example of a bearish pinbar candlestick pattern on the chart of Nifty. It appeared exactly at the day's high (in the selling wick of the first candle) and then the price swifty rallied on the downside.

Image 14.42 shows an example for a bullish pinbar candlestick pattern on the chart of Nifty Bank. It appeared exactly at the previous swing low and then the price swifty rallied on the upside.

However, it is important to note that pinbars should not be used in isolation and should be considered within the broader context of the market and other technical indicators.

Candlestick patterns and support and resistance levels are two widely used technical analysis concepts in the trading world. Candlestick patterns are visual representations of price movements that provide valuable insights into the psychology of market participants. On the other hand, support and resistance levels are price points that the market tends to respect as either a floor or a ceiling for price movements. By combining these two technical analysis concepts, traders can gain an in-depth understanding of market dynamics and make more informed trading decisions.

Here are some reasons why a combination of these two helps:

1. **Confirmation of trend reversal:** Candlestick patterns can identify potential trend reversals, and support and resistance levels can be used to confirm the reversal. For example, if a bullish reversal candlestick pattern forms at a key support level, it may indicate that the market is likely to turn bullish.

2. **Entry and exit points:** Support and resistance levels can be used to identify potential entry and exit points for a trade.

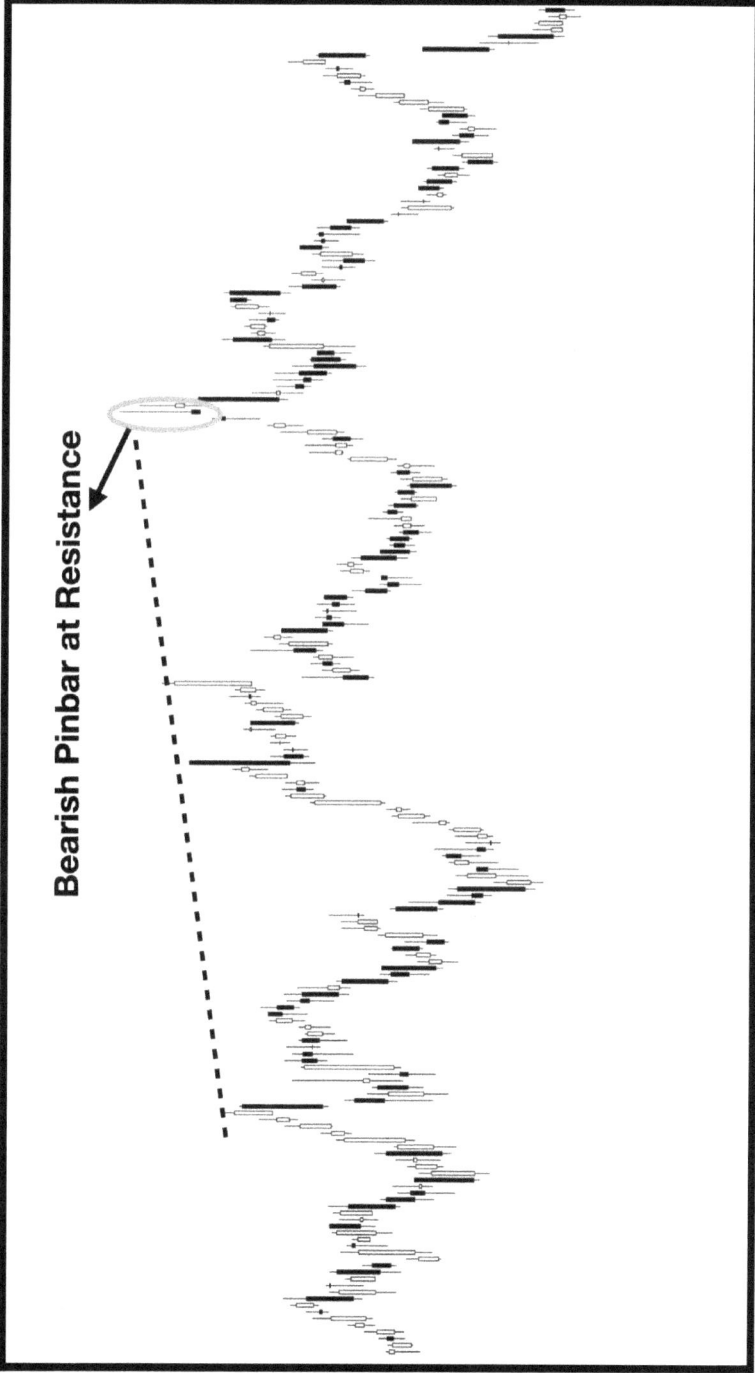

Bearish Pinbar at Resistance

Image 14.41: Bearish pinbar on the chart of Nifty

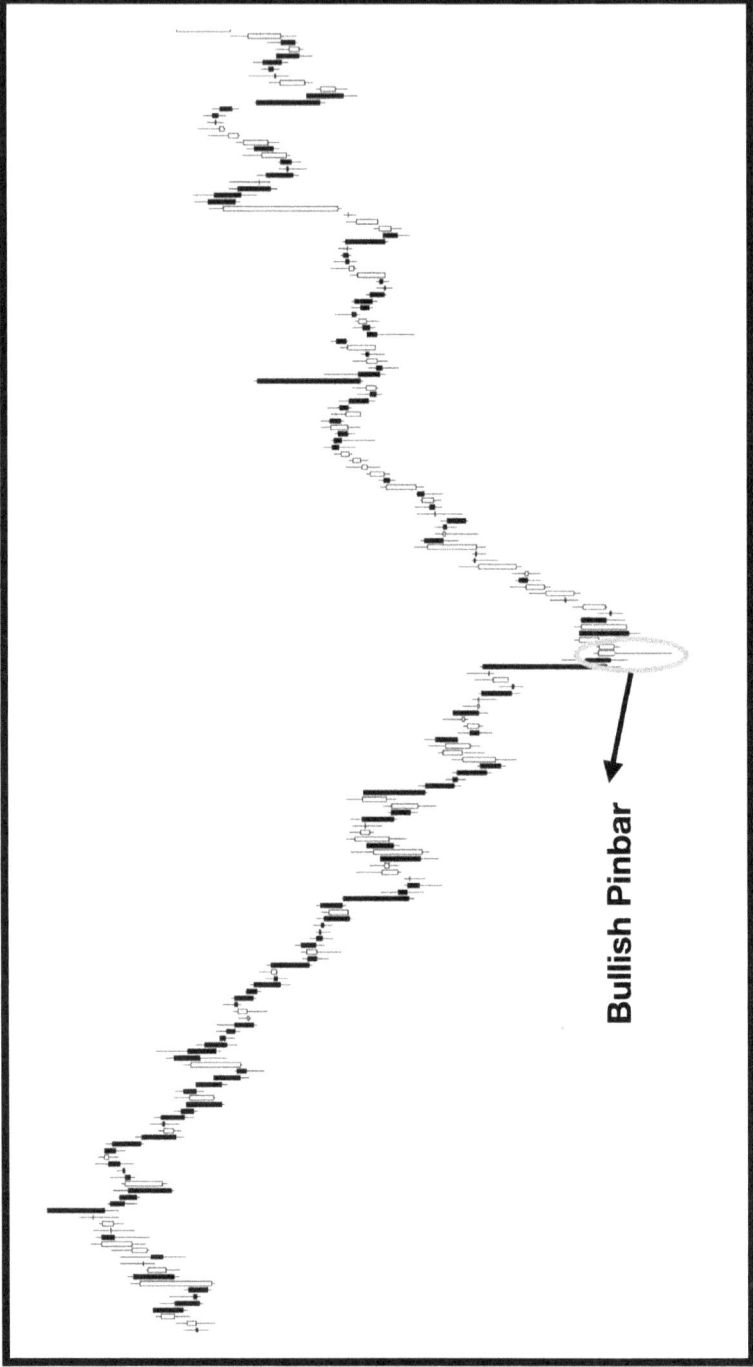

Image 14.42: Bullish pinbar on the chart of Nifty Bank

At the same time, candlestick patterns can provide further confirmation of the trade setup. For instance, if a bearish candlestick pattern forms at a key resistance level, it may indicate a good time to sell or exit a long position.

3. **Risk management:** Combining candlestick patterns and support and resistance levels can also be helpful in managing risk. For example, suppose a trader enters a long position at a key support level and sees a bullish candlestick pattern forming. In that case, it may indicate that the trade has a higher probability of success. Conversely, suppose a bearish candlestick pattern forms at a key resistance level. In that case, it may indicate that the trade has a higher probability of failure, and the trader may consider placing a stop-loss order to limit potential losses.

Overall, using candlestick patterns along with support and resistance levels or other technical analysis concepts can help traders better understand market dynamics and make more informed trading decisions.

TECHNICAL INDICATORS

Many people think only beginners use technical indicators in the market, and experts use price action concepts. But this is a highly debatable topic because the market does not care whether a person uses price action or technical indicators to take his trades. If the person's trades are correct, the market rewards him with some profits; if his trades are wrong, it punishes him with some losses.

Price action is undoubtedly one of the most efficient ways to analyse price movements. However, it is not the only way to make profits in the stock market.

As the name suggests, technical indicators only give an indication of future price movements based on their values. Most of these indicators are derived from price and volume, which are the essential parts of price action.

Most beginners may have trouble understanding naked price action concepts. Besides, their emotions might trouble them in the live market. When they use any indicator, it acts as a backup to support their views. At the same time, it helps them avoid revenge trading in the live market as they have default rules.

There are thousands of indicators in the technical analysis domain, and discussing all of them is not practical. So I will explain only some of the popular, yet powerful indicators used in trading.

1. Moving Average

Moving average (MA) is one of the most famous indicators. It helps smooth out price data by creating a constantly updated average price over a specific time period (depending on the timeframe a person chooses). This makes it easier to see a stock's overall trend without being distracted by short-term fluctuations.

For example, image 14.43 shows a price chart and a 50-period moving average indicator. This is a daily chart, so when we opt for the 50 MA, it calculates the average price over the last 50 days and plots that as a line on the chart. As each new day passes, the average is recalculated by including the latest day's price and dropping the oldest.

There are different variations of moving averages, but two widely used MAs are the simple moving average (SMA) and the exponential moving average (EMA) (image 14.44). The SMA gives equal weight to all the prices in the period, while the EMA gives more weight to recent prices, making it highly responsive to recent price changes.

If you are an investor who uses longer timeframes, like weekly or daily charts, then the simple moving average is more than enough. Suppose you are a trader who uses shorter timeframes, like an hourly or 15-minute chart, an exponential moving average is better.

People use moving averages to identify the direction of a trend

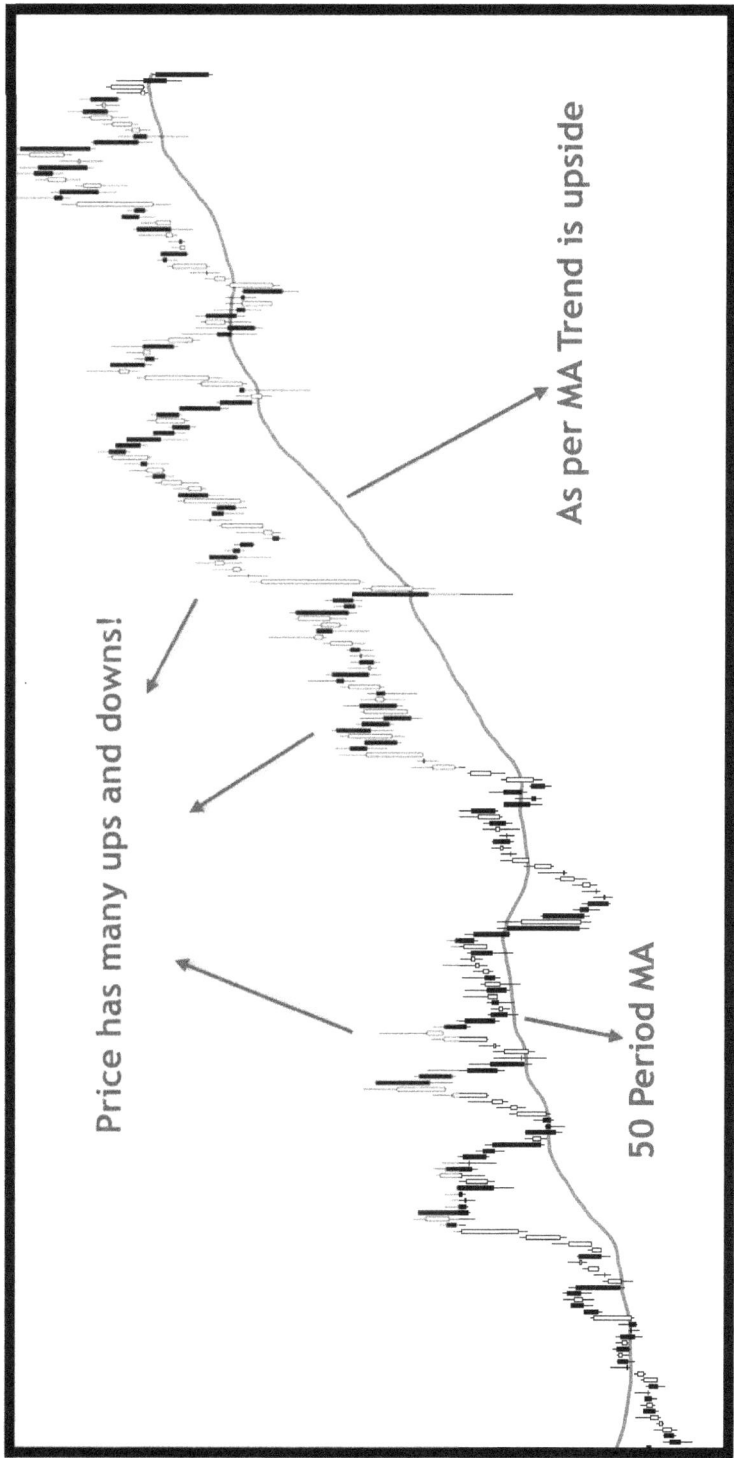

Image 14.43: Moving average (50 period) on a daily chart

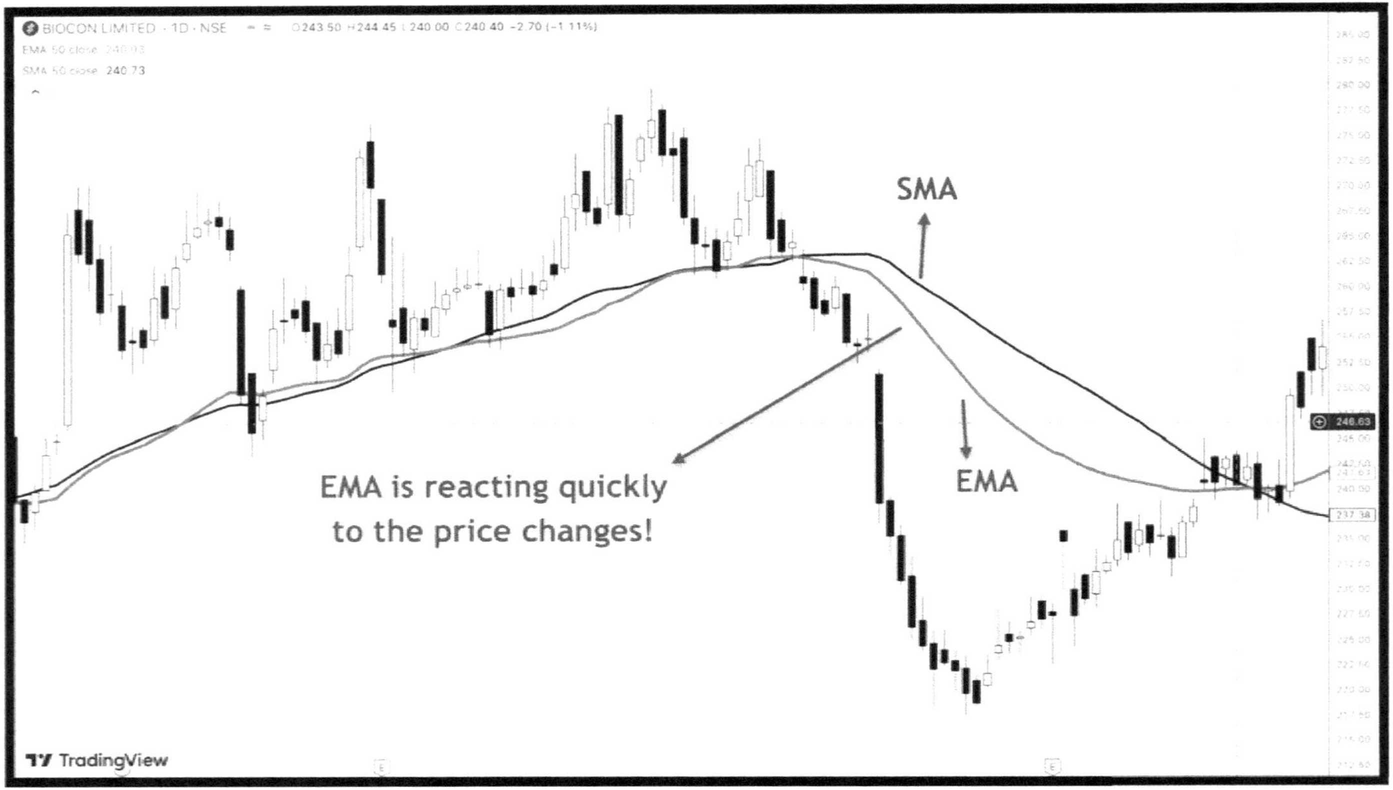

Image 14.44: Exponential moving average vs. simple moving average on the daily chart of Biocon Ltd.

(whether upward, downward, or sideways). For example, suppose a stock's price is above its 50-day moving average. In that case, it is generally seen as an uptrend, while a price below it might indicate a downtrend.

MA crossovers are the most popular technique widely used by many traders and investors. In crossovers, a short-term moving average crosses over a long-term moving average, signalling a buying or selling opportunity.

For instance, if a 50-day MA crosses above the 200-day MA, it is called a golden cross (image 14.45) and is seen as a bullish signal. Conversely, a death cross happens when the 50-day MA crosses below the 200-day moving average, signalling potential bearish momentum (image 14.46).

Traders use a smaller version of the same logic in a lower timeframe. For example, an intraday momentum trader might use a 5-MA crossover with a 50-MA to take trades in a 15-minute or 30-minute timeframe.

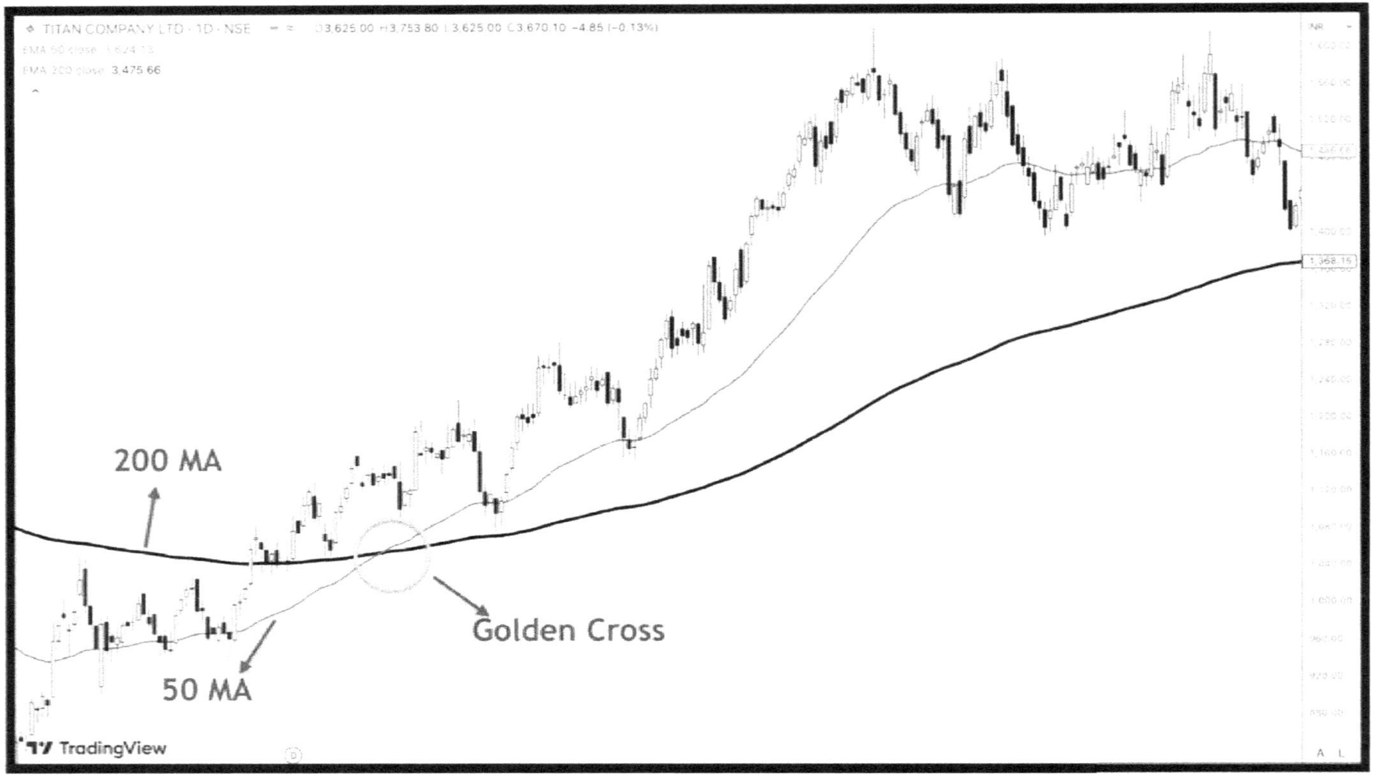

Image 14.45: A golden cross MA on the daily chart of Titan Company Ltd.

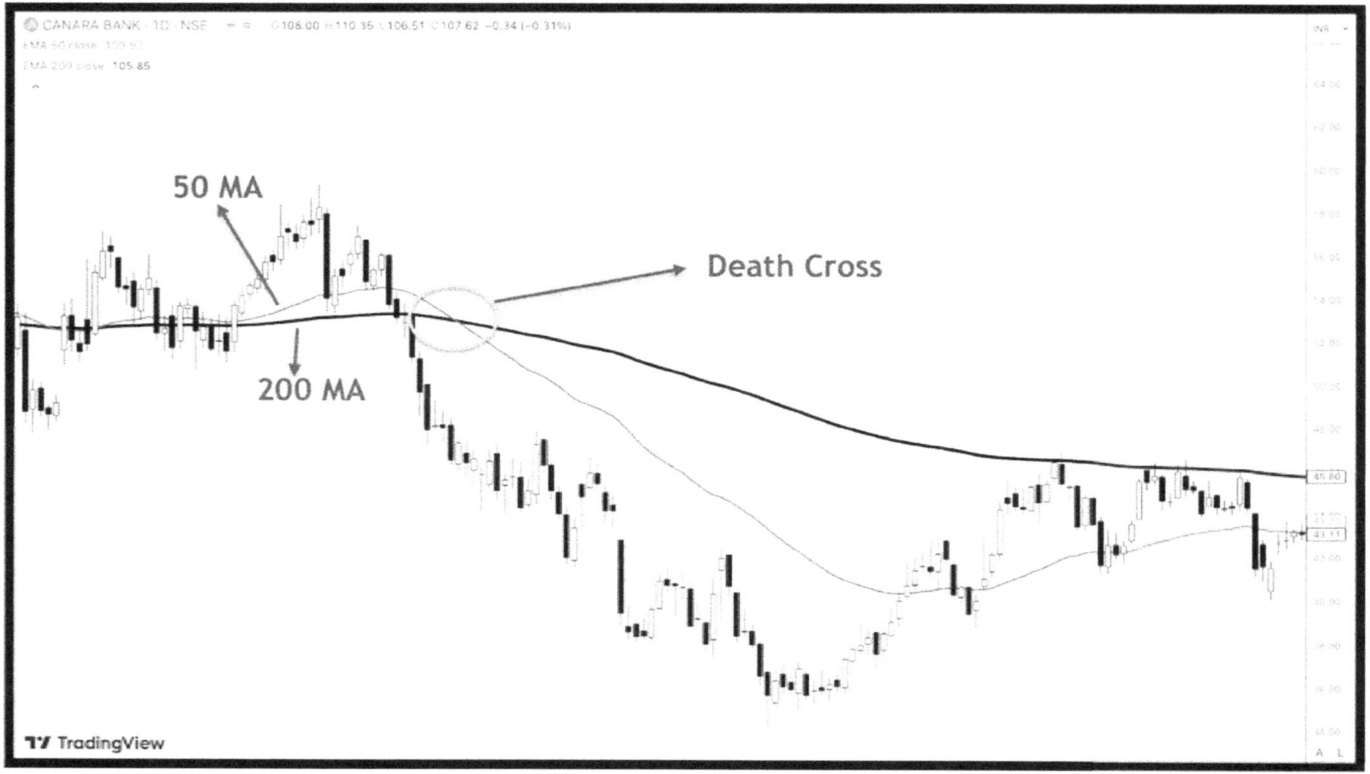

Image 14.46: A death cross MA on the daily chart of Canara Bank Ltd.

2. Relative Strength Index

The relative strength index (RSI) is a popular technical momentum indicator used in trading to measure the speed and change of price movements. The RSI value ranges from 0 to 100. It is typically calculated over a 14-day period. Any value of the RSI above 60 indicates a bullish trend, below 40 indicates a bearish trend, and between 40 and 60 indicates a sideways trend.

By default, most charting platforms highlight the values of 70 and 30, which are nothing but oversold and overbought scenarios. But these overbought and oversold scenarios fail miserably in a trending market. For example, RSI can stay above 70 for a long time in a strong uptrend market. Similarly, it can stay below 30 for a long time in a strong bear market.

In image 14.47, when the price was in a strong uptrend on the daily chart of JSW Steel Ltd., RSI stayed above 70 for a longer duration. If you take a short trade thinking it is an overbought scenario, you would have faced many losses.

Look at image 14.48. When the price was in a strong downtrend on the daily chart of Tata Motors Ltd., RSI stayed below 30 for a longer duration. If you take a long trade thinking it is an oversold scenario, you would have faced many losses.

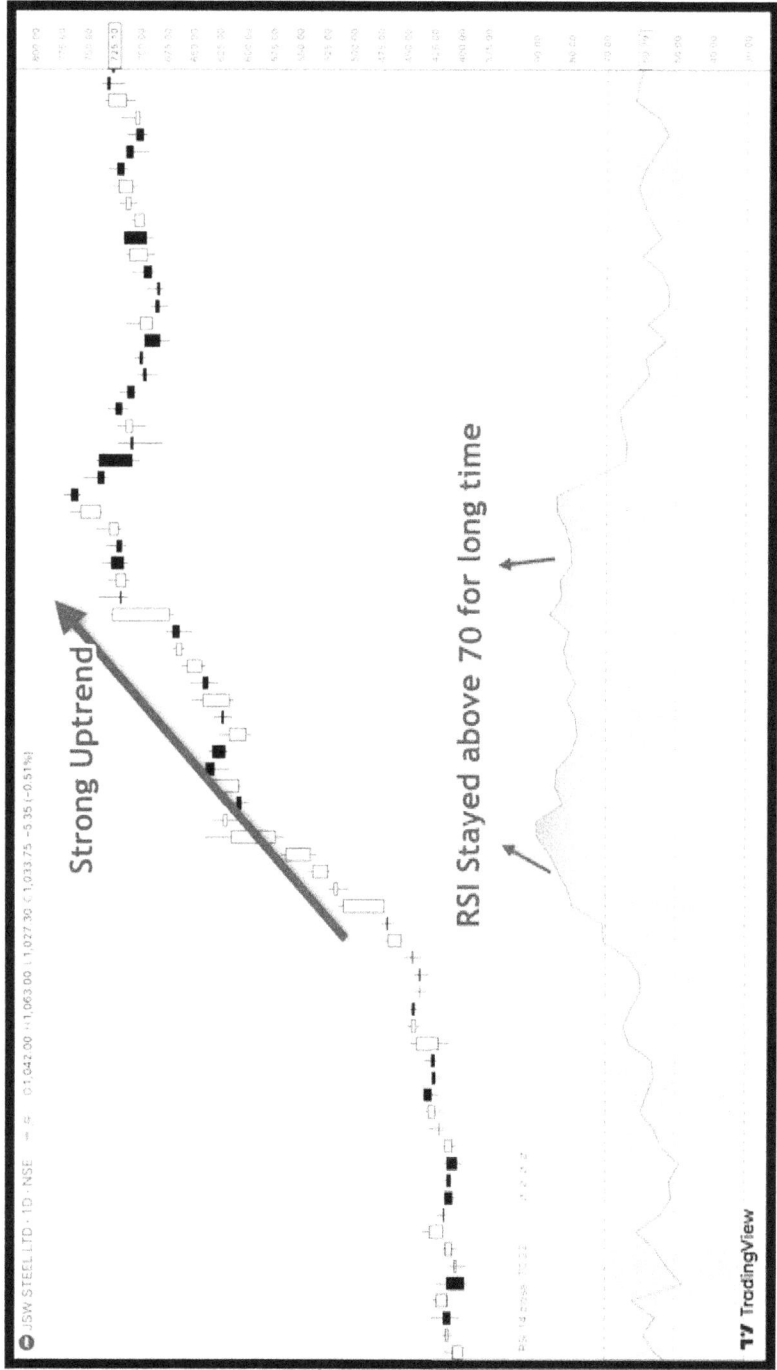

Image 14.47: RSI 70 overbought rule failure on the daily chart of JSW Steel Ltd.

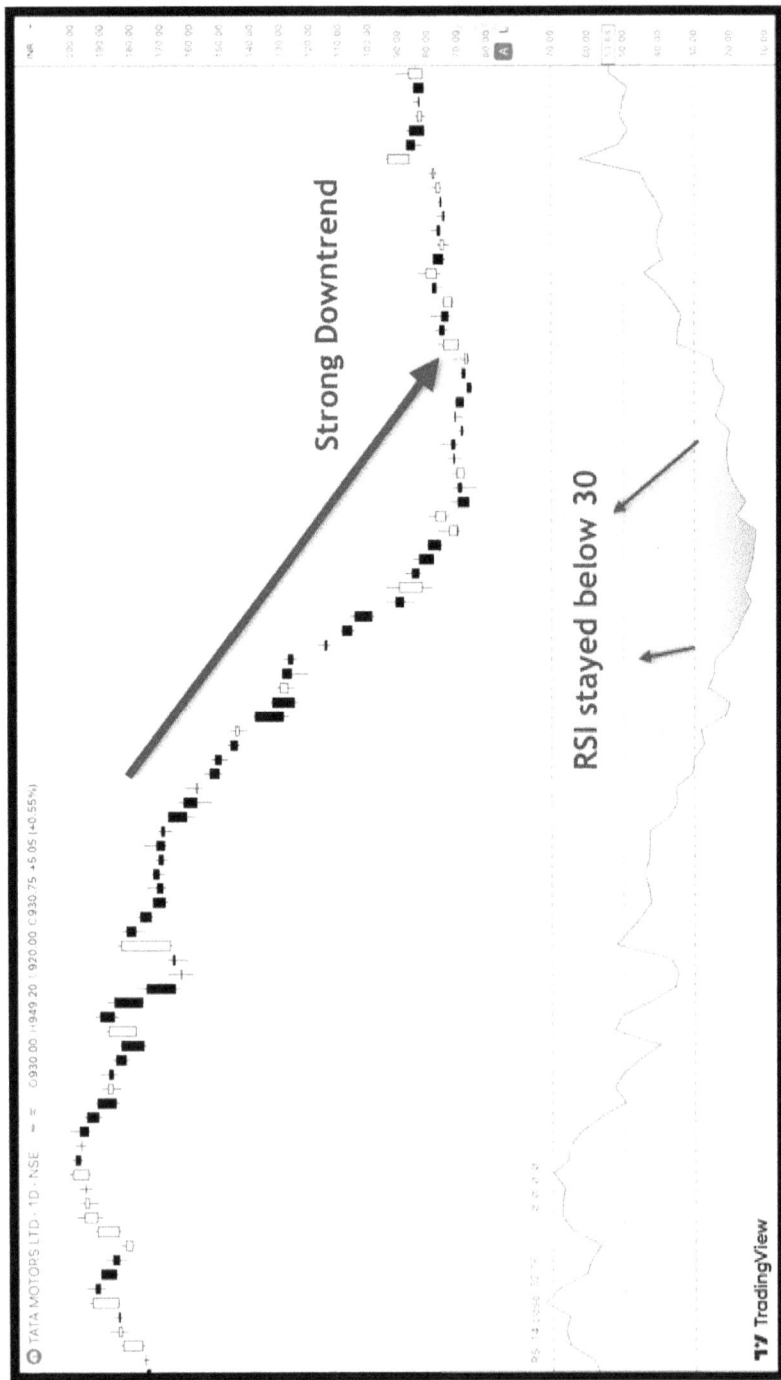

Image 14.48: RSI 30 oversold rule failure on the daily chart of Tata Motors Ltd.

When you use the RSI 40-60 rule, that is, above 60 is bullish, below 40 is bearish, and 40-60 is a sideways zone, then this logic works in both sideways and trending markets.

Image 14.49 shows RSI above 60 in an uptrend on the daily chart of Tata Motors Ltd.

Image 14.50 shows RSI below 40 in a downtrend on the daily chart of Tata Motors Ltd.

Image 14.51 shows RSI between 40 and 60 in a sideways trend on the daily chart of Tata Motors Ltd.

So if you prefer to use RSI, it is better to change the highlighted values from 70, 30 to 40, 60.

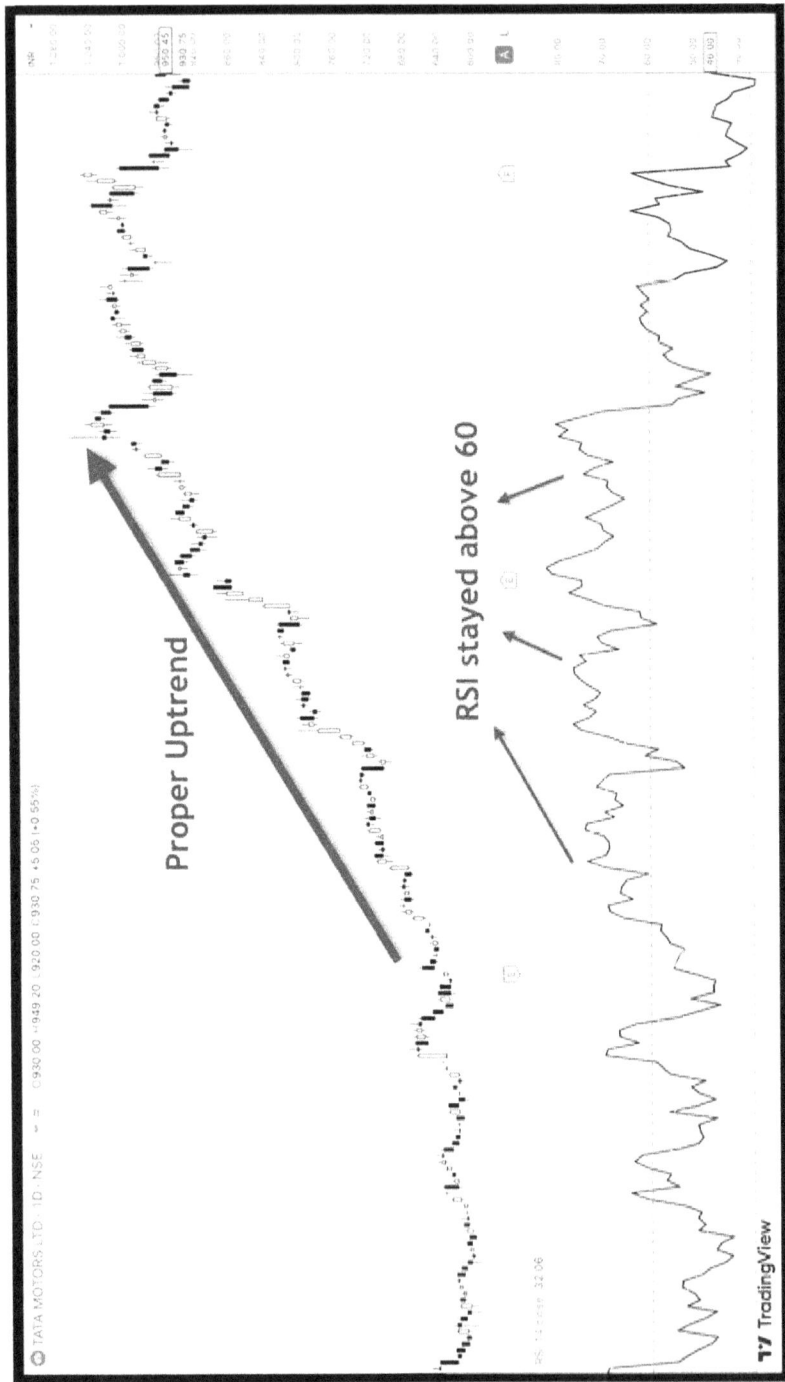

Image 14.49: RSI above 60 in an uptrend on the daily chart of Tata Motors Ltd.

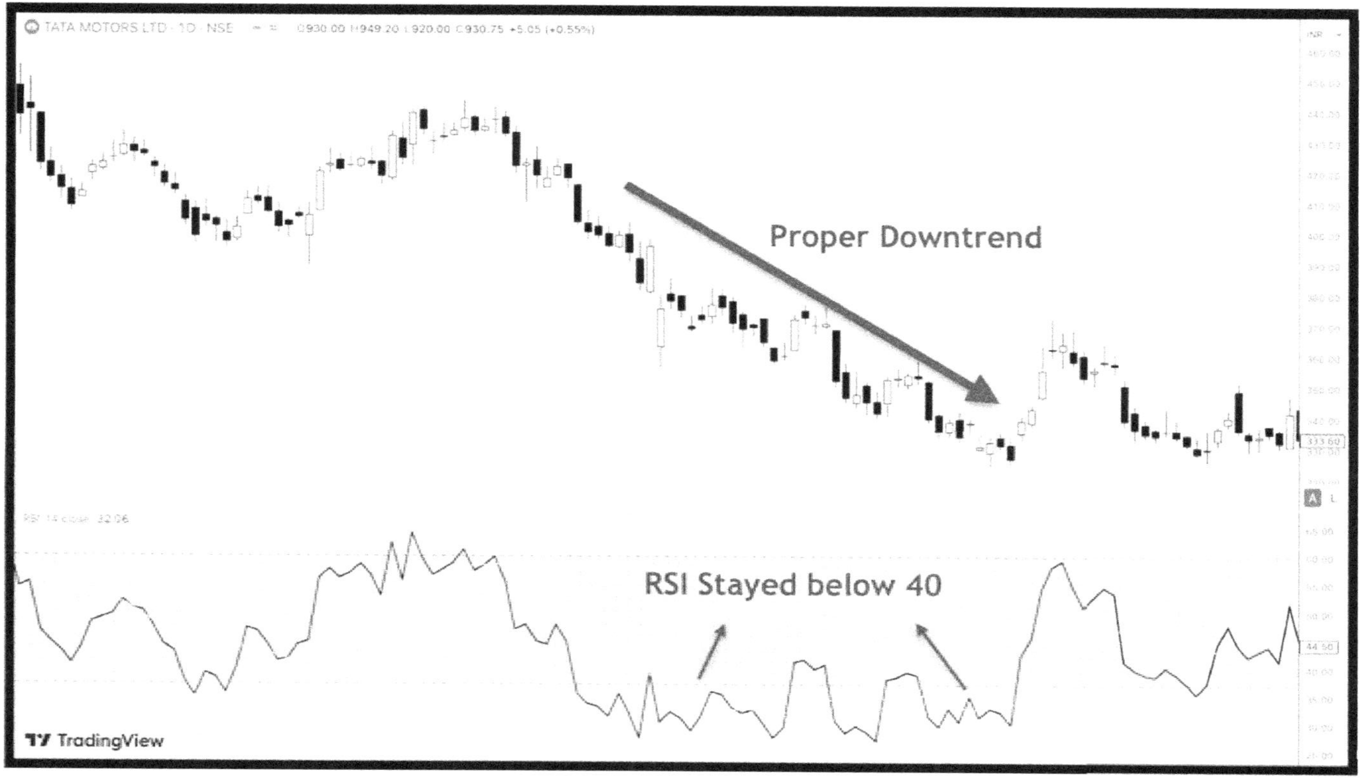

Image 14.50: RSI below 40 in a downtrend on the daily chart of Tata Motors Ltd.

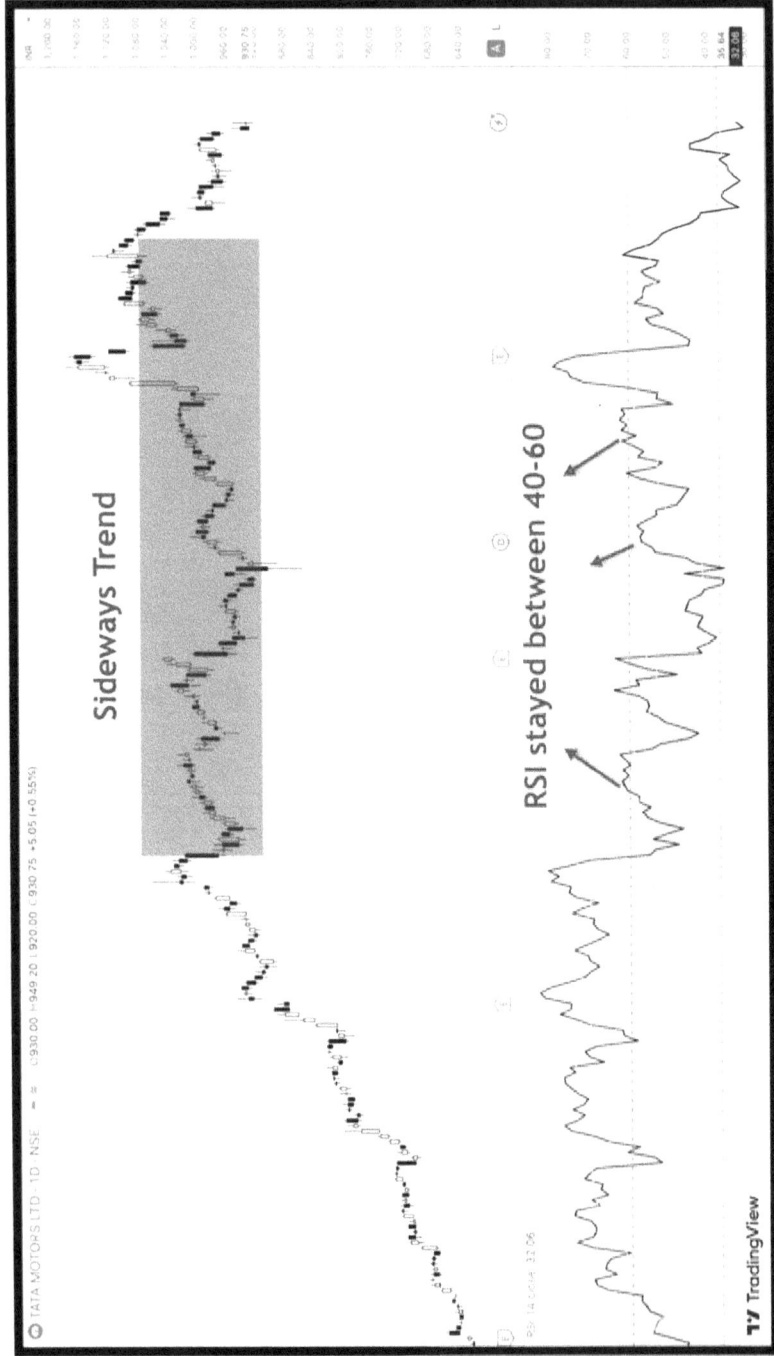

Image 14.51: RSI 40-60 in a sideways trend on the daily chart of Tata Motors Ltd.

3. Average Directional Index

The average directional index (ADX) indicator has three components: ADX line, + Directional Movement Index (DMI), and –DMI.

An ADX line above 20 is considered a strong trend (either uptrend or downtrend).

If the +DMI line is above –DMI, it is a bullish trend. Similarly, if –DMI is above +DMI, it is a bearish trend.

A trader can plan a long trade only if the ADX line is above 25, +DMI is above –DMI and the price takes support at the trend line or displays a breakout of the resistance line.

Similarly, he can plan a short trade only if the ADX line is above 25, –DMI is above +DMI, and the price takes resistance at the resistance trend line or breaks a support trendline.

Traders should understand that the ADX indicator works well as a trend-following system. Hence, holding successful trades until the end of their trend is essential to maximise profits. Besides, it is better to note that it does not work well in a sideways market.

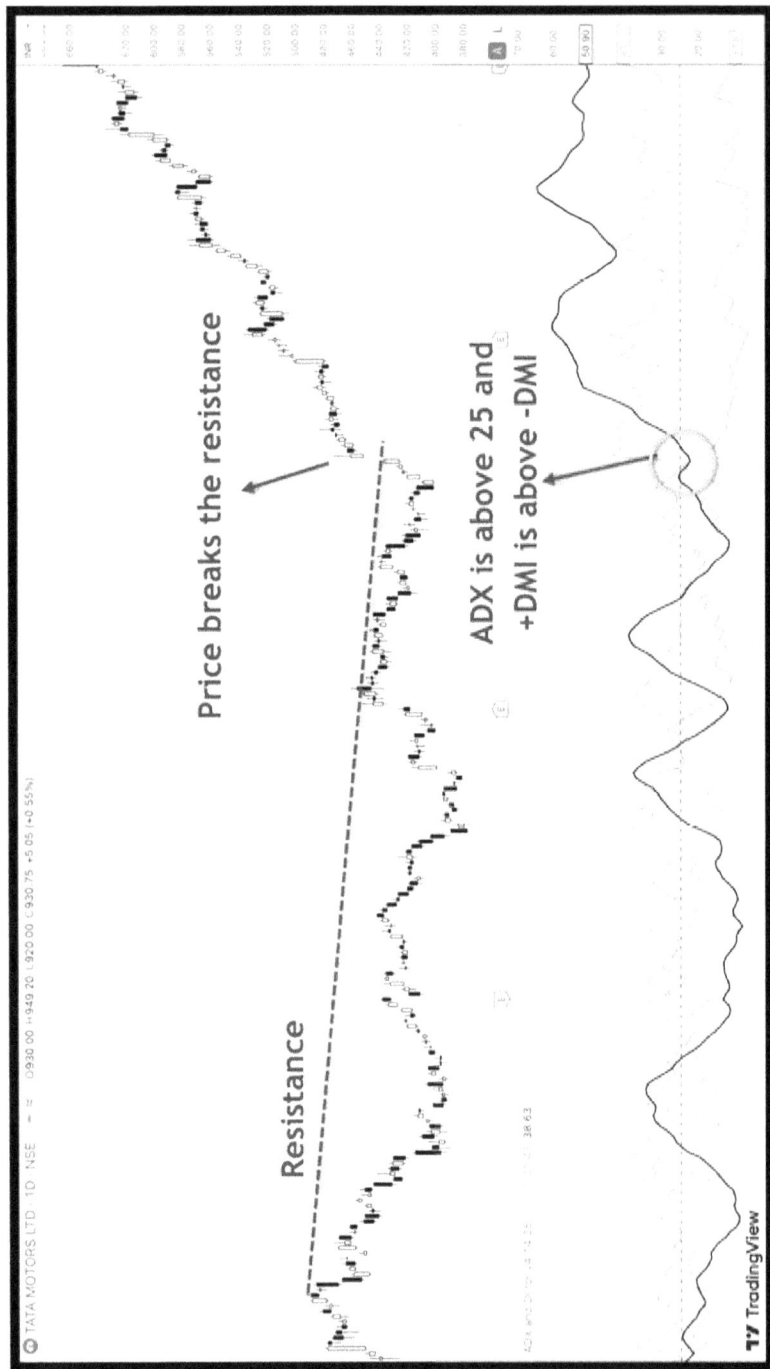

Image 14.52: ADX indicator on the daily chart of Tata Motors Ltd.

4. Bollinger Bands

John Bollinger developed Bollinger Bands (BB) in the mid-1980s. BB consists of three different lines:

1. A 20-period SMA as midline
2. Two lines as two standard deviations above and below the midline

The distance between these bands is based on the standard deviation (sd); hence, they contract and expand based on price fluctuations, nothing but volatility (image 14.53).

If volatility is high, the band will expand automatically, and if volatility is low, the band will contract. Hence, these bands can also identify overbought and oversold conditions in any stock.

When the band squeezes due to low volatility, there is a high probability of a sharp and quick price move in any direction (image 14.54). This method is recognised as the 'Bollinger Band Squeeze Breakout' trading method, and some traders use it. As the price moves in any direction, the bands expand slowly.

In a robust trending environment, the price keeps hugging any band (upper or lower). In case of a sideways move, the price rotates between upper and lower bands.

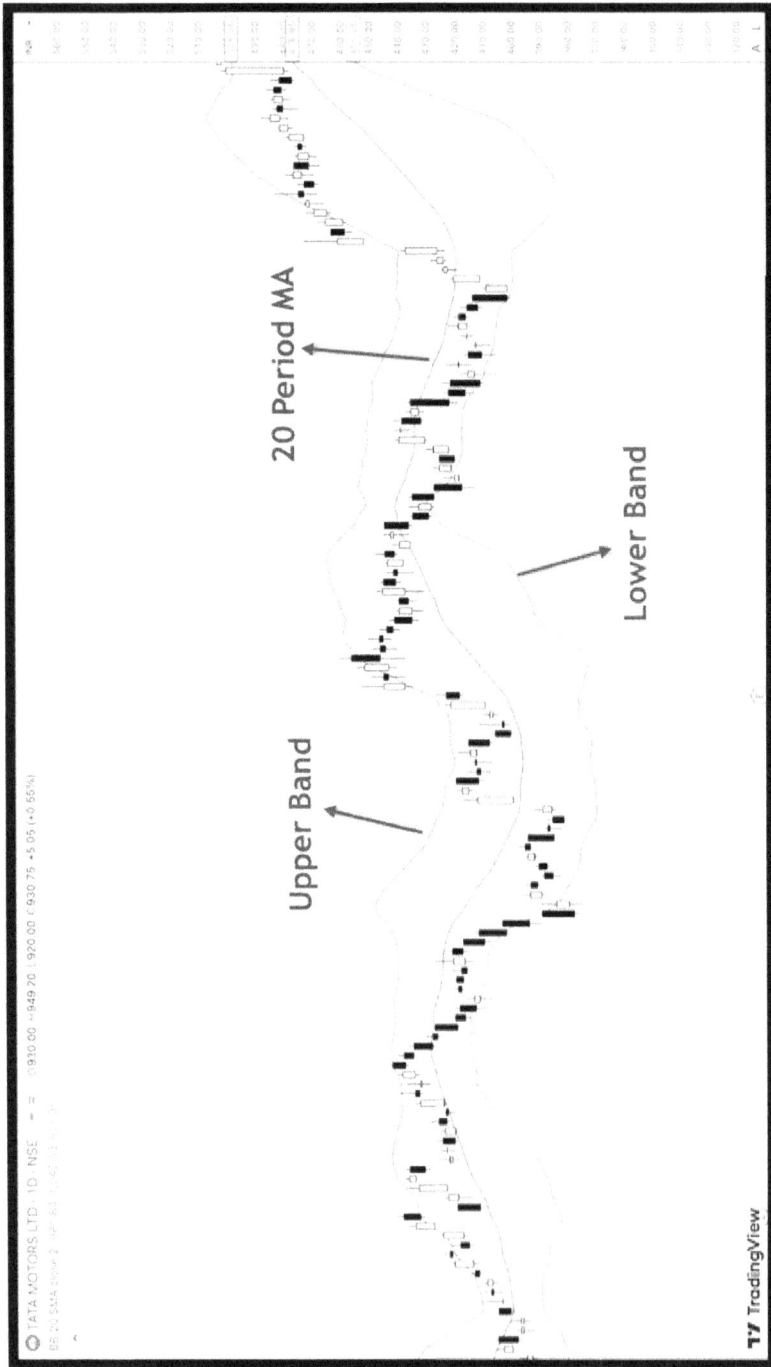

Image 14.53: Bollinger band indicator on the daily chart of Tata Motors Ltd.

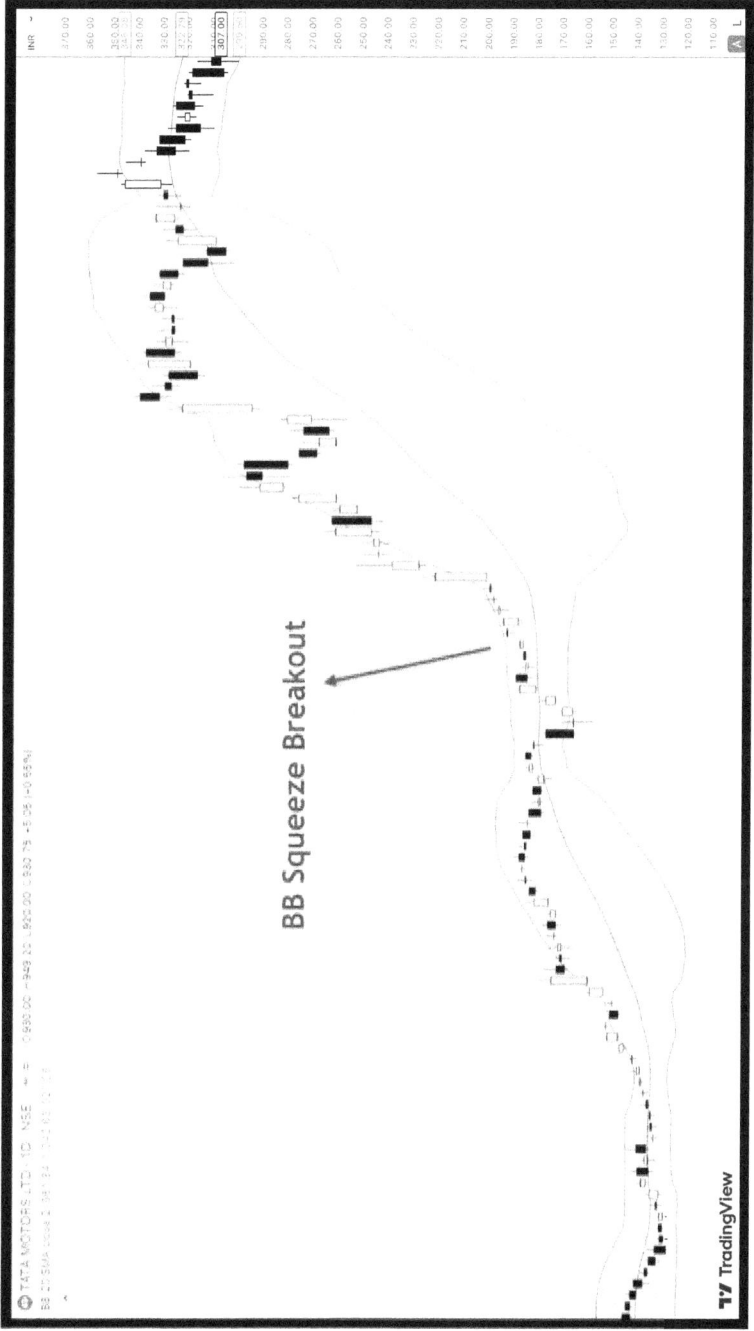

BB Squeeze Breakout

Image 14.54: Bollinger band squeeze breakout

5. Parabolic Stop And Reverse (PSAR) indicator

J. Willes Wilder first introduced the PSAR indicator in 1978 in his book *New Concepts in Technical Trading Systems*. This indicator is a simple series of dots above or below the price candles. These dots are calculated using a formula that considers the extreme price (EP), the acceleration factor (AF), and the previous PSAR value. It appears below the price candle if the stock is in an uptrend and above the price candle if it is in a downtrend.

The point at which the PSAR dots change from above to below the price candle is considered the reversal point (end of downtrend), and traders plan their 'long' trades accordingly. They trail their stop-loss along with the PSAR dots until it stops out (price trades above PSAR dots levels). Image 14.55 shows the PSAR indicator on the daily chart of Tata Motors Ltd.

The PSAR indicator helps identify the price direction and trail the stop-loss. Hence, it gives good results in a trending environment. However, it produces false signals in the sideways zone of the market. Traders can avoid these false signals by picking only strong trending scenarios with momentum oscillators such as RSI or stochastics.

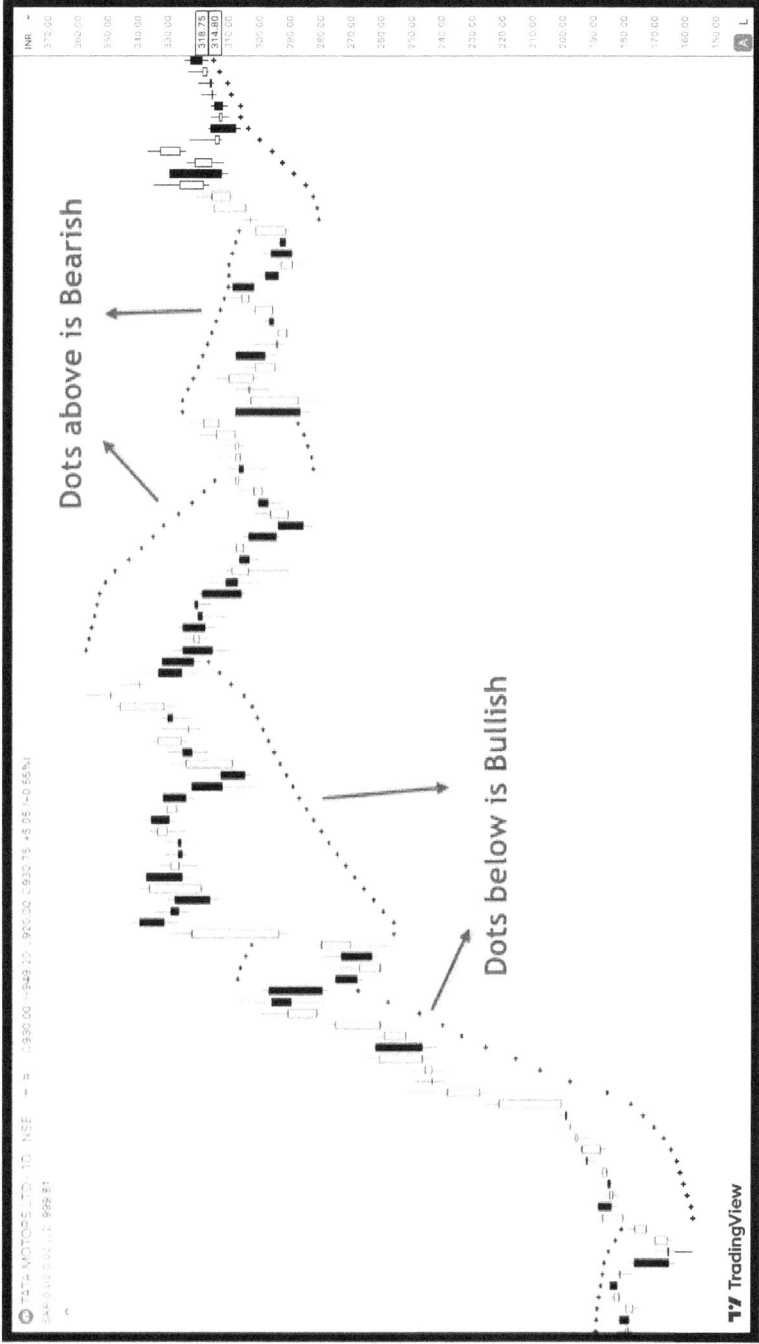

Image 14.55: PSAR indicator on the daily chart of Tata Motors Ltd.

GLOSSARY

American option
An option that can be exercised at any time before its expiration date.

assignment
When an option seller is required to fulfill the obligation of the contract, either by delivering the underlying asset (call) or buying the asset (put).

at-the-money (ATM)
When the strike price of the option is equal to or very close to the current price of the underlying asset.

bear market
A market condition where prices are falling or expected to fall, often accompanied by widespread pessimism.

break-even point
The point at which a trade neither makes nor loses money. For call options, it is the strike price plus the premium, and for put options, it is the strike price minus the premium.

bull market
A market in which prices are rising or expected to rise, characterised by optimism.

butterfly spread

An options strategy combining two spreads (bull and bear) to bet on low volatility. This involves buying and selling multiple options at different strike prices.

call option

A contract that gives the holder the right to buy an underlying asset at a specified price (strike price) within a certain period.

candlestick chart

A price chart that displays the high, low, opening, and closing prices of a security for a specific period.

circuit breaker

A mechanism that halts trading on an exchange for a period if the market moves by a large percentage in a single day.

covered call

A strategy where a trader holds a long position in an asset and sells call options on the same asset to generate income.

Delta

A measure of how much the price of an option is expected to change when the price of the underlying asset changes by Re 1 or $1.

derivative

A financial contract whose value is derived from the performance of an underlying asset (such as stocks or indices). Examples include futures and options.

dividend

The portion of company earnings distributed to shareholders, usually in cash or additional shares.

European option

An option that can only be exercised on its expiry date.

exchange-traded fund (ETF)

A marketable security that tracks an index, commodity, or asset basket like an index fund but trades like a stock on an exchange.

exercise
The process of invoking the right to buy (in the case of a call) or sell (in the case of a put) the underlying asset at the strike price.

expiry date
The last day on which the option can be exercised or traded. After this date, the option contract becomes void.

extrinsic value
The difference between the premium and the intrinsic value of an option. It represents the time value and volatility factors.

fundamental analysis
A method of evaluating a security by attempting to measure its intrinsic value by examining related economic, financial, and other qualitative and quantitative factors.

futures and options (F&O)
Futures and options are derivative contracts based on an underlying stock or index, allowing traders to speculate or hedge.

Gamma
A measure of how much the delta of an option changes in response to price movements in the underlying asset.

greeks
The variables that are used to assess risk in the options market are commonly referred to as "the greeks." They are a set of calculations you can use to measure different factors that might affect the price of an options contract. A Greek symbol is used to designate each of these risks.

historical volatility
A statistical measure of the price fluctuations of the underlying asset over a specific time period in the past.

implied volatility
A forecast of a likely movement in the price of the underlying asset, derived from the current price of options.

index
A statistical measure of the changes in a portfolio of stocks representing a portion of the overall market, such as Nifty50 and Sensex.

initial public offering (IPO)
The process through which a private company issues shares to the public for the first time.

in-the-money (ITM)
When a call option's strike price is below the current price of the underlying asset, or when a put option's strike price is above the current price.

intrinsic value
The real value of an option if it were exercised today. For example, a call option has intrinsic value if the current price is higher than the strike price.

iron condor
A neutral strategy using four options: buying a call and a put, and selling two calls and two puts at different strike prices. It benefits from low volatility and small price movements.

liquidity
The ease with which an option can be bought or sold in the market without affecting its price.

lot size
The minimum quantity of shares required to trade in a derivatives contract like options or futures.

margin
The collateral that the holder of a financial instrument has to deposit to cover the credit risk to the broker.

naked call
Selling a call option without owning the underlying asset. This is riskier as the potential losses can be unlimited if the stock price rises sharply.

open interest
The total number of outstanding (open) options contracts in the market for a particular asset at any given time.

options chain
A listing of all available options contracts (both calls and puts) for a given security, organised by strike price and expiry date.

options
A financial contract giving the buyer the right, but not the obligation, to buy (call) or sell (put) an asset at a predetermined price before or on a specified date.

out-of-the-money (OTM)
When a call option's strike price is above the current price of the underlying asset, or when a put option's strike price is below the current price.

premium
The price paid by the buyer to the seller for acquiring the option contract.

premium spike
A sudden increase in the premium of an option due to high demand or rapid changes in implied volatility.

put option
A contract that gives the holder the right to sell an underlying asset at a specified price (strike price) within a certain period.

relative strength index (RSI)
A momentum indicator that measures the speed and change of price movements, used to identify overbought or oversold conditions.

resistance

A price level where a stock or index faces selling pressure, preventing the price from rising further.

Rho

It measures the sensitivity of an option's price to changes in interest rates.

SEBI

Securities and Exchange Board of India, the regulatory body for securities markets in India.

short selling

The practice of selling borrowed stocks with the expectation that their price will fall, enabling the seller to buy them back at a lower price for a profit.

slippage

The difference between the expected price of a trade and the actual price at which the trade is executed.

spot price

The current market price of a security, used in contrast with the price of future contracts.

stop-loss order

An order placed with a broker to buy or sell once the stock reaches a certain price, used to limit potential losses.

straddle

A strategy involving the purchase of both a call and a put option at the same strike price and expiry date, profiting from significant movement in either direction.

strangle

A strategy where the trader buys a call and a put option with different strike prices, profiting if the price moves significantly in either direction.

strategy
A trading strategy is the method of buying and selling in markets that is based on predefined rules used to make trading decisions.
strike price
The price at which the holder of an option can buy (in the case of a call) or sell (in the case of a put) the underlying asset.
support
A price level where a stock or index tends to find buying interest, preventing it from falling further.

Theta
It represents the time decay of an option, or how much the value of the option erodes as the expiry date approaches.
time decay
The rate at which the value of an option decreases as it approaches its expiry date.

Vega
It measures the sensitivity of an option's price to changes in the volatility of the underlying asset.
volatility
A measure of how much the price of the underlying asset is expected to fluctuate over a specific period of time. Higher volatility increases option prices. Higher volatility indicates higher risk and greater price swings.
volume
The number of shares or contracts traded in a security or an entire market during a specific time frame.

ABOUT THE AUTHOR

INDRAZITH SHANTHARAJ is a trader, investor, and bestselling author with extensive experience in the stock market. He has helped thousands of traders through his books, YouTube videos, and insightful market analysis. His website, https://indrazith.com, provides high-quality content on trading strategies, market profile, and investing.

He is a former IT professional with over a decade of experience. He voluntarily chose to pursue a full-time career in the stock markets, driven by his passion and expertise in the field.

With a deep understanding of market behaviour and price action, Indrazith has guided numerous traders in refining their strategies and enhancing their trading psychology. His work continues to empower traders and investors to navigate the markets with confidence.

www.ingramcontent.com/pod-product-compliance
Lightning Source LLC
Chambersburg PA
CBHW071536200326
41519CB00021BB/6503